Refugees and Development in Africa

The Case of Eritrea

Gaim Kibreab

THE RED SEA PRESS
Publishers & Distributors of Third World Books
556 Bellevue Avenue
Trenton, New Jersey 08618

This book is dedicated to
African refugees
and to the
individuals and organizations
which are trying to alleviate
their plight.

THE RED SEA PRESS, INC.
556 BELLEVUE AVENUE
TRENTON, NEW JERSEY 08618

First Printing, September 1987

Cover Design by Adjoa Jackson-Burrowes

Typeset by TypeHouse of Pennington, Inc.

Library of Congress Catalog Card Number: 86-63776

ISBN: 0-932415-26-1 Cloth
0-932415-27-X Paper

Contents

Acknowledgements

I have incurred many debts in completing this study, more than I can acknowledge here. A number of individuals and institutions, however, provided assistance without which this project would not have been possible.

This work is part of a research project called 'Refugees and Development in Africa', which is coordinated by the Scandinavian Institute of African Studies (SIAS). Dr. Michael Stahl and my colleagues in the project, Dr. Peter Nobel and Mekuria Bulcha, have been sources of inspiration and support throughout the project. Dr. Stahl's critical comments on earlier drafts were of inestimable value.

A great debt is due to the staff of the Sudanese Commissioner for Refugees in Khartoum, Showak, Gedaref and various settlements, to the staff of the SCC/EsRP in Gedaref and the settlements, and to the Euro Action Acord staff in Khartoum and Qala en Nahal. Great thanks are also due to the Economic and Social Research Council in Khartoum and to the UNHCR Office in Geneva, the branch office in Khartoum and the subbranch office in Gedaref.

My greatest debt is to the refugees and to the resident committees (Legina) in the settlements for their warm welcome and for sharing with me their inexhaustible wealth of knowledge about their conditions of existence. Without their cooperation this work would have never been completed. Without the generous hospitality and brotherhood that was extended to me by the refugees, by the SCC/ESRP, by EA-A and by the project administration's employees, the task of carrying out the field work in the harsh physical conditions would have been very difficult. This hospitality made my stay at the settlements with the refugees one of the happiest experiences of my life. My thanks are also due to Kuflom Tsegai and his wife Nigesti, with whom I stayed in Khartoum.

I am grateful to Professor Bo Gustafsson, Docent Kersti Ullenhag and Dr. Eskil Ekstedt, who with admirable, scrupulous and clear-sighted objectivity and inexhaustible patience led this work away from many errors. I am also grateful to Dr. Lars Magnusson's invaluable comments on earlier drafts. My deep appreciation is also due to Professor B. Nindi who read the final manuscript critically. Without the inspiring and harmonious atmosphere that prevails at the Department of Economic History, all these efforts would have been in vain. I am therefore grateful to all my colleagues at the postgraduate seminars. I am also grateful to Dr. Ashok Dar for his critical comments and constructive suggestions.

I wish also to acknowledge a special debt to my friend, Mohamed Mazeem, for his help in processing the data, to Omer M. Yasuf for redrawing the maps and the diagrams, and to Nigel Rollison and Lynn Karlsson for proofreading the manuscript. Thanks are also due to Karl Eric Ericsson, Ingrid Dahlqvist and the library staff at SIAS. My appreciation is also due to Karin Berg, who cheerfully typed the various drafts and the final manuscript with great efficiency.

None of these efforts would have been sufficient without the financial assistance from the Swedish Agency for Research Cooperation with Developing Countries (SAREC), and the Faculty of Social Sciences of the University of Uppsala. Travel grants were also received from SIAS.

I am indebted to my wife, Senait Tsegay, for her patience, understanding and encouragement. Needless to say, none of these benefactors is responsible for the views expressed or any shortcomings in the study.

Gaim Kibreab
Uppsala, 1986

Editor's Note

This book was first presented to The Red Sea Press as a doctorate thesis. To turn it into a book that the more general reader would find accessible, we have made several changes. The methodology of the study was moved from Chapter 1 to Appendix 1. References to some of the unpublished and more unattainable sources of information have been removed from the text to make reading easier; they remain all fully referenced in the bibliography. References to sources have been removed from many of the tables. Where there is no source indicated, it is usually the questionnaire upon which this study was based and which Gaim Kibreab describes in Appendix 1.

We hope that these changes make this important study into a well-organized, accessible and informative book.

Abbreviations

COR	Commissioner's Office for Refugees - Sudan
EA-A	Euro Action Acord
GOS	Government of Sudan
IRC	International Rescue Committee
NCAR	National Committee for Aid to Refugees
NGOs	Non-Governmental Organizations
SCC/ESRP	Sudan Council of Churches/Eastern Sudan Relief Program
THS	Tractor Hire Service
UNHCR	United Nations High Commissioner for Refugees
WFP	World Food Program
WLDH	Wide Level Disc Harrows

Meshrua— is a square of 1000 feddans within which 100 hawasha (holdings), each consisting of 10 feddans, are located.

Seluka— digging stick (plough stick)

Legina (Arabic)— Residents' committee

Sheikhs (Arabic)— Clan leaders

Shimaghele (Tigrinya)—Residents' committee

1 feddan = 1039 acres

PART I

The Background

CHAPTER 1

Refugees

> Uprooted, often powerless to influence his fate, torn between the hope of return, which makes him a perpetual wanderer, and the desire to integrate himself in the society which is sheltering him so as to become something other than a recipient of aid, an alien without any protection other than that of the High Commissioner—valuable as it is—the refugee remains a fragile being, whose chances of self-development are cruelly jeopardized, even on the assumption—often theoretical—that his material needs would be looked after.
>
> L. Tindemans, President of ICARA II, July 1984

> There is a tendency in the world to tackle problems piecemeal rather than at their roots.
>
> G.J. von Heuven Goedhart, UN High Commissioner for Refugees

One of the most dramatic events of our time is the large extent of population movements within and across national boundaries. The causes of these movements include economic hardship due to natural calamities such as earthquakes, droughts, famine and floods, as well as economic hardship due to lack of income-generating opportunities at the population's place of origin. Political instabilities also force population movements at both national and international level.

Nowhere in the world have these movements been as dramatic as in Africa. Of the world's estimated 12.6 million refugees and internally displaced persons, about 50% are Africans. Africa's refugee crisis is a symptom of the more general political, economic, ecological and social crises with which the continent is gripped.

> It is estimated that 150 million people in Africa are affected by hunger as a consequence of drought and unsolved political and military conflict.

> This has led to a decline in food production while at the same time Africa's population is constantly increasing. (FGR representative's statement in ICARA II, 1984)

REFUGEES IN TODAY'S WORLD

Unlike the post-war refugee problem in Europe which was immediately followed by high rates of economic growth, the massive population movements and the politico-socioeconomic crisis in Africa today are occurring at a time when the world economy has failed to maintain an acceptable growth rate and when there is serious unemployment worldwide. These developments have detrimental effects on refugees, because the economic crisis in the developed world will lead to cutbacks in humanitarian and development aid. Furthermore, the world economic crisis has created a parallel crisis in African countries which has reduced the absorbing capacity of countries of asylum and aggravated the political instability in refugee-generating countries.

The provision of assistance to African refugees has not kept pace with the magnitude of the problem, but the international community has scored commendable achievements in meeting the need for emergency relief in situations of new influxes and repatriations.

Long-term approaches to refugee crises have been less satisfactory, however. Current programs are designed to benefit only refugees to the neglect of the local population and assistance to refugees is not provided beyond the level of subsistence. The inadequacy of this approach is now being recognized by the international community and a new and imaginative approach is being called for, whereby humanitarian refugee assistance must address the development needs of the areas affected by the refugee influx and not only the needs of the refugees themselves.

But whatever new approach is taken, it will not eliminate the problem of refugees in Africa. An end to the African refugee problem will come only when the international community at large and the African governments in particular address themselves to its root causes. The All Africa Conference of Churches and World Council of Churches in ICARA II correctly noted that up to now, perhaps for political reasons, the root causes have been ignored.

> The tendency that most of us are guilty of is to treat merely the symptoms of refugee movements rather than deal with their root causes; to consider such movements on a piecemeal, short-term basis; to overlook the uncomfortable fact that the presence of refugees anywhere indicates that something has gone wrong; to ignore the evidence and here we shall be very frank—that while many Africans may be refugees from natural disasters like the present drought or from

> white minority regimes, the vast majority are refugees from the countries represented at this conference.
>
> Statement of All Africa Conference of Churches and World Council of Churches in ICARA II, 1984

DEFINING REFUGEES

How do refugee movements differ from general population movements (migration)? Although a refugee movement is part of a general population movement, it is necessary to recognize the fact that refugees are a special category of migrants. A refugee, as noted by Sir J.H. Simpson is

> distinguished from the ordinary alien or migrant in that he has left his former territory because of political events there, not because of economic conditions or because of the economic attractions of another territory.
>
> (Simpson: 1939, 4)

Unlike the immigrants, a refugee is forced to leave his country of origin by forces which he cannot control. Refugees move against their will. It is their unwillingness to move that above all distinguishes them from other immigrants.

There are also social and demographic differences between refugees and immigrants. Immigrants often tend to be male and young. Unlike immigrants, refugee movements are usually not often sex and age selective, and they are socially and demographically rather heterogeneous. In his study of Angolan refugees and immigrants, A. Hansen found that the refugees were older than the immigrants. (Hansen: 1982, 187) The Eritrean refugees in Eastern Sudan, for instance, include not only both sexes and all ages but also all rural social groups. (However, it must be noted that the social and demographic characteristics of the Eritrean urban refugees vary radically from the socio-demographic features of the rural refugees. Many of the urban refugees are mainly young men and women.)

Available psychiatric investigations also indicate that sudden flight in panic traumatizes more than a calm departure based upon a conscious decision. The refugee

> although all his ties, especially primary group ties, are broken during exile plans to return to his native country after 'liberation'. Hence, his orientation differs from that of a normal immigrant . . .
>
> (Kolaja: 1952, 289)

Unlike the immigrant, who can maintain contacts with his kith and kin and who can return for a visit or stay, 'in general the refugee cannot return without danger to life or liberty . . .' (Simpson: op.cit., 4) Sometimes the dream to return can block the refugees' possibility to integrate into the country of asylum. Pfister-Ammende, for instance, points out that

> there were many refugees whose sole purpose in life was the reality of their home country . . . Consumed by great nostalgia they were in danger of fixation . . . while clinging to the elusion of return, block their way to a new life in a new country.
>
> (Pfister-Ammende: 1973, 9)

This psychological factor can be a cause of failure if not taken cognizance of by policy makers and organizations involved in refugee work.

Legal Definition

Even though the problem of refugees has existed since antiquity, international efforts to alleviate the plight of refugees were for the first time mobilized after World War I. Even then the problem of refugees and displaced persons was perceived as an ephemeral phenomenon and all the measures suggested were of temporary nature. Not only this but a consensus on the definition of the term refugee was difficult to achieve. This entire question was politically sensitive. Provision of a sanctuary by one member state for refugees fleeing from another member state was considered as an act of hostility. On 3 December 1949, a decision was passed by the General Assembly to create the Office of the High Commissioner for Refugees as of 1 January 1951. The Statute of the Office was adopted on 14 December 1950. According to Art. 6 A (ii) only persons who became refugees 'as a result of events occurring before 1 January 1950' were covered by it. Art. 6 B defined the term refugee as,

> Any other person who is outside the country of his nationality, or if he has no nationality, the country of his former habitual residence, because he has or had well-founded fear of persecution by reason of his race, religion, nationality or political opinion and is unable or, because of such fear, is unwilling to avail himself of the protection of the government of the country of his nationality, or, if he has no nationality, to return to the country of his former habitual residence.
>
> (Art. 6 B of the Statute)

Art. 1 (2) of the 1951 Convention defined the term refugee similarly and contained the same time restriction as in Art. 6 A (ii) of the Statute. The fact that both the Statute and the Convention excluded those persons who were driven from their native countries as a result of events occurring after 1 January 1950 again shows that the refugee phenomenon was perceived as transient phenomenon that would cease after World War II. However, the developments that occured in the 1950s and 1960s clearly indicated that the refugee problem would not come to an end as the international community had hoped for and the deadline set by the Statute and the Convention was deleted by the 1967 Protocol relating to the Status of Refugees. Article 1 (3) of the 1967 Protocol also eliminated the geographic limitation.

As a result of the elimination of the limitations of time and place, a large number of refugees, including Africans who were formally outside the realm of UNHCR activities, could now enjoy legal protection and assistance afforded to their counterparts in Europe. (However, it must be made clear here that despite limitations of time and place, UNHCR's assistance to African refugees dates back to 1957 whereby about 200,000 Algerian refugees in Tunisia and Morocco received UNHCR assistance.)

Both the definitions embodied in the Statute and the Convention place emphasis on two important elements, i.e., for a person to seek a political asylum, he or she must have a 'well founded fear of being persecuted' and must be 'outside the country of his/her nationality or habitual residence'. There is no problem with the second criterion, but the first criterion is very vague and difficult to test objectively. What is a 'well founded fear'? How is it to be measured? Is the psychological disturbance generated by 'fear of persecution' as to necessitate flight the same for all people? The criterion of well foundedness can probably be objectively tested in countries where people risk no persecution for expressing themselves or organizing themselves according to their constitutions, but in situations where people flee to escape the ravages of war and where flagrant violations of human rights are part of everyday life, fear of persecution is partly subjective and cannot easily be tested objectively in every individual case.

This is further complicated by the fact that the movement of most African asylum seekers is characterized by mass-scale influxes which render the application of procedures established for the determination of a refugee status of individual asylum seekers impractical because of the massive nature of the problem and due to lack of a developed machinery and infrastructure which can allow strict scrutiny by the country of asylum of every individual case.

One thing that must be borne in mind is the fact that refugee status cannot be claimed as a right by the asylum seeker. The right to a refugee status does not exist. It is the prerogative of the government of asylum to grant it.

However, in order to protect the asylum seeker against expulsion, the principle of '*non-refoulement*' is included in Art. 33 (1) of the 1951 Convention whereby it is provided that,

> No contracting state shall expel or return ('refouler') a refugee in any manner whatsoever to the frontiers of territories where his life or freedom would be threatened on account of his race, religion, nationality, membership of a particular social group or political opinion.

The principle of 'non-refoulement' does not apply to refugees for

> . . . whom there are reasonable grounds for regarding as a danger to the security of the country in which he is or who having been convicted by a final judgement of a particularly serious crime, constitutes a danger to the community of that country.
>
> (Art. 33 (2) of the Convention)

Like granting of asylum, it is the government whose borders have been crossed which decides whether the refugee in question 'constitutes a danger to the community of that country' or not.

Because the Organization of African Unity (OAU) felt that there were some aspects that were specific to the problem of African refugees not explicitly covered by the 1951 Convention, it passed in 1969 a regional supplementary Convention known as the 'OAU Convention Governing the Specific Aspects of the Problem of Refugees in Africa'. (Art. VIII (2) specifically states that 'the present convention shall be the effective regional complement in Africa of the 1951 United Nations Convention on the status of refugees'.) Owing to the restrictive nature of the definitions of the term refugee in the UN Convention, the OAU tried to overcome this restriction by adding to the definition adopted by the UN Convention the following clause,

> Every person who, owning to external aggression, occupation, foreign domination or events seriously disturbing public order in either part or the whole of his country of origin or nationality is compelled to leave his place of habitual residence in order to seek refuge in another outside his country of origin or nationality.
>
> (Art. 1 (2) of the OAU Convention)

Unlike the UN Convention, this definition is extended to include people who flee from war or disturbance and seek refuge outside their country. A refugee under the OAU Convention is not required to prove 'well founded fear of persecution'. It is enough that his country is subjected to foreign 'aggression, occupation, domination' or there are 'events' that result in serious public disorder. This is an objective criterion. The OAU Convention does not provide the right of asylum either. However, the principle of '*non-refoulement*' which was already laid down in the UN 1951 Convention was included. (Art. II (3)) of the OAU Convention) Like in the UN Convention, the OAU Convention also leaves the determination of the status of refuge to the discretion of the 'contracting state'. (Art. I (6) of the OAU Convention)

THE PROBLEM OF REFUGEES IN AFRICA

Until the 1960s Europe and Asia were the major producers of refugees. There were few refugees in Africa for most of the continent was then under relatively stable colonial rule. The phenomenon of refugees was seen by the international community as a European problem and it is for this reason that almost all of the international instruments concerning refugees were specifically designed to meet the need of European refugees. Refugees were also viewed as a transitory problem to be solved on a case by case basis. Since the 1960s, however, the focus has shifted to the Third World, especially to Africa where up to 50% of the world's refugees and internally displaced people are found. (See Table 1.1)

TABLE 1.1 Estimated Distribution of Refugees (1981) and Internally Displaced Persons by Regions.

Region	Refugees	Internally Displaced Persons	Total	Per cent of total
Africa	3,589,340	2,735,000	6,324,340	50.0
Asica & Oceania	1,994,500	170,000	2,164,500	17.1
Latin America	189,600	50,000	239,000	1.9
ME & SE Asia	1,962,200	1,600,000	3,563,000	28.2
Europe	354,600	–	354,600	2.8
Total	8,090,240	4,555,000	12,646,040	100.0

Source: Adepoju, *Refugees in Africa, Problems and Prospects,* 1984.

At the heart of the African refugee problem is the violation of human rights, and it is an amazing fact that the overwhelming majority of African refugees are produced by the independent African states. There are now about 6,324,340 refugees and internally displaced persons in Africa. Out of this figure about 2,662,700 are refugees, a large minority of whom (45%) come from Ethiopia and are to be found mainly in Somalia (700,000), Sudan (460,000) and Djibouti (35,000) (*Refugees,* 1983).

The causes of mass movements in Africa have varied across history—from civil wars caused by internal strife as in the Congo (Zaire), Sudan, Chad, Nigeria and Uganda, to wars of national liberation as in Algeria, Guinea Bissau, Angola, Mozambique, Zimbabwe, Eritrea, Namibia and Western Sahara, to national oppression as in Burundi, Rwanda and South Africa.

Out of the total number of displaced people in Africa, about 43% are internally displaced. Internal displacement tends to be caused mainly by natural disasters such as drought, flood, severe food shortages and shortages of water for human consumption and animal husbandry, but it can also be caused by armed conflicts and wars of liberation. A recent ECA (Economic

Comission for Africa) Conference of Ministers on Africa's economic and social crisis stated:

> The emergency situation . . . aggravated the movement of persons in search for food and water. Water for human consumption and animal husbandry, particularly in the rural areas, has been drastically reduced as the result of the drought. Wells and boreholes which support the livelihood of thousands of small communities have dried up.
>
> Quoted in Adedeji, 1984

In the post-World War II period, the problem of refugees was overcome either by voluntary repatriation, local integration or by resettlement in third countries. The demand for labor in the US and Oceana led to the resettlement of many refugees. The need for reconstruction and rehabilitation of the ravaged European economies and infrastructures also created a demand for labor which enabled the spontaneously settled refugees to integrate themselves into the host communities.

Such opportunities do not exist in today's world. Furthermore, most of the African countries face severe economic and social crises caused by drought, epidemics, inadequate water supplies, food shortages, underdeveloped physical and social infrastructures, and severe shortages of foreign exchange due to declining productivity, the deteriorating terms of trade and the increasing external public debt and debt service payments. Most of the African countries cannot meet their own development needs, yet many of them have to provide for hundreds of thousands of refugees and returnees. About 80% of African refugees are hosted by countries that are classified by the UN as least developed. Most of these countries have overstretched their already inadequate economic and social infrastructures and are unable to absorb the large refugee populations into their labor force or to feed them.

Solutions for Refugees

Traditionally there have been three solutions to the problem of refugees—voluntary repatriation to the country of origin, settlement in the country of first asylum, and resettlement in a second country of asylum. There is no doubt that voluntary repatriation is the most durable and most desirable solution. However, voluntary repatriation should occur only when the root causes of refugees are eliminated (*see* Kibreab, 1983). Africa has a considerable history of voluntary repatriation. For example, following the achievement of national independence by the former Portuguese colonies of Guinea Bissau, Angola and Mozambique, hundreds of thousands were voluntarily repatriated to their countries of origin. In 1979-80, after amnesty was declared by the Zairian Government, about 190,000 refugees voluntarily returned from neighboring countries. In 1980 about 200,000 refugees returned to Zimbabwe following independence. A program of voluntary repatriation of Ethiopian refugees from Djibouti began in 1983. These large numbers of returnees are evidence of African refugees' strong desire to return to their homeland when the cause of flight is eliminated.

The second most durable solution to the problem of African refugees is local integration of the refugees into the host society. This can be done either by creating organized settlements or by letting the refugees settle spontaneously among the local population. African countries of asylum in collaboration with the United Nations High Commissioner for Refugees (UNHCR) and non-governmental organizations (NGOs) establish organized rural refugee settlements which provide the refugees with land. Administrative input comes from the host governments; physical and social infrastructural services are provided by the UNHCR and NGOs, and food rations by the World Food Program (WFP) during the establishment period. Where there is adequate land, the transfer of refugees to agricultural settlement schemes gives refugees the opportunity to become self-supporting; it also can prevent the generation of a dependent refugee mentality which can stifle the refugees' productive capacity. Furthermore, if properly planned and successful, settlement projects can reduce the burden imposed on the local population, the host government and the international community, as well as generate spillover effects at a regional level which can create additional opportunities for both the refugees and the local population. Through the provision of capital for investment by the international organizations, refugee settlements can also develop of an underdeveloped and neglected area which may contribute to the development of the region as a whole.

The third traditional solution to the refugee problem is resettlement in a third country. Some countries admit refugees on the basis of annual quotas. However, it seems that these countries prefer to admit refugees from certain areas, especially Eastern Europe and South East Asia. (See Melander, 1982, 36) Resettlement in a second country of asylum has been a major solution for the post-war European refugees and recently for the South-East Asian refugees, but it has been either non-existent or exceptional for African refugees. The American Refugee Resettlement Program is accepting Ethiopian and Eritrean refugees from the Sudan for resettlement. However, compared to the total number of these refugees in Sudan (three-quarters of a million), an insignificant number are affected by this program (See Table 1.2).

STUDYING ERITREAN REFUGEES

This book is a study of the second option—the settlement of refugees in the first country of asylum. One of the most ambitious programs to settle refugees locally with the aim of enabling them to become self-supporting is being carried out in Eastern Sudan in Kassala Province. This book is an assessment of that program. It highlights some of the complex problems of linking refugee

TABLE 1.2. Resettlement of Ethiopian and Eritrean Refugees in Third Countries of Asylum 1981-March 1983.

Country of Resettlement	Number of Refugees
U.S.A.	1,495
Canada	27
FRG	52
UK	4
Sweden	63
Switzerland	8
Denmark	1
Somalia	5
Norway	1
	Total 1,656

Source: UNHCR Branch Office, Khartoum, 1983.

assistance with development and of creating structures that can enable refugees to become self-sufficient and reduce or eliminate the financial and managerial burden on host governments and international donor agencies. Furthermore, since such settlement programs exist in a number of African countries, this study may provide a useful comparison.

This study looks at the rural land settlements of Eritrean refugees in the Kassala Province in the period 1967-1983. In particular, it assesses the land settlements' progress to date by identifying the factors and problems that affect their performance, such as the host government's policies, the socio-economic backgrounds of the refugees, their opportunity to participate in decisionmaking processes, and the households' resource base—land, labor and capital.

We have tried to follow the refugees from their areas of origin to the settlements. This is because of our belief that the refugees' socioeconomic backgrounds, the problems confronted during flight and life in the transit camps are important factors that can influence their economic performance in the settlements. However, it must be admitted here that the refugees' life in the transit camps received only marginal treatment and that this is because firstly, the majority of the refugees in the six villages of Qala en Nahal were transferred to the permanent settlements without delay and secondly, we wanted to give more space and time to the refugees' socioeconomic situation in the settlements.

Out of the 14 land settlements inhabited mainly by Eritrean refugees, six villages were selected systematically: Umsaqata, Umbrush, Dehema and Adingrar from the six villages in Qala en Nahal, and Aburakham and Wad Awad outside of the Qala en Nahal area. In particular, we examined:

1. The demographic characteristics and occupational structure of the refugee households.

2. Land availability, population density, land use, climate, soil, rainfall, the methods of maintaining soil fertility and land tenure. We paid special attention to the organizational aspects of land distribution and to the level of economic differentiation within the framework of the existing legal restrictions in regard to land possession. The refugees are by law prohibited from owning land and immovable property.

3. The availability and utilization of family labor, and the way farm households organize their family labor among the different tasks.

4. Mechanization and its impact on the achievement of self-sufficiency. The ability of the farm households to generate the necessary management and technical skill and to accumulate capital for the maintenance and replacement of the agricultural machinery and for new investments.

5. Distribution of income among the settlers and the components of total income, namely income from sorghum, sesame, wage labor, trade, remittance, assistance. This is important in order to see the level of income in refugee households and to see the significance of the non-farm income-generating activities.

On the basis of our findings, we look in depth at the economic viability of the settlements.

The problem of refugees in Africa almost always involves enormous human suffering, and it calls for immediate action. It is hoped that this book will contribute to making that action informed and sensitive to the needs of refugees and affected local populations.

(For a detailed account of the research methodology used, see Appendix 1.)

CHAPTER 2

Eritreans Flee To Sudan

Towards the end of the 1960s, the Eritrean countryside, especially the western lowlands, was subjected to severe violence often deliberately directed against the civilian population and their means of subsistence—mainly their livestock. Towards the end of the 1960s and early 1970s, the eastern lowlands were also subjected to pacification campaigns by the Ethiopian army which resulted in serious losses of lives and property. Later, during the 1970s, especially the mid-1970s, practically the whole of Eritrea, including all the cities, was affected, and there was more devastating damage to both lives and property. The result of such violence was that thousands of people were forced to leave their villages either temporarily or permanently. Some hid themselves in caves and trenches during the day time and worked on their farms during the night in the moonlight. Others remained in their villages despite the threat. Others moved to less affected areas (internal displacement), yet others crossed into the Sudan to seek protection.

This chapter argues that although wars, political persecution, and the violation of human rights are the major causes underlying the flight of refugees, flight is not just a physical reaction to actual or perceived threat of violence or persecution. Whether people become refugees or stay in their country of origin is determined by an inter-play of structural and socio-cultural factors. Some refugees have no choice but to flee or to lose their lives. For the majority, however, flight involves a deliberate decision based on comparisons between alternatives. (*See* Hansen: 1982, 190) When groups or individuals are threatened, they tend to weigh alternative measures against each other and to decide either to face the consequences or to leave their country of origin. An empirical study of the socioeconomic background of those Eritreans who, despite the threat of death or persecution, decided not to flee and of those who did decide to flee, reveals that the decisions were not determined randomly. The aim of this chapter is therefore to identify the different groups that were affected by the war and to attempt to explain the structural and socio-cultural factors that either countervailed or reinforced their flight. The main reinforcing and countervailing factors appear to be first, the distance to the possible country of asylum; second, the conditions of existence in the affected peoples' places of origin, and third, the perceived conditions of existence in a nearby country of asylum.

THE FLIGHT BEGINS—1967

The first refugees came to the Sudan in February-March 1967. Most of these refugees were pastoralists, but some were agropastoralists whose means of subsistence mainly depended on livestock herding. They were exclusively Moslems from the Beni Amer and Maria ethnic groups.

The Eritrean Liberation Front (ELF) took to arms in September 1961 in the western lowlands (Fig. 2.1). According to the village elders, some of the youth around Tokombia (the place of origin for some of the refugees) started to join the front from 1963 onwards. Some of them secretly visited their villages to recruit new fighters and collect contributions. They also came to Tokombia to buy commodities for the ELF. This was reported to the army headquarters in Barentu which in 1967 dispatched a unit to Tókombia. The troops marched

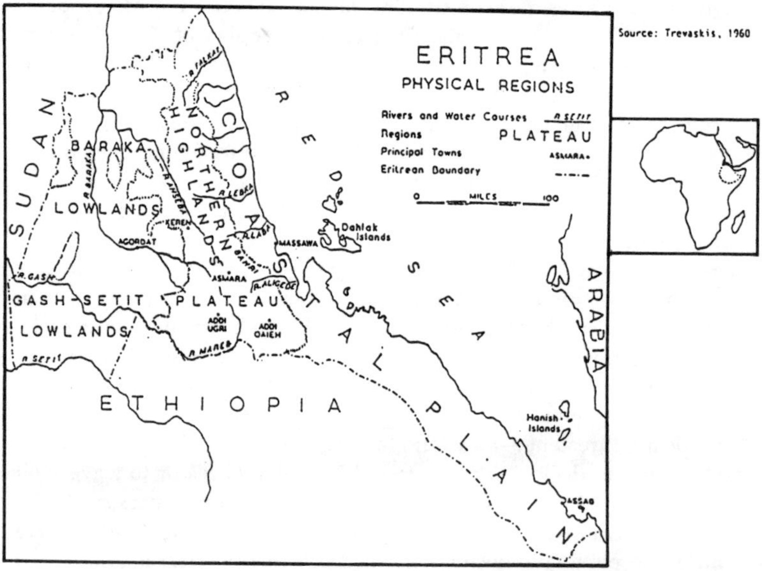

Figure 2.1

into Ad-Ibrahim, a village near Tokombia, and killed about 42 people and burned the village to the ground. Then they returned to Tokombia and called the *sheikhs* (village leaders) to a meeting and killed ten of them. This killing and burning created panic and most of the people in Tokombia and the surrounding region fled to the Sudan. According to the village elders, this news spread throughout the Gash area with a 'lightning speed' and most of the people in the area fled to the Sudan. The refugees gathered in a transit camp called Genre near Mount Galsa in the outskirts of Kassala, Sudan.

> According to Sudanese Goverment estimates about 7000 Eritrean nationalists who demanded self-determination for Eritrea had fled to the Sudan up to mid March as a result of military operations carried out by the Ethiopian government in Eritrea.
> (Keesing Contemporary Archives: June 24-July 1, 1967, 22104A)

Most of the refugees were women, children and old men of semi-nomadic origin (Holsborn: 1975, 1337). In February 1967, the Ethiopian Emperor, Haile Selassie, visited the Sudan and an agreement on the Eritrean refugees was reached with the Government of Sudan. At the end of his visit,

> . . . it was announced that both governments had reaffirmed their adherence to the treaties governing the boundaries between the two countries and had agreed to conclude a treaty on refugees, which would give the latter the option of repatriation or removal from the frontier.
> (Keesing Contemporary Archives, June 24-July 1, 1967, 22194 A)

Following this agreement, six temporary camps were set up in May 1967, south of the city of Kassala to accommodate a total of 25,503 refugees. (See Karadawi: 1977, 100)

According to the refugees, the military attacks tended to occur during daytime when most of the livestock were not present in the villages and were therefore not seriously affected. Those refugees whose flights were less dramatic managed to take their livestock with them to the Sudan, while the rest of the animals were later taken to the Sudan by people who remained behind. There were also many refugee families who were forced to abandon their livestock and who fled with only the clothes they were wearing at the time.

Besides people of the Beni Amer and Maria groups, there were also some people from the Saho national group who fled to the Sudan after this first group. However, these Saho people had been living in the western lowlands when they fled the country, having migrated to the western lowlands with their livestock when their villages in the eastern lowlands were subjected to repression. In the western lowlands, they settled in four villages called Sanda Lauda, Hamed shekai Mai Anbesa and Koroken in the western lowlands. In

December 1966, the Ethiopian army set fire to the first three villages and killed 27 civilians.

The village elders stated that the rest of the population fled to the mountains, leaving the dead bodies and livestock behind. Later the army established two 'strategic hamlets' in Shambko and Bushuka, into which all the peasants and the pastoralists were to be herded. The army ordered them to join the 'hamlets' lest they face the danger of being wiped out by air raids. The people had no choice but to comply. After they had gathered, the army forcibly removed them to the towns of Ginda, Massawa, Adikeyih and others which were wrongly believed to be their places of origin . (These were rural people who were residents of the province of Samhar and Eastern Akeluguzai, not of the cities to which they were forcibly taken.) They were not allowed to take their livestock with them. During the initial phase, the Ethiopian Government supplied them with food, but probably owing to lack of housing, health services and food, an epidemic broke out and many died. The rest fled in small groups to the western lowlands and temporarily settled in the vicinity of Agordat and at Obel in upper Barka. They were again subjected to violence and forced to flee to the Sudan in 1967. They joined the other refugees in Genre near Mount Galsa outside Kassala, where they subsisted on rations provided by UNHCR.

News of the military operations that led to the uprooting of thousands of people rarely reached the rest of the world, but sometimes it did. The Swedish evening paper, *Aftonbladet*, for instance, stated on March 13, 1969:

> In Eritrea, which has been united with Ethiopia since 1952 in what the Eritreans consider an unpopular federation, a guerilla war has been in progress for many years. There are rumors of napalm bombs being dropped in the area along the Sudan border, of brutal repressions by the Government, of people being forcibly moved from their homes, and of pacified villages.
>
> (Aftonbladet 13.3 1969)

Another newspaper, *Svenska Dagbladet,* also reported that:

> The activities of the Eritrean Army of Liberation have caused Ethiopia to bomb the area, mainly villages in rural areas which are controlled by the liberation movement, and the population has been forced to flee over the border into Sudan.
>
> (Sv.D. 24.4 1969)

It was further noted in the same paper that:

> On several occasions Addis Ababa has attacked the civil population

> from the air. About 30,000 civilian Eritreans have fled over the border to the Sudan.
>
> (S.D. 27.4 1969)

The cause of flight of these refugees was also succinctly stated by the commissioner of Kassala province in the Sudan:

> As a result of the sweeping operations against villages near the border near Kassala, large numbers of Eritreans crossed the border in order to escape the looting and destruction caused by Ethiopian army'.
>
> (Quoted in Karadawi: 1977, 98)

It would have been interesting to find out the proportion of the people who fled compared to those who remained in their place of origin, but due to lack of statistics this cannot be done.

THE SECOND INFLUX—1969

Towards the end of the 1960s, guerrilla activities were intensified along the eastern lowlands and Eastern Akeleguzai. In 1969 a partial curfew was imposed by the Ethiopian army, of whose total strength of 40,000, about two-thirds was employed in Eritrea.

At this time refugees were mostly from Semhar and Di-ot in Eastern Akeleguzai. In April and May 1970, these areas were subjected to infantry and air raids that led to the death of many civilians. The refugees were mainly Saho pastoralists and when they went to wells for water for their livestock and themselves, they became an easy target for air and military attacks. It was also claimed that the Ethiopian army was poisoning wells. News and rumors about these incidents spread throughout the area and the people fled to escape the imminent perceived danger. Their flight took different forms. Some walked from their villages to Ginda and took a bus to Aligidir outside Tessenei near the Sudanese border. Others walked or travelled by camel all the way to the Sudan. Those from Aligidir went to Wadhileu in the Sudan. Others went to Tokar, Port Sudan and Kassala. Many stayed in sheds outside Kassala for six months and some of them were later transferred to the Rahad river. In October 1970, the latter group was transported to Umzurzur, Umbrush and Adingrar in Qala en Nahal.

THE THIRD INFLUX—1970

This category of refugees, although relatively few in number, mainly came from the villages around Keren following the massacre of hundreds of innocent civilians including women and children in 1970. Towards the end of the 1960s, the Ethiopian troops, as we noted earlier, had launched a pacification campaign. The villagers were forcibly moved from 'sensitive' areas and herded into heavily guarded larger villages known as 'strategic hamlets'. In order to discourage them from returning, their villages were burned down. In order to frustrate the campaign, the ELF launched a counter-offensive by destroying five bridges and the railway communication between Massawa and Tessenei.

In 1971 Professor Knutsson from the University of Stockholm was doing fieldwork in Eritrea, studying land tenure in the countryside. After witnessing the atrocities committed against the civilian peasantry, he decided to interrupt his research and write about what he saw for the Swedish daily, *Dagens Nyheter*. According to his report, a skirmish between the ELF and the Ethiopian army near Keren was followed by the massacre of the population of a nearby village. After the retreat of the ELF unit, he reported,

> . . . a village in the immediate vicinity of Keren met its Song My. 460 corpses of women and children were counted when people from the neighboring area after two days dared to enter the ruins to bury the dead.
>
> (Knutssons: DN 1971)

In mentioning Song My, Knutsson is referring to the massacre of five to six hundred peasants in Vietnam by American soldiers on March 16, 1968. He further notes that about ten villages were burned and thousands of people lost their means of subsistence. In another incident not far from this site, villagers gathered in a mosque to hide from an air attack, but the army sealed the mosque and killed hundreds of them. These incidents are not the only ones that occurred; they are simply some of the few that reached the world press.

Despite these gruesome atrocities, only a small number of people from around Keren fled to the Sudan. In this area, sedentary farming is the dominant basis of subsistence and the inhabitants are overwhelmingly Bilen.

FLEEING THE DERGUE—1974-75

In September 1974, the Ethiopian Emperor, Haile Selassie, was overthrown and power passed into the hands of the Provisional Military Council (PMC), known as the Dergue. One of the measures the PMC undertook upon seizing power was to act forcefully against the Eritrean movements. In October 1974, a dusk-to-dawn curfew was imposed on the city of Asmara and a number of military incidents were reported in the vicinity of the city. In December a number of civilians were found strangled with steel wire. They were thought to have been killed by army units for suspected contact with the ELF.

The PMC pursued repressive measures, while speaking publicly of resolving the Eritrean problem through peaceful means. On December 28, the Ethiopian Minister of Information together with the Minister of Commerce and others started talks with 345 Eritrean representatives in Asmara. But these talks were discontinued. The Eritrean representatives forwarded certain demands at the resumed talks which proved to be incompatible with the offer made by the PMC. (The demands forwarded by the Eritrean representatives were (a) the withdrawal of the Ethiopian army from the city of Asmara to their barracks: (b) genuine negotiations with the representatives of the rebels, whom the Eritrean representatives regarded as the sole representatives of the Eritrean people; (c) cancellation of the students' campaign as far as Eritrea was concerned; (d) release of all political prisoners; (e) publication, in the national press in Addis Ababa, of full information on the current negotiations and the situation in Eritrea. The representatives also called for a referendum to be held on Eritrea's future and for official discussions of the province's status before international organizations. In contrast, the PMC offer was limited to (a) giving the Eritrean representatives authority to make contact with the fronts; (b) an order to soldiers to exercise maximum restraint; (c) a promise to review the cases of all political prisoners; (d) the issue of special instructions to people taking part in the students' campaign and, (e) an assurance that all subsequent talks between government representatives and prominent Eritreans would include religious and community leaders. **Note:** Immediately after its seizure of political power in 1974, the provisional Military Government proclaimed a student campaign (Amharic-Zemetcha), whereby all students in the university, colleges and in the senior high schools (above grade 10) were sent to the countryside to 'educate the masses' for a period of two years.)

Despite its limited attempts at peaceful negotiation, on December 18, 1974 the PMC announced its decision to 'eliminate those who fight against the unity of the country'. This declaration marked the end of peaceful attempts to resolve the Eritrean conflict. To forestall the Government's offensive, some guerrilla units infiltrated the city of Asmara and attacked military posts. 'On February 2, the Ethiopian Air Force began to raid guerrilla strongholds in villages around Asmara' (Keesing's March 24-30, 1975, 27031). All journalists were banned from Eritrea. Moreover,

> church and relief workers estimated that over 1600 people had been killed and thousands more wounded, while Eritrean community and religious leaders continued to accuse government troops of committing acts of atrocity and terror against civilians. Some 16,000 refugees were accommodated in camps set up by church workers.
>
> (Keesing's: op.cit., 27032)

On February 15, 1975, the state of emergency was extended to cover the whole of Eritrea. Almost all of the military activities were concentrated in the Eritrean highlands, and the populations there were subjected to unprecedented forms of violence. Mary Dines, from War on Want (a British humanitarian organization), who visited Eritrea during this period noted:

> On the morning of 13th March, 1975, a group of 300 Ethiopian soldiers on their way from Asmara to Keren passed through the village of Woki (population about 2500) at 7 a.m. They rounded up the villagers on a piece of waste ground and shot 37 dead. After this, most of the people fled into the hills, but the rest, believing there was nowhere safe to go or that nothing else would happen, remained.
>
> (Dines: 1980)

According to her, the troops also killed a number of people in Woki on March 14, 1975. She also states that the army 'killed all the livestock and set fire to the houses'. Dines gives further examples of villages, farms and livestock being destroyed. 'In the summer of 1975,' she states, '110 people in the village of Wokiduba were herded into an orthodox church and massacred'.

Despite these gruesome atrocities, few peasants from the Eritrean highlands crossed into the Sudan to seek refuge. We shall try to explain this later. However, it must be mentioned here that sedentary farming has been the basis of subsistence in these areas for hundreds of years and over 90% of the population is Christian.

On March 3, 1975, Um Hajer, a small town near the Sudanese border, was set on fire and practically all the residents of Um Hajer, Golouj, Garguf, Shunuteshreb, Aligidir and other nearby towns and villages fled to Hafir and Hamdait on the Sudanese side of the border. After 20 days they were transferred to Wad Hileu, a transit camp not very far from the border. The attack on Um Hajer was so sudden that it caught the residents unawares, and very few of them had time to take property with them. One of them described their flight as 'flight in blind panic'. The total number of the refugees who crossed into the Sudan from these areas was estimated in May 1975 to be about 40,000.

What is most interesting for us here is why these areas, unlike the highlands, produced 40,000 refugees as a result of one week's repression, while the highlands, despite repeated acts of repression, produced few or no refugees at all. This is a question we will look at in depth a little further on.

MORE REFUGEES FROM FIGHTING—1977

The ELF launched an offensive on April 4, 1977 to capture Tessenei, succeeding in doing so on April 6. Many of the residents fled to the Gash area. They fled suddenly and took no property with them, so the ELF had to provide them with relief assistance. After a while this placed a serious strain on the

ELF's meager resources and the leadership of the Front advised the displaced persons to cross into the Sudan temporarily.

The refugees arrived at Kassala on April 8, 1977 and were later transferred to Qala en Nahal on May 25, 1977, mainly to Umbrush. The majority in this category were urban refugees, whose basis of existence was mainly wage labor. Most of them worked on the cotton plantation of Aligidir and on other farms.

THE FINAL GROUP—1978

By 1977 the national liberation movements controlled the Eritrean countryside as well as most of the cities, except Asmara, Assab, Barentu and part of Massawa. In 1978, however, the Ethiopian forces fully backed by the Soviet Union, carried out a large-scale counter-offensive to recapture the Eritrean cities and towns. Napalm and cluster bombs were used against towns held by the liberation fronts, and,

> According to the ELF-RC there were, at the end of April, 115,000 Ethiopian troops ready for an offensive comprising 30,000 men (with 100 armored vehicles and 35 tanks) at Adowa (80 miles south of Asmara, Eritrea's capital which was besieged by secessionist forces), 30,000 men poised to attack the Barentu area (75 miles west of Asmara), 15,000 near Humera (on the Sudanese border, 160 miles southwest of Asmara) and 40,000 men deployed against Decamere (20 miles south of Asmara).
>
> (Keesing's Contemporary Archives: December 15, 1978, 29356)

During July and August 1978 the offensive resulted in the recapture of most of the towns which had been controlled by the liberation movements. It made 122,000 people homeless, some of whom had crossed into the Sudan but most of whom remained in Eritrea.

The withdrawal of the liberation movements from the cities and towns was accompanied by mass internal displacements and flight across the border. Those who crossed into the Sudan in large numbers were mainly from the border towns of Um Hajer, Tessenei, Aligidir, Golouj, Haikota, and others. A smaller number of refugees were also reported to have left Agordat, Barentu and the surrounding areas to enter the Sudan. The overwhelming majority of the residents of the highland cities such as Mendefera, Dekemhare, Adi Qala, Segeneiti and others were internally displaced and did not cross into the Sudan.

These six groups could generally be said then to represent the major refugee influx in the Sudan during the period of our concern, 1967-1983. However, the inflow of urban refugees still continues unabated and, from 1984 to the present day, drought and famine in Eritrea has driven many thousands of Eritreans into the Sudan.

DECIDING TO FLEE

There are important differences between refugees and normal immigrants, therefore most theories of migration cannot be applied to refugee movements without some modification. Most importantly, the decision to migrate is based on the desire to positively improve one's conditions of existence. In contrast, the decision to flee is based on the desire to escape from drastically deteriorating conditions of existence. In essence, emigration is a movement *towards something perceived to be better and attractive,* while flight is a movement *away from something perceived to be dangerous or expulsive.* An emigrant, for instance, leaves his place of origin as a result of a deliberate decision and leaves for a definite area of destination. He is often 'pushed' by lack of income-generating opportunities (if the cause of migration is economic or social pressure) in his place of origin and/or is 'pulled' by perceived or actual better earning opportunities or a more positive atmosphere in the area of destination. Refugees, on the other hand, are forced to leave their country of origin by forces external to themselves (see Fig. 2.2). Their move is involuntary, and this is what distinguishes them from immigrants. (Bernard: 1976; Kunz: 1973; Prins: 1955; Murphy: 1955; Kolaja: 1952; Etinger: 1973; Petersen: 1958)

An emigrant tends to be confronted with alternative options—to stay, to move to another place within his country or to emigrate. This introduces a considerable deliberation and voluntariness into the decision. In contrast, a refugee tends to be confronted with a very restricted set of alternatives, which narrows the scope for deliberation and voluntariness. (See Fig. 2.2)

Most migration theories are based on the so-called 'push-pull' factors, in which the motivations to migrate are inferred from structural factors. This model is not adequate to enable us to describe and explain refugee movements. (See Taylor: 1969, 99.) Deteriorating socioeconomic conditions at the place of origin constitute the 'push' factors, while perceived or actual socioeconomic conditions at the place of destination constitute the 'pull' factors. *Improvement of socioeconomic conditions is believed to be the driving force behind people's decision to abandon their place of origin in favor of new temporary or permanent residence.*

In the case of refugees, deteriorating political conditions, which may actually or probably lead to the destruction of lives and property or to political persecution at the place of origin, are factors that force people to flee. The refugee's immediate concern is to find a country where his or her life will be safe. Therefore, the 'pull' factor is either minimal or totally absent at the time of the decisionmaking.

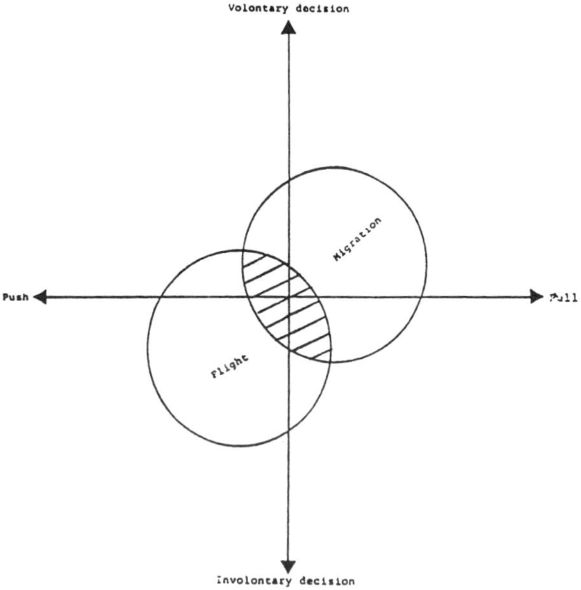

Figure 2.2

But how external to him are the forces that set the refugee in motion? Does the refugee retain any residual power to decide whether or not to flee when exposed to a situation which to his judgement constitutes a serious danger to his safety? Or is his power of decisionmaking proportionally reduced with the intensity of the outside force or pressure applied? If the flight of refugees can be perceived as a sheer physical response to external pressures, why do some people flee while others do not? Does not the fact that people in extreme situations adapt different strategies imply the presence of some kind of residual power? The decision to flee or to stay must be conditioned also by factors other than the intensity of the pressure applied.

According to E.F. Kunz, 'It is the reluctance to uproot oneself and the absence of positive original motivations to settle elsewhere which characterizes all refugee decisions . . .' (Kunz: 1973, 130) There seems much that is sound in this description. But the problem arises when Kunz extends his argument and compares 'acute refugee movements' with the movement of a billiard ball, which is characterized by

> . . . a singular absence of self-propelling inner forces. Their progress more often than not resembles the movement of the billiard ball: devoid

of inner direction, their path is governed by the kinetic factors of inertia, friction and the vectors of outside forces applied on them.

(Kunz: op.cit., 132)

Kunz believes that an inner self-propelling force is absent in refugee movements. But does the lack of 'positive original motivation to settle elsewhere' imply an absence of an intention and will to flee in the face of an ensuing or perceived danger? The positive desire to settle elsewhere may be absent, but cannot the intention to flee still be present, without having the motivations to settle elsewhere and despite the reluctance to uproot?

A distinction has to be drawn between the intention to flee and the desire to accept the consequence of such an act which often turns out to be temporary or permanent settlement elsewhere. It is difficult to determine whether the refugee who chooses flight as a survival strategy is at the time of decisionmaking aware of the consequences of his or her act, i.e., whether or not his state of mind at that time includes an awareness that his action may bring about an undesired consequence—settlement elsewhere and hence social uprooting. In resorting to flight, the involuntary migrant often believes and hopes that his flight will come to an end soon and is, no doubt, mentally opposed to uprooting and 'settlement elsewhere'. But that does not alter the fact that he has, to save his life, taken the risk of being uprooted and of being temporarily or permanently settled elsewhere despite the strong reluctance to uproot.

In any case, flight is a physical expression of the refugees' feeling of relative helplessness and powerlessness to protect themselves against persecution, moral insult, physical assault and so on. However, both the perceived powerlessness in the face of a stronger enemy and the perceived danger represented by an approaching outside force involve some uncertainty—hence both are partly subjective judgements. The would-be refugee cannot predict with certainty how troops will behave towards him unless he or other members of his community have experienced violence before from the same military force. Hansen, in his study of Angolan refugees in Zambia, argues that . . . refugees are people who choose to leave and are successful in doing so. Their flight is neither automatic nor inevitable'. He further notes that 'although some people flee in blind panic without any forethought . . . to most refugees, flight and the destination are chosen as the result of more deliberation'. (Hansen: 1982, 190)

The author, himself a refugee, lived under extreme conditions with his friends who were in the same predicament in Eritrea in 1975. To be a youth and an Eritrean in Asmara was at that time very dangerous. Most of us were aware of the danger that awaited us if we fell into the hands of the security forces. Yet, only a few of us chose flight as the only viable strategy for survival (though many others followed later). There were some who remained behind due to political commitments, there were others who remained behind with no political commitments but conscious of the risk of being liquidated (several of them were, in fact, killed), and there were others who joined the liberation movements. This variation in response—(especially among those who thought that the risk of staying was higher than the risk of leaving, and among those who did not have other reasons, political or social, to outweigh the risk of staying)—was not due to different evaluation of the danger of staying, but rather was due to an interplay of various subjective and objective factors which were important at the time of decisionmaking. When we discussed our situation, all of us agreed that our safety depended on flight, but when it came to deciding to leave, we found various excuses to rationalize our unwillingness to be uprooted, even if we were aware of the fact that staying could entail death. (It should be noted that since most of the Eritrean cities under the Ethiopian forces were sealed, exit was severely restricted and escape at times involved higher immediate risk. A person caught while fleeing was severely punished and sometimes killed. It is possible that this fact might have deterred some from fleeing.)

One is struck by the similarity of the state of mind that precedes the decision whether or not to flee that exists among would-be anticipatory refugees. (Anticipatory refugees are those who 'leave their home country with transport prepaid and with a knowledge of destination before the military or political situation prevents orderly departure'. In our case we were anticipatory, not in the sense that we left our country with transport pre-paid before the deterioration of the situation, but because we had a clear knowledge of our destination. But still we were very uncertain about our safe arrival) S.A. Prins, describing the circumstances and the state of mind that existed in himself and his friends during the Nazi occupation of Holland, notes that,

> it is strange fact that of all my friends and acquaintances I was almost the only one who took the full consequences of quitting Holland . . . Doubtless many others knew what was going to happen just as well as I did, but I think a certain preparedness of mind was needed to make the decision.

He further notes that,

> I wanted to go away from the dangerous vicinity of the enemy, certainly, but in the first place I wanted to flee from myself. There existed a psychological coincidence of inner and outer causes which made flight an imperative necessity for me that others in a similar position did not feel. People who lacked this peculiar state of mind did not want to go, but found all sorts of excuses to delay their actual departure.
>
> (Prins: 1955, 25)

These two quotations show that the decision to flee in the case of anticipatory refugees is not a mere reaction to external forces. Individuals, no matter how pressured by forces outside themselves, exercise some degree of residual power that can enable them to decide whether or not to flee. (It should be noted that anticipatory refugees tend to be more educated urban dwellers.)

These two cases throw some light on the process of decisionmaking with regard to urban or individual refugees, but they represent a digression because they say little about the decisions behind mass flights, and most of the refugees in the rural settlements under study came as a result of a mass flight.

This being said, let us try to link this conceptual scheme to the actual experience of the Eritrean rural refugees in Eastern Sudan—the object of this study.

THE SAMPLE FAMILIES

The sample families were asked to identify the three major reasons for leaving Eritrea. The results are presented in Table 2.1 below.

As can be seen from Table 2.1, the major causes of flight reported by the refugees are fear of massacre, destruction of homes and villages and fear of air attack: 90% or 266 families gave fear of massacre as the major cause of flight, and 212 families also mentioned destruction of homes and villages. Fear of air attack was mentioned by 58 families. Only 19 families mentioned destruction of crops as constituting a cause, while four families mentioned mass behavior. This refers to those who fled their place of origin because they see others fleeing in blind panic without knowing the reason for flight. Out of the total sample, only three reported having abandoned their country in search of better economic opportunities in the Sudan. The two families out of the three are in Aburakham and their place of origin is not Eritrea but Tigrai in Northern

TABLE 2.1. Reasons for Leaving their Country.

Reasons	Number of times reasons mentioned by a sample of 294 household heads
Fear of air attack	58
Fear of massacre	266
Destruction of homes and villages	212
Destruction of crops	19
Mass behavior	4
To look for a job	3
Total of mentioned reasons	562

This table gives the number of causes mentioned, since the sample families could give up to three reasons.

Ethiopia. These people are best referred to as economic refugees. Only a few families named destruction of crops as a cause for leaving. This might be because the events that led to their flight occurred during the dry season (due to transportation problems, military movements usually occur during dry seasons), but it may imply that destruction of crops alone would not have resulted in their flight.

The majority has given 'fear of massacre' as one of the three major reasons for leaving. Whether this 'fear of massacre' is well founded cannot be determined objectively. Most of the refugees probably did not risk persecution as individuals, but were subjected to violence collectively.

The circumstances that prevailed during and after their flight are incontestably in keeping with the provision of the OAU and UN conventions governing refugee status. The reported reasons for leaving tell us, however, very little about the factors that enter into the decision to flee. Most of the refugees who were interviewed have been in the Sudan for more than ten years, and their memories are likely to be blurred and to focus on a certain dramatic event thus overlooking other factors that might have influenced their decision to flee. It is also very difficult to distinguish between what is stated as a reason for leaving and the actual reason. Due to these problems and to gain a deeper insight, we shall relate the reported motives with the structural factors that, directly or indirectly, seem to enter into the decision to cross borders with the aim of seeking asylum. A fuller understanding of the determinants of flight cannot be achieved without going beyond that which is stated by the refugees themselves.

ALTERNATIVES TO FLIGHT

Did the refugees have alternatives to flight? If so, could they have resorted to them, if they wished to, in the face of the perceived or actual danger to their lives?

If the violence or the perception of it were a necessary and sufficient cause for their flight, the response of the people in all of the affected areas would have been the same, i.e., all who were physically fit would have fled. That some areas produced very few refugees despite being exposed to similar military pressures as those areas that produced tens of thousands, indicates that real or perceived military violence was not a sufficient cause on its own for flight.

The alternatives to flight for the Eritrean rural refugees were several. First, the refugees adopting a 'wait and see' attitude could have stayed in their residence of origin. There were many who did that despite the risk it entailed. Second, they could have moved behind the lines of the liberation movement, i.e., to the base areas. Third, they could have migrated to the unaffected areas so as to escape detection by the army. Fourth, since the Ethiopian government was forcibly moving people to 'strategic hamlets' often established in the outskirts of various towns, the refugees could have obeyed such orders. Fifth, they could also have joined the liberation fronts. Flight was but one of six alternatives, therefore.

Why some groups resorted to one alternative and not another is a very difficult question. Possibly, it is determined by an interplay of various social, economic, political, geographic and military factors. Different individuals and groups attach different utilities and costs to different alternatives. Many variables enter into the decisionmaking process.

For people to stay in their place of origin, the commitment to their original environment must be so overwhelming as to induce them to accept the consequence of staying even if it be the cost of their lives. Resorting to the second alternative, i.e., moving behind the lines of the liberation front, is again a function of many variables. The front must have liberated areas and must be able to defend them and provide relief assistance to those who are displaced. Second, the civilian population must have confidence in the ability of the liberation front to defend it or must have the political commitment to accept the risk. Third, the liberation organization must have a policy that discourages people from resorting to flight or encourages people to stay in spite of the risk involved. Such opportunities and policies did not exist in the 1960s, and it was only after the birth and consolidation of the Eritrean People's Liberation Front (EPLF) that such an alternative developed fully. Then the areas where it operated (Northern Highlands) were, relatively speaking, the least refugee-producing areas despite their structural similarity to the Barka lowlands.

The third alternative, i.e., to move from their places of residence to less affected or unaffected areas, is also determined by the availability of such areas, by the willingness of the affected people to move and by the attitude of the people in the receiving areas. This in turn is a function of various objective obstacles and opportunities and the affected people's perception of such alternatives as a viable strategy for survival.

The fourth alternative, i.e., moving to 'strategic hamlets' established by the government, can only take place if the people do not politically sympathize with the national liberation movement, if they oppose the liberation movement and are too afraid of it to stay in their villages, if the government enforces a coercive policy of moving people from their areas of origin, or if the people, despite their sympathy with the liberation movement, do not see a better alternative.

This alternative was the least attractive to the Eritrean peasants and pastoralists, because they deemed it very unnatural to submit and move closer to what they believed to be the major cause of their disturbance and unrest. Many of those who were forcibly moved into such 'strategic villages', according to the elders, seized every opportunity to escape. Some succeeded, but others lost their lives. Removal from their habitual environment also meant loss of their means of livelihood—livestock and land.

Joining the liberation fronts instead of fleeing required serious political commitment and a certain degree of physical fitness which many of those who decided to flee possibly lacked, due to bad health, old age and poor nutritional status. The capacity of the fronts to accept new recruits, especially sudden influxes, might have been limited as well.

Whether the refugees chose the Sudan as a place of refuge or went there as a result of random movement is also difficult to determine. This question involves issues such as the distance to the border, the nature of the conditions that gave rise to flight and the amount of information that the community had about the country of destination. African refugee movements even under the most threatening pressure seem to follow a discernible pattern of movement and this is supported by the map showing where major refugee movements have occurred. (See Fig. 2.3)

Until the beginning of 1974, the Ethiopian government always denied the existence of a problem in Eritrea, therefore it is unlikely that it had a deliberate policy of wanting people to cross into the Sudan. Their presence in the Sudan would seem to embarrass the government and refute its claim to tranquility in Eritrea.

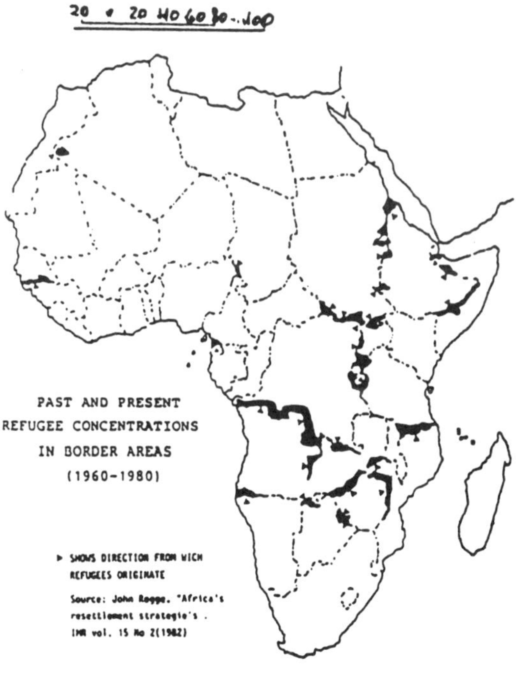

Figure 2.3

However it must be noted that the Ethiopian government could have a deliberate policy of chasing people out of the country and yet deny their existence or deny that it pursues such a policy. It can be argued that driving Eritreans into the Sudan was not only a direct consequence of its military actions but also part of its military policy. The Ethiopian government's military strategy against the guerrilla fronts was based upon the logic that since the guerrillas depend for food, water and information upon the peasantry, clearing the countryside of people could deprive the guerrillas of their lifeline. Hence, the government's military actions involved the forcible removal of people, the burning and bombing of villages, and the killing of civilians. The result of these actions was the destruction of lives and property, refugeeism, internal displacement and a disruption of normal rural life. This disruption had catastrophic economic and social consequences. Owing to air bombings, the peasantry could not grow crops. In the Barka lowland sowing has to take place within a few days after the first rains. If those days are not utilized, due to military operations or air attack, the annual crop is lost, leading to famine and mass dislocation. The military movements and air raids also had a negative effect on the ecosystem, often leading to accelerated erosion and overgrazing.

Naturally, the result of all this was, directly or indirectly, to force people to resort to flight. Whether the people affected crossed the borders or not was, as we shall show, conditioned by many other factors.

The Dynamics of Flight

As pointed out before, despite the whole Eritrean countryside being subjected to military pressure during different periods of time, not all the rural population became refugees. Responses to the external pressure included flight, internal displacement and remaining in the place of origin.

The refugees in the rural settlements in Eastern Sudan include people from the various geographical regions and national groups, but the overwhelming majority are the Tigre national group from the western lowlands and the Saho national group from the eastern lowlands, particularly Eastern Akeleguzai (See Fig. 2.4) The majority were pastoralists and to some extent agropastoralists. A considerable proportion of the refugees who were settled in Qala en Nahal in 1978-80 and of those in Aburakham and Wad Awad included people from the Tigrinya national group but their places of origin just before their flight were the border areas and not the Eritrean highlands. They had migrated to these areas in the late 1950s and throughout the 1960s in search of better economic opportunities. They were 'pushed' from the *Kebessa* region by shortage of cultivable land resulting from overpopulation, colonial land alienation, overfragmentation and unequal distribution coupled with soil erosion and decline in fertility.

That the majority of the Eritrean refugees in the settlements come from the western and eastern lowlands is very interesting and throws some light on our problem. The reason why the western and the eastern lowlands produced

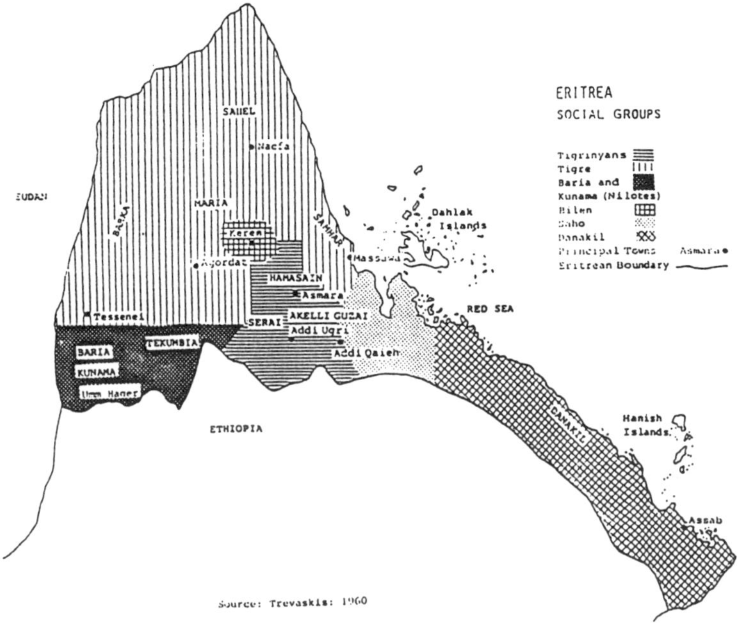

Figure 2.4

more refugees than the plateau, in spite of being exposed to similar severe violence, was not due to a different perception and evaluation of the danger involved, but was mainly due to other factors.

The western lowlands and later the eastern lowlands were the first areas to be affected by war, mainly because of the discriminatory policy pursued by the Ethiopian army whose aim was to divide the Eritreans along religious lines, but also because these areas, especially the western lowlands, were the birth place and center of military activities of the liberation movement during the 1960s and early 1970s. Later all Eritreans, irrespective of their ethnic identity or religion, became targets of periodic military and air attacks which often resulted in the destruction of lives and property.

Since the 'refugee' phenomenon, as Beijer points out, often 'conceals a great variety of reasons for flight' (Beijer: 1969, 18), the experience of different groups of refugees is likely to vary depending on the conditions that give rise to flight and the problems encountered on the way to the country of asylum. To throw some light on this we shall discuss some of the conditions that gave rise to a refugee situation.

The Eritrean rural highlands, despite the intensity of the violence they were exposed to, produced an insignificant number of refugees, whereas the western and eastern lowlands and the border areas produced the largest number of refugees. There is no evidence which indicates that the latter areas were subjected to more violence than the rest of the country. The fact that there is considerable variation in people's behavior despite the similarities of the pressure that they are exposed to, is a clear indication that refugee movement is a multivariate phenomenon.

In the following we shall look into the factors that either countervail or reinforce flight across international borders.

DISTANCE AND FLIGHT

The significance of distance as a factor countervailing or reinforcing migration was recognized in the literature as early as the end of the 19th century. In 1885, Ravenstein formulated what he called seven laws of migration and noted that,

> ... the great body of our migrants only proceed a short distance ... Migrants enumerated in a certain centre of absorption will consequently grow less with the distance ...
>
> (Ravenstein, 1885, 198-199)

Stouffer in 1940 argued that 'there is no relationship between mobility and distance' and he instead introduced the concept of intervening opportunities at the place of origin and existing opportunities at the distance. According to him, 'the number of persons going a given distance is directly proportional to the percentage increase in opportunitites'. (Stouffer; 1940, 846) In his theory of migration, Lee introduced the complementary concept of 'intervening obstacles'. (Lee: 1969, 290) In refugee movements, how does geographic distance affect the decision to flee in the face of a perceived or actual danger?

The overwhelming majority of the Eritrean rural refugees in the organized rural refugee settlements in Eastern Sudan have only 'proceeded a short distance' to cross into the Sudanese border. To estimate the distance between the area of origin and the area of destination (the border), we asked the refugees to state the number of days the journey took them. Despite the imprecision of this method of estimating distance, it is the only one that could be used with people who do not think of distance in kilometers or miles. The problem is that some families, owing to their age composition, might have walked slower or faster, while others may have walked day and night or only at night, and so on. Almost all of the refugees have travelled on foot. (See Table 2.2) As can be observed from Table 2.2, only about 2% in Umsaqata, 2% in Umbrush, 2% in Dehema, 4% in Adingrar, 7% in Aburakham, and 6% in Wad Awad fled their areas of origin by car. Since some of the refugees in Aburakham and Wad Awad include former commercial farmers in the Gash-Setit area, it is possible that they took their own cars or tractors with them. But

TABLE 2.2. Percentage Distribution of the Sample Refugees, by Means of Transport to the Country of Asylum.

Means of transport	Umsaqata	Umbrush	Dehema	Adingrar	Aburakham	Wad Awad	All villages
On foot	85.2	95.2	97.9	92.0	89.8	87.5	91.8
By car	1.6	2.2	2.1	4.0	6.9	6.2	3.8
By animal	13.1	2.2	–	4.0	3.4	6.2	5.1
Total	99.9	100.0	100.0	100.0	100.1	99.9	100.7

the other refugees who travelled by car (buses and trucks) in the other villages are those who fled under less dramatic circumstances, i.e., they are refugees who have fled with a clear intention and for a definite destination.

The overwhelming majority of the Eritrean rural refugees in the organized rural refugee settlements in Eastern Sudan only travelled a relatively short distance to arrive at the border of the country of asylum.

As can be seen from Table 2.3, 38% of all the refugees travelled between 1 and 5 days to arrive at the Sudanese border. In fact, out of this group the majority have made the journey in less than 2 days. This is mainly true of those refugees who fled from Um Hajer and the surrounding areas, which is reflected in the figures for Dehema and Aburakham where the majority of the refugees are from the small towns near the border area. The majority of the refugees, i.e., 65% of the sample households, walked between 1 and 10 days. Considering the demographic and sex composition of the refugees, which included people from all age groups (children and old people of both sexes), the distance they covered per day could not have been considerable. Since these movements often involved whole villages, it is natural that even the sick and those with physical handicaps also went along—further reducing the distance covered per day. Only 13% of the total sample took more than 20 days. These are probably the refugees whose place of origin is the eastern lowlands and Eastern Akele Guzai. These are the Saho refugees, the majority of whom are settled in Dehema, Adingrar, and Umzurzur. The latter village is not included in the sample. This is relatively reflected in the figures, where 1% in Dehema and 20% in Adingrar have travelled for more than 20 days. Most of the refugees in this category reported that it had taken them between 25 and 30 days to arrive at the border area.

In our discussion above, we used the number of days taken during the journey to measure the distance between the refugees' place of origin and the Sudanese border. It may be argued that some of the refugees, owing to their age, sex and health conditions, might have walked faster or slower than others. However, this argument cannot be valid in light of the existing communal solidarity among the rural refugees. It is inconceivable to envisage a situation where the most fit individuals would walk alone leaving the women, children and the aged behind.

In addition, we tried to measure the distance between the refugees' places of origin in Eritrea and the Sudanese border on a map, taking account of some problems which affect the accuracy of the measurement. Since the refugees did not travel by trains or buses, it is very difficult to identify the course they followed to come to the Sudan. The actual distance was also conditioned by the obstacles confronted on the way, for example police or army stations.

The accuracy of the measurements on a map is also affected by the nature of the terrain the refugees have to pass through. Even by using this measurement, the overwhelming majority of the refugees have travelled short distances. The first group of the refugees that entered the Sudan in 1967 from the Gash-Setit

TABLE 2.3. Percentage Distribution of the Sample Refugees, by Number of Days Spent on the Journey.

Number of Days	Umsaqata	Umbrush	Dehema	Adingrar	Aburakham	Wad Awad	All villages
1-5	34.4	28.9	40.4	22.0	69.5	21.9	38.1
6-10	36.1	37.8	19.1	22.0	18.6	31.2	27.2
11-15	16.4	13.3	15.0	24.0	1.7	25.0	15.0
16-20	6.6	6.7	8.0	12.0	3.4	6.3	7.1
Over 20	6.6	13.3	17.0	20.0	6.8	15.6	12.6
Total	100.1	100.0	99.5	100.0	100.0	100.0	100.0

province travelled about 80 km. The refugees in the fourth group, i.e., those who came from the small towns of Um Hajer, Golouj, Garguf, Aligidir, and Haikota, only travelled between 5 and 30 km. Those in the fifth group, i.e., the refugees from Tessenei, Aligidir and the surrounding areas, travelled short distances varying from 35 to 5 km. The refugees in the sixth group, from the border cities and towns, had travelled insignificant distances varying from 5 km to 35 km. Following the recapture of cities such as Barentu (about 160 km from the border) and Agordat (about 220 km), some refugees from these cities and the surrounding areas had travelled a considerable distance. But these are relatively few and are mainly of urban origin. Those in the third group who came from the surroundings of Keren had travelled a considerable distance. But these are relatively few and are mainly of urban origin. Those in the third group who came from the surroundings of Keren had travelled about 290 km to arrive at the Sudanese border. However, as noted earlier, despite the gruesome violence these areas were exposed to, the number of the refugees who came from these areas was very small. One of the reasons why there were so few refugees from these areas is probably because of the long distance between the Sudan and the areas of origin. The Eritrean rural highlands produced no or very few refugees and this is probably because of the long distance (over 400 kms) from the Sudanese border.

The major exception to the general trend is the second group of refugees whose flight was not hampered by long distances. These were mainly the Saho from the eastern lowlands and Eastern Akeleguzai, which is roughly over 450 km from the Sudanese border. We shall discuss later other factors which could account for the behavior of this group of refugees.

The above discussion clearly shows that distance is as important countervailing or reinforcing factor in refugee movements to the extent that it has always been significant in voluntary migrations. In fact, in voluntary migration, it is only beyond a certain remoteness that distance becomes a factor because in peace time, people can often avail themselves of the opportunities that exist in a nearby area by commuting without abandoning their area of origin.

The hypothesis that flight is a decreasing function of geographical distance is further strengthened by the nature of refugee movements that have occurred in the last two decades in Africa. A casual look at Figure 2.3 shows that almost all rural refugee movements in Africa invariably originated from and around the border areas. This is true of the refugees in the Sudan, Somalia, Angola, Djibouti, Cameroon, Zaire, Tanzania, and other countries. In the majority of cases this has occurred despite the fact that all the regions in these countries are directly or indirectly affected by the crises that generate refugees.

Distance and Impediments

Distance has another feature to it and that is the impediments or obstacles likely to be encountered during the journey. These will increase proportionally with geographical distance, and include the risk of being detected or attacked, starving due to lack of food and water, falling sick, and others.

If one's place of origin is near the border of the country of asylum, these impediments are few and constitute no major obstacle.

The majority of the refugees in Aburakham and to some extent in Wad Awad and Dehema are originally from the border areas, i.e., from Um Hajer and the surrounding towns and other small settlements. In Aburakham, only 20% of the sample households claimed that one or more of their family members fell sick during flight and 31% in Wad Awad. (See Table 2.4) The highest figures reported are in Umsaqata and Umbrush, where most of the refugees, especially in the former, originated from the Barka lowlands. Some of the refugees in Adingrar and Dehema originally come from remote areas and, although the figures reported are higher than those in Aburakham and Wad Awad, they are slightly less than those in Umsaqata and Umbrush. The fact that the number of sick persons reported is higher for those who travelled longer distances shows that impediments increase with distance.

Table 2.5 shows the two major problems encountered by the refugees during flight. The majority of the refugees faced shortages of food and water, and there seems to be no significant difference between those who covered long or short distances. It is obvious why. If the supply of food and water was interrupted even for one day, the refugees would have felt hungry and thirsty, and they did not have to go hungry for weeks in order to report hunger and thirst as the major problems encountered.

The second problem encountered by the refugees was the possibility of military attack. Those from distant places, who invoked military attack or fear of it as a second impediment, are referring to the dangers represented by the various police stations and military positions that existed throughout the country. The fear of being detected and subsequently attacked is also likely to increase with the uncertainty about the route to the country of asylum. Those who reported disease as a problem encountered during flight were mainly those who set out from the relatively remote areas (see Aburakham, Dehema, and Umsaqata).

Generally, the refugees from the Um Hajer areas did not emphasize the obstacles they had to overcome to cross into the Sudan. Most of them claimed that the problems encountered were easily surmountable.

Distance and Shock

Lee, in his theory of migration, argues that the psychic pressure among voluntary migrants increases with distance (see 1969), but our evidence shows the opposite, i.e., the 'push' pressure radically decreases with distance, assuming that the refugees are not physically chased from behind all the way to the border. In other words, distance gives refugees a chance to recover from their state of shock, and the movement that was being governed by blind panic at the beginning is now brought under the control of the subject. At this stage, the people in flight are able to take a decision by comparing different alternatives. If they have already lost their means of subsistence—crops on the farm, in stores, livestock—the economic factor then becomes an overwhelming

TABLE 2.4 Percentage Distribution of Sample Refugees, by Number of Families with Members who Fell Sick during Flight.

Percentage of Sample Families	Umsaqata	Umbrush	Dehema	Adingrar	Aburakham	Wad Awad	All villages
	43	49	40	40	20	31	37.3

TABLE 2.5. Frequency Distribution of the Sample Households according to the Two Major Problems Encountered during Flight.

Problems encountered	Number of times type of problems mentioned						
	Umsaqata	Umbrush	Dehema	Adingrar	Aburakham	Wad Awad	All villages
None	6	3	1	2	6	1	19
Fear of military attack	10	12	14	11	14	4	65
Lack of food & water	47	37	39	40	38	27	228
Disease	3	3	1	5	3	2	17
Total of mentioned reasons*	60	52	54	56	55	33	310

*Excluding those who faced no problems of any kind.

variable in the decisionmaking process. In any case, whether or not they continue their flight across an international border is determined by the number of opportunities that exist within the country or outside it. Opportunity in this case means both exist within the country or outside it. Opportunity in this case means both economic and physical safety.

If the refugees had to travel a short distance, it is likely that they would cross over the borders of the asylum country without being able to get respite to recover from their shock. The sudden and abrupt change of events that occurred during 1975 and 1978 in the Eritrean border areas forced people to cross into the Sudan, most of them without even knowing that they had reached the border.

Distance and Information

Information about the conditions in the country of destination is likely to increase in proportion to proximity. This is even more so where the major source of information, in the relative absence of radio and newspapers, is personal contacts.

The information is often carried by black market traders across the borders, by herdsmen, by seasonal laborers, and others. This is precisely the case in the border areas of Eritrea. That there was such a border crossing by the people inhabiting the Western Eritrean lowlands is well documented. Nadel, for example, states that 'In winter the camel herds move to Khor Hombol and into the Sudan'. (Nadel; 1945, Appendix A) Lipsky also notes that some of the western lowlanders 'travel seasonally to the Sudan to pick cotton'. (Lipsky: 1962, 48) No matter how sporadic these movements were, they were enough to carry information back and forth between the two sides of the border. The people in the remote areas had no access to such information.

Distance and Historical Contacts

The likelihood of historical contacts based upon migration is higher between short distances than long distances. In the Eritrean lowlands the pastoralists inhabiting these areas had a long tradition of migration to the Sudan in search of pasture (Nadel: 1945) and/or earning cash by working either in Gezira, Tokar, or Kashm El Girba. (Lipsky: op.cit., 87; Bushra: 1982, 5) The inhabitants of the border areas,

> ... form the core of a rigorous trading network between the grain producing centres of the Eastern Sudan and Eritrea; this network, however, has gone through drastic modifications in recent years, but it still continues.
>
> (Bushra: op.cit., 5)

This movement can be traced back to the pre-colonial history. The present day African national states are the artificial creation of colonial powers. Eritrea in its present day geographic shape was created by Italian colonialism and Anglo-Egyptian. Eritrea's colonial boundary with the Sudan was demarked between 1901 and 1902. (Goitom: 1980, 17) Until this period, though the Nabtab class headed by the Deglel (paramount chief of the Beni Amer), enjoyed full autonomy, most of the Eritrean western lowlands were at least formally under the Fung Kingdom of Senar (Paul: 1950; Trevaskis: 1960) and later under the Egyptian rule.

> In 1885 Egypt lost its Eritrean province to Italy on the advice of the British government and then vacated the Red Sea and Kassala provinces, again on the advice of the British government.
>
> (Balamoan: 1976, 25)

Because of the establishment of the colonial boundary during the Italian occupation in Eritrea, and the Anglo-Egyptian reoccupation of the Sudan after the defeat of the ,Mahdists in 1898, the population inhabiting the border areas was divided into two;

> . . . by administrative boundary agreed upon by the occupying powers, about two-thirds being left in Eritrea, and a third, containing only a few of the Nabtab caste in the Sudan.
>
> (Paul: op.cit., 226-227)

Although the establishment of the colonial boundaries implied restriction on freedom of movement across the border, colonial policies did not radically restrict the movement of Africans as long as they behaved themselves.

The policy was reversed after the achievement of national independence but, as noted by Balamoan, despite the African national government's attempt to restrict movement, by modern means of transportation, the automobile and the airplane they did little to restrict the movement of pedestrians across the borders. This was probably due to their lack of the means to patrol the long borders, especially between the Sudan and Eritrea. (The governments on both sides were at least formally trying to restrict unauthorized movements. The refugees from the border areas at Qala en Nahal, for instance, told the author that they were moving back and forth across the borders not because they were allowed, but because of the large size of the border they could easily escape detection. If an Eritrean Beni Amer was caught in the cities in the Sudan before 1967, he was put in jail for three months and was later deported to Tessenei. Having one's coethnic group in the Sudan was no defense. Often a Beni Amer in such a situation could easily escape persecution by claiming that he was from the Sudan and to show this he often gave a name of faked village and sheikh in the Sudan.)

Along the border areas there has always been seasonal treks between the two countries. Whenever there was a drought, the cattle herders migrated to

Gash, Atbara, Tekeze, and the Rahad areas. During the survey we met Eritrean cattle herders from the western lowlands (near Tessenei) around the Rahad river a few miles from Aburakham. These are not refugees but Eritrean pastoralists who migrate to the Sudan to take advantage of water and grazing land. They return to Eritrea during the rainy season and consider Eritrea their country. This movement, according to them, happens without the knowledge of the authorities on either side. Smock also states that,

> even before refugees from this war began to cross into the Sudan in 1967, a sizeable group of Eritreans found the Sudan to be attractive for a variety of reasons. The Beni Amer moved from one side of the border to the other, grazing their herds and marketing their produce.
>
> (Smock, 1982, 451)

The alienation of land in Eritrea during the Italian colonial period, coupled with the introduction of veterinary medicine which had the effect of doubling the number of livestock between 1905 and 1938, exacerbated the problem of overgrazing so that some of the pastoralists were seasonally pushed beyond the colonial boundaries. (See Table 2.6.)

This historical movement was also further increased by the introduction of cash crops, such as cotton and sesame, in the Gash-Setit area in the 1950s and the 1960s, which disturbed the transhumance routes and the seasonal pattern of migration of the lowland pastoralists. Vast stretches of land were brought under cultivation. This restricted grazing areas of the pastoralists which in turn led to overgrazing, forcing some pastoralists to cross into the Sudan seasonally in search of water and pasture. To this was added the military threat which increased with the gradual escalation of the war.

The uninterrupted historical ties that exist between the peoples on both sides of the Eritrean and Sudanese border are, no doubt, one of the most important factors that enter into the refugees' decision-making process when they consider flight as a viable strategy for survival.

Distance and Cultural Gap

Social distance increases in proportion with geographic distance, i.e., the cultural gap between the country of origin and the country of asylum is likely to increase with the distance. This is shown by the cultural shock experienced by the urban refugees from the Eritrean highlands. This cultural distance often stems from linguistic and religious differences. The arrival of refugees with diverse cultures and religions in the Sudan has,

> ... resulted in what a Sudanese official called problems of 'cultural incompatibilities'. Such 'cultural incompatibilities' may result from linguistic, religious or ethnic differences between the refugees and the local population.
>
> (News from the UNHCR cited in Kibreab: 1983, 88)

TABLE 2.6. Estimated Number of Livestock 1905-1946.

Year	Cattle	Goats and Sheep	Camels	Horses, Mules and Donkeys	Pigs	Total
1905	296,000	736,000	47,000	30,000	–	1,109,000
1928	747,000	1,896,743	78,742	59,700	–	2,784,485
1938	591,000	1,491,000	68,000	51,000	–	2,201,000
1946	1,200,000	2,200,000	105,000	83,000	25,000	3,613,000

Source: Rapport de la Commission des Nations Unies: Economia quoted in Leonard: 1980, Table 4.

In the Eritrean situation there is a clear relationship between geographic distance and social distance measured in religious, ethnic and linguistic differences. It is assumed, therefore, that social distance can be a countervailing factor in accepting flight as a viable alternative.

Climatic Differences

Another countervailing factor closely linked to distance is the question of climate. There is a tremendous difference between the hot and dusty climate of the Kassala province in the Sudan and the very cool and pleasant climate of the Eritrean highlands, whereas the climate of the Eritrean lowlands does not differ dramatically from that of Kassala province. The peasantry in the highlands has always been reluctant to migrate to the lowlands even when faced with serious economic problems. When the Italian Colonial Government and later to some extent the British administration alienated large tracts of cultivable land in the high plateau, the peasantry was faced with two alternatives. Either to

> ... expand or to starve; and in this plight, the spacious and thinly populated lands of the Moslem tribes beckoned invitingly. Any mass migration to these lowland prairies was precluded by the Abyssinians (highland peasantry's) distaste for the intense summer heat and their fear of malaria.
>
> (Trevaskis: 1960, 55)

This being the case, it is possible that the harsh climate in the Sudan is also one of the factors that countervails the highland peasantry's decision to flee or which reinforces their decision to stay.

THE WORLD THEY CAME FROM

In order to explain variations in the propensity to flee, it is necessary to investigate the socioeconomic and cultural conditions of the populations in the affected areas. For force (actual or perceived) to result in mass exodus, certain conditions must be present and these conditions depend upon the economic basis of a society and its sociocultural values.

Sedentary Agricultural Areas

The psychological disturbance generated by a threat that creates a refugee situation and the social costs of the flight that results will vary from people to people. This is because the socioeconomic and cultural forces that bind potential refugees to their villages of origin are not the same. This point can be illustrated by a comparison of the peasant communities of the Eritrean Highlands (Tigrinya-Kebessa) and the pastoral and agro-pastoral communities of the eastern and the western lowlands.

In the Eritrean plateau, sedentarized agricultural group life began some time after the arrival of the Sabaeans between 1000 and 700 B.C. (Longrigg: 1945, 11). It concentrated people in villages which became a focus of traditional social life.

The attachment of the peasants to their plots of land as a focus of social status and kinship identity and the village as focus of social life has always been paramount and has created the base from which all social and political status evolved. In a brilliant article on land tenure on the Eritrean plateau, Nadel, an anthropologist and a British colonial officer, states that,

> *It has been said of the African that he does not possess his land but is possessed by it.* The attitude of the Eritrean peasant towards his land cannot be more aptly described. *Indeed, his preoccupation with his landed possession shows a depth and passion not often parallelled among African races.*
> (Nadel: 1946, 1) (Emphasis added)

He further notes that this attitude emanates from various roots,

> The possession of land is intimately linked with the whole structure of Eritrean society; it enters, as a paramount factor, into distinctions of social status and forms of social unity . . . Political factors, finally, have lent to the titles and claims to land an almost disproportionate importance; for the various political forces which were at work in historical Eritrea invariably centers around land—its acquisition, expropriation, or redistribution land rights thus became rights which needed to be jealously defended and backed by physical force.

There are three types of land ownership in the Eritrean Highlands. These are (a) individual ownership by the heads of individual families; (b) *Resti*—family ownership, i.e., ownership by the *Enda* (Kindred); and (c) *Diesa* or *Shehena* where land is common property of the whole village. According to Nadel, the family ownership of land or *Resti* is the

> paramount land title in Eritrea and one which is deeply rooted in the social structure. Indeed, the people speak of *Resti* as a 'fundamental' right and a 'sacred possession'.

The concept of *Resti* is originally based upon the principle of first occupation which in the highlands is traced back to ancient times often, a semi-mythical happening yet it still determines in many ways the conception of present day *Resti*. *Resti* starts as an individual ownership by the family that first occupied it and as the family grows in number, every married member is given a plot or plots not only for his livelihood, but as a sign of kinship identity.

The allotment does not confer on the individual recipient a title of ownership but rather the right to usufruct. If the *Enda* (kindred) increases as a result of natural growth, the *Resti* is divided among the married men, conferring a title of ownership on every recipient. This is known as *Tselmi,* while the first category where every *Enda* member by virtue of kinship identity enjoys usufruct, is known as *Resti. Resti* is administered by democratically elected family councils. The land of a deceased member is restored to the land bank of the *Enda* and is in turn allocated to newly married couples.

In most cases *Resti* land cannot be an object of transaction, but when it is allowed, the *Enda* members have a pre-emptive right and it is only when they explicitly declare their intention not to exercise this right that land can be sold to outsiders. Still, purchased land never confers the same social status as that enjoyed by the descendant of the original occupant—*Restenya* (owner of *Resti*). Even the *Restenya* who has sold his land still enjoys a respectable social status by virtue of belonging to the original occupants.

> *Resti* represents much more than merely an economic benefit. Its derivation from an original first occupation lends it an important social significance, that of a qualification for enhanced social status. The social status founded on *Resti* possessions is permanent and inalienable, more so than are the possessions themselves. The owner of *Resti* land can sell it or let it; but the fact that he once owned *Resti* will rarely be obscured. It invests him almost for ever with the status of a member of the hereditary families, almost of landed aristocracy *which looks down upon 'new comers' (MaKelaialet)* who have come later and had acquired land by purchase or lease.
>
> (Nadel: op.cit., 9)

Among the privileges stemming from being a *Restenya* is that only the latter can be a member of the village *Shimagele* (village committee), a position which entitles him to supervise and administer the affairs of the village, and only a *Restenya* can be a village chief (*Chikka Adi*).

Individual ownership of land is based upon purchased land (grat worki). The possibility for a new comer to purchase land is very limited because an outsider can only buy land if the *Enda* members are unwilling to buy the land in question, and land is rarely for sale.

Under village ownership (*Diesa* or *Shehena*), land is owned by the village and all residents are guaranteed access to it provided they have a house of their own (*Tisha*). Nadel notes that in the past 'new comers' could easily get access to land, but now owing to shortage they are excluded and even widows are allotted only half a share. As a result of pressure exerted by the 'new comers' and by colonial intervention, *Resti* land ownership has often developed into *Diesa* land. But although the *Resti* land holding system is weakened at the economic level, its social aspect is still intact. Nadel states that,

> even in the communities where diesa has existed as far as memory goes, a sharp distinction is still drawn between 'strangers' (though they may

have immigrated several generations ago) and the families of original inhabitants.

In the *Diesa* system it was not possible to own more than one share of a particular quality of land. To accommodate new claims made by newly married couples, to ensure equality of access to all members and to avoid an entrenchment of a vested interest group or individual, a periodical redistribution of the village land took place by lot. The lot was cast in the presence of all male members of the community. To guarantee equal access, the village land was graded according to fertility and distance and lots were drawn for each category of land and each community member received a plot from each category.

In these communities, possession of land provides an identity and social cohesion with one's clan and family members. But the commitment of the peasants to their place of origin stems also from their attitude towards their village which was founded by their forefathers. The present generation is bound to maintain and transfer this to the coming generation. Even those who live outside the traditional home or village often return to maintain their ties. They maintain land rights. These are maintained not for their income-generating potential, but as a means of maintaining a link without which one is considered to be rootless. Highlanders that live outside their place of origin frequently return to their villages, pay land tax, build houses and prefer to be buried there. This commitment is difficult to understand unless one looks at the social pull of the village manifested in *Resti*, *Tabot* (village church), village cementry, *Tisha* (stone house) and the social cohesion stemming from communal and kinship life that binds peasants to their place of origin. 'Territorial organization and village centers were the focal points of social living in these sedentary agriculturalist Coptic Christian communities.' (Gehre-Medhin: 1984, 54)

Such a structure has a strong natural inertia that binds the inhabitants to it even at the cost of their lives and property. They are disinclined to resort to flight, first, because the minimum amount of psychological disturbance that produces refugees is probably higher among them and because of the social costs that flight entails. A community that has always looked down upon immigrants is less likely to resort to flight even in the face of an actual and present danger. As was pointed out earlier, after the killing of 37 people in Woki, some of the people 'believing . . . that nothing else would happen remained. On their return . . . the Ethiopians slaughtered . . . 500 people'. (Dines: op.cit., 309) And after the death of 500 people, Woki is still there. The people have rebuilt their stone houses despite constant fear of another attack. There are villages in the highlands that have been burned down 2 or 3 times, but still the population has not crossed into the Sudan.

Pastoral and Agropastoral Areas

How do the socioeconomic and cultural structures that have produced refugees differ from the structure that prevails in the highlands? The refugees from the eastern lowlands and Southern Akeleguzai are mainly from the Saho national group who before their flight lived in the 'coastal depression between Massawa in the north, the Gulf of Zula in the east and the escarpment of the Akeleguzai in the west'. These are the second group of refugees who came to the Sudan, the majority of whom are herdsmen. According to 1943 statistics, out of the 41,000 Sahos, 31,000 lived in the escarpments of Akeleguzai, of whom about 93% were 'nomadic'. (Longrigg: 1974, Appendix C) Trevaskis also notes that the majority of the Saho '. . . are pastoral nomads or semi-nomadic. A few on the plateau are settled agriculturalists'. (Trevaskis: 1960, 15) It was only during the last hundred years that the Saho started taking to sedentary livelihood 'amidst the plateau population'. (Nadel: 1946, 3)

The Tigre national group that inhabits the Barka lowlands, the northern highlands, and the eastern lowlands are described by Trevaskis as '. . . mostly pastoral nomads or at least of semi-nomadic habits'. (See also Lipsky: 1967, 48; Silkin: 1983, 910; Smock: 1982, 451; Gebre-Medhin: 1984) However, some combine pastoralism with agriculture. (See Nadel: 1945, Appendix A; Paul: 1950; Seligman: 1912) In these areas the

> . . . geographical and climatic features determine the annual cycle of tribal life. Largely nomadic, the Beni Amer move with the grazing, from the dried up river beds in the north to the winter pastures in the southern river valleys.
>
> (Nadel: 1945, 52)

The Beni Amer are a section of the Tigre national group and are dominant in most of the rural settlements in eastern Sudan, especially in Qala en Nahal. Unlike in the Eritrean plateau, where large villages are the focal point of all social, political and economic life, the Tigre group tends to live in scattered settlements, and the social pull of village life seems to be absent among them. As Nadel notes,

> Indeed not even the Beni Amer clan grazes its herds collectively; clan sections and kinship groups may choose widely scattered pastures: even individual families and herdsmen move independently. The economic habits foster a kindred outlook and mentality. The individual male is born into a scattered and broken up group. From the age of 12-14 he lives with the herds, guided solely by their needs of grazing and watering. He knows intimately his few neighbors on the pastures or in the nearest camp. His knowledge of the rest of the clan . . . is by comparison, of indirect and of secondary interest.
>
> (Nadel: 1945, 60)

This social organization of limited interaction is diametrically opposed to that of the sedentary peasants in the highland plateau where there is territorial unity and a collective social life evolving around large villages.

The two small national groups, the Baria and the Kunama, occupy the south-western Eritrean lowlands known as Gash and Setit. They are bounded by the Beni Amer in the north and partly by the highland plateau (Serae) in the east, and are settled agriculturalists. (Nadel: 1945; Trevaskis: 1960, 16; Lipsky: 1962, 50) 'Among the Kunama descent is matrilineal; amongst the Baria it is patrilineal as elsewhere in Eritrea.' (Trevaskis: op.cit., 16; Lipsky: op,cit., 50) Except in the case of the Baria, the overwhelming majority of the rural refugees have come from the pastoral and agropastoral communities. How do we explain the deviation of the Baria national group from the general discernible pattern which we identified above?

In the pre-colonial period, there were no chiefs in the social organizations of the Baria and Kunama communities. When the Egyptians extended their rule to these areas towards the end of the 19th century, they appointed a Baria chief called Totil to collect 'taxes and execute their orders'. Later the Italian colonialists converted the 'position held by the Totil into a hereditary chieftainship extending to Kunama as well as to Baria'. (Trevaskis: op.cit., 16) This was 'deeply resented by the Kunama who are now culturally very much less close to the Baria than they once were'. He further notes that 'The Baria are now all moslems and have largely become assimilated to their Tigre neighbors whose customs they have in many respects adopted'.

Nadel also speaks of the 'feud' that once arose between the Beni Amer and the Kunama which may have benefitted the Baria in their strife against the Kunama. The Baria had allied themselves with the Tigre, and it is natural that they fled with the latter with whom they have a religious and cultural affinity. The refugee elders reported to the author that the Ethiopian troops treated the Kunama communities favorably and exploited these differences. For instance, villages belonging to the Baria were set on fire, whereas villages belonging to the Kunama were left alone. Refugees even reported that some Kunama chiefs collaborated with the Ethiopian army in its pacification campaign against the ELF.

The above evidence suggests that some economic and social structures generate more or less mobility-prone cultural values. Quite a mobile society has been necessitated by the ecosystem in which most pastoralists and agro-pastoralists live. This environment is characterized by seasonal drought, by pasture spread over wide areas and by a shortage of water. Hence, to take advantage of seasonal variation in rainfall, the pastoralists have to move from one place to another. Therefore, the propensity to flee when faced with a threat, is higher among pastoral and agro-pastoral communities than among peasants with a long history of sedentary life tied to the land.

The capacity of people who inhabit arid and semi-arid areas to deal with outside pressure also seems to be less, because the pastoralist, unlike the sedentary peasant who depends on his annual crop saving, mainly depends on milk which is supplied daily. Hence the pastoralist's life can very easily be disturbed. Pastoralists also lack a collective and cohesive social organization to resist natural or man-made disaster. On the other hand, unlike the sedentary peasant whose food supply can be destroyed if his house is set on fire, the pastoralist avoids this easily by moving his base of subsistence—livestock—to escape detection and destruction.

During the dry season in the areas where the pastoralists live, water comes only from a few water holes. The simple act of poisoning and sealing a well easily disturbs the transhumance routes and can even force pastoralists to abandon their places of origin. Peasants in the highland plateau, in contrast, have alternative water sources even during the dry season. All this suggests that the factors discussed above reinforce or countervail the decision to flee or to stay.

Our research also suggests that there may be a relationship between mass exodus and lack of economic, political and social development in the places of origin. The people living in the relatively more developed Eritrean plateau were evidently more resistant to the onslaught of military violence than the pastoralists and agropastoralists in the lowlands. To throw some light on this, we shall look at the historical developments of the Eritrean highlands and the Eritrean western lowlands.

During the successive colonial periods, the western lowlands were always peripheral with respect to political participation, the provision of infrastructural services and integration into the colonial economy. In taking over Eritrea towards the end of the 19th century, Italy intended to establish a permanent colony, to settle its surplus population and to use the colony as a springboard from which it could expand its colonial territory in East Africa. To wage its colonial wars against the young Ethiopian Empire and to facilitate the settlement of the colonists, the colonial state invested heavily in building the physical infrastructures. This created a considerable labor demand. To secure the supply of cheap labor and meet the demand for cultivable land of the colonial settlers, the colonial power alienated large tracts of land. Those who lost their means of production were forced to migrate to the towns where there were employment opportunities. And finally, to further induce the peasants to respond to the demand for labor and to the call for soldiers and to raise part of the capital necessary to finance the building of the infrastructures, the colonial government imposed taxes which had to be made good in cash. Peasants were forced to work for wages to raise the cash income. According to Trevaskis, 'Italian law had empowered the Governor to declare certain specified types of land *demeniale* (state domain) provided he gave adequate notice of what he proposed to do.' (Trevaskis: 1960, 54) However, 'in practice, the provisions of the law were often ignored, or unwittingly misapplied by *commissari* (provincial governors) who, in their zeal to further Italian agricultural development often allocated land to Italian agriculturists which had never been declared *demeniale*. (Ibid.)

The number of the colonial settlers and investments in infrastructure increased tremendously following Mussolini's rise to power, and in 1935, fascist Italy had taken over Ethiopia from its base areas—Eritrea and Somaliland. The question which interests us here is the impact of the colonial economy on the pre-capitalist socioeconomic structures that prevailed in the different parts of the country.

Most of the investment and land alienation occurred in the Eritrean highlands. Land alienation according to Trevaskis was 'largely exercised from the few cultivable acres of the plateau, since it was there alone that the climate favored Italian settlement'. (Trevaskis: op.cit., 54) There the response of the sedentary peasants to the new market, employment and conscription opportunities was more positive than in the lowlands:

> Because they were nearer and were by nature more gregarious, the Abyssinian peasantry had responded to the call for soldiers, clerks, artisans, and laborers in very much larger numbers than the Moslem tribesmen. Their exodus from the plateau valleys brought about important changes in the local economy, society and land tenure.
> (Trevaskis: op.cit., 52)

These changes modified the pre-capitalist socioeconomic structures in the plateau although these older structures still co-exist with the capitalist mode of production in articulated form and to a great extent hamper technical progress and capitalist development in agriculture.

In contrast, capitalist penetration into the pre-capitalist socioeconomic structures of the western lowlands was less dramatic. The colonial economy never succeeded in subordinating the nomadic population of the western lowlands. First, the colonial government did not have expansionist ambitions towards the Sudan because Italy's occupation of Eritrea was partly facilitated by Great Britain which was ruling the Sudan in the form of the Anglo-Egyptian Condominium. (Balamoan: 1976, 25) Italy's expansionist ambitions were directed against the newly created Ethiopian Empire and in order to eliminate any possibility of political alliance between the Eritrean feudal lords and the church on the one hand, and the aristocracy of Tigrai on the other, the colonial Government had to weaken the former by confiscating the estates of the church and of the highland landlords. Since there was no such fear in the West, and in order to concentrate its efforts on the highlands, the colonial Government pursued a policy of indirect rule in the western lowlands.

Second, because there was unlimited land supply in the western lowlands and owing to the inhospitable climate for European settlement, the extent of land alienation in this area was insignificant and could not radically modify the existing socioeconomic structure.

Third, not only did abundance of land minimize the effects of capitalist penetration, but pastoral life was by its very nature more flexible than sedentary life. The creation of a few plantations and the improvement of veterinary services, which had the effect of increasing the size of the livestock, no doubt created new opportunities for the nomads by opening their hitherto isolated areas to the international markets. But one should not overstate the disintegrating effects of the capitalist mode of production on the pre-capitalist mode of production and social relations.

One of the major obstacles which paralyzed colonial political control over the western lowlands was, in contrast to the highlands, lack of institutions and the existence of scattered patterns. Nadel, for instance, notes that,

> One of the causes of the weakness of political control lies, as I have already suggested, in the nomadic habits of the tribe. The very fact of physical dispersion makes for looseness of organization. Widely scattered, and each intent upon its own varying needs of securing the holding vital grazing land, the clans are not amenable to unitary command.
>
> (Nadel: 1945, 60)

Gebre-Medlin also notes that 'relatively speaking, the western lowlands were not as heavily penetrated as those of the Kebessa (highland) regions'. (Gebre-Medhin: 1984)

The few social services provided by the colonial Government were almost wholly concentrated in the cities and, to some extent, in the highland plateau. No efforts were made either by the Italians, British or Ethiopians to improve the pastoralists' access to physical and social infrastructural services. When Britain took over the territory at the beginning of World War II, its policies were to maintain the status quo, and the law of uneven development was left to operate as before.

AID AS A PULL FACTOR

Given a crisis situation, underdevelopment becomes a factor that reinforces mass exodus. By the same token, development policies which aim first at the elimination of social injustices, increased supply of social and physical infrastructural services such as housing, clean water, health, and education, second, at the improvement of the material life of the inhabitants, and third, at the creation of structures through which the inhabitants can participate in the decision-making process may, no doubt, have countervailing effects on mass exodus.

But does provision of relief and development assistance on the other side of the frontier represent a 'pull' factor for refugees? This is a tricky and indeed an elusive issue. However, it must be admitted that the four million or more refugees in Africa are not only a result of the political problems and violations of human rights that are now part of everyday life in the continent, but also of the structural economic crises that have gripped the continent. African refugees are generated by the interplay of political, economic, ecological and social crises. This is exacerbated by the formal principles under which most of the inter-governmental agencies and non-governmental organizations are operating. The international organizations usually provide relief and development assistance only if requested by the governments, which formally claim sovereignty over the territory where assistance is required. However, in reality, it may be opposition forces which control the area. Thus assistance directed through the official channels may not reach the affected people for 'security reasons'. The majority of international organizations are reluctant to direct their assistance through unofficial channels for the mere reason that these channels are not recognized by the Organization of African Unity or by the United Nations.

It is possible that the large-scale influx of refugees that occurred after October 1984 in to Eastern Sudan would not have been of such magnitude if relief assistance had reached the victims of famine in their areas of origin and internal displacement. When relief assistance failed to reach the victims of famine, mainly due to political problems and due to lack of long-term response acceptable to the former, the alternative was either to perish or to flee to a neighboring country where the perceived conditions of existence were better than in the areas of origin. This suggests, therefore, that it is only when the conditions of the affected areas are humanly unbearable that people flee. However, it must be emphasized that as long as the conditions of existence in the affected areas remain expulsive, people will be forced to cross international borders even without knowing what is on the other side of the frontier.

According to van Praag,

> . . . during April and May some 40,000 people who had crossed the border . . . to the Sudan from Ethiopian Province of Tigray, began the long trek back to their farms and villages.
>
> (van Praag in Refugees: July, 1985)

The return of many Tigreans to their country in spite of an unchanged political situation indicates that those who returned were primarily victims of famine and not political persecution. Their flight could have been avoided had there been proper policy and long-term responses to the ecological disaster, which is one of the causes of crop failure in the area. Even under these circumstances it is the expulsive and unbearable conditions of existence at the refugees' place of origin, caused mainly by the Government's wrong policy priorities, that is 'pushing' the refugees, and there is no evidence which indicates that the refugees in the Eastern Sudan are 'pulled' by the handout which is often only the minimum necessary to sustain a life.

However, rural life is disturbed by political and social upheaval which obstructs normal economic activity, if there is no provision of relief in the affected peoples' place of origin, if relief and development assistance are provided across the border, and if the affected people are informed about it and infrastructural services provided, these factors may, no doubt, reinforce their decision to flee their country of origin, even when they do not directly risk death or persecution.

This chapter has attempted first to identify the various groups that fled to the Sudan and were later placed in the rural refugee land settlements, and second, to discuss the causes underlying their flight. The adjustment of the refugees to the new situation in the settlements is partly linked to their old mode of existence. Therefore, an investigation of the socioeconomic structure of their areas of origin is important for a better understanding of the refugees' situation in the refugee rural land settlements. The following chapters will examine the country of asylum and the conditions and progress of the settlement programs.

PART 2

The Study

CHAPTER 3

Sudan: Country of Asylum

The aim of this chapter is to discuss the physical factors of the area where the refugee land settlements are situated, the history of refugees in the Sudan, Sudan's refugee and settlement policies and to describe the settlement process itself.

THE SETTLEMENT AREA

The Gedaref area where the refugee land settlements are situated is located southeast of Khartoum between latitudes 12°45′ and 14°45′ N and is bounded by Atbara river on the east and Rahad river on the west and south-west. The area has good transport links and is suitable for internal and external trade. It is a flat plain

> . . . at an altitude of approximately 600 m above sea level. A gentle slope of 5% to 1% is common, giving the impression that the area is well suited for large-scale mechanization.
>
> (Agabawi: 1968: 72)

There are isolated hills and rocky outcrops throughout the area, and some of the refugee villages in Qala en Nahal are located below small hills. (For the topography of the Qala en Nahal refugee settlement, see Fig. 3.1.) The soils in the Central Plain rainfed area are dark-colored and strongly cracking and have a characteristic coarse structure in the upper 30 to 40 m. (Van der Kevie & Buraymah: 1976; Agabawi: op.cit., Suliman: 1977; SCC/ESRP: 1980) Due to the high clay content of the soil, which varies from 61% to 73%, the danger of soil erosion should be very small, but soil erosion is not uncommon. According to Agabawi, the soils in the area are

> alkaline in reaction and the soluble salt content is uniform and always below 1% which is the critical limit for crop growth. Both potasium and phosphorus supplies are adequate but nitrogen may become deficient when continuous cropping of exhaustive crops is practiced.
>
> (Agabawi: ibid.)

Waterlogging is a serious problem, especially in the low-lying areas. The nitrogen deficiency suggests the need for artificial fertilizers, however, '. . . recent research still shows major applications of artificial fertilizers to be uneconomic'. (Spooner: 1981, 23)

Climate

The province covers about 125,120 square kilometers, lying between latitudes 12°40′ and 17°57′ N and longitudes 33°34′ and 37°01′ E. The greater part of the province is in the desert, semi-desert or arid climate zones where there is inadequate rainfall for rainfed agricultural production (see Figure 3.2 (a)). In the arid zone, there are large irrigated schemes such as Kashm el Girba, Gash delta and Rahad. Most of the dry areas are used for grazing, mainly by camels. (Van der Kevie & Buraymah: 1976, 7) The southern part of the province (see Figure 3.2 (a)) with a semi-arid or monsoon climate has more than 450 mm annual rainfall (see Figure 3.2 (c)) and both modern mechanized rainfed and traditional agriculture are widely practiced. This area is often referred to as the 'Granary of the Sudan'. The area is also widely used for grazing livestock.

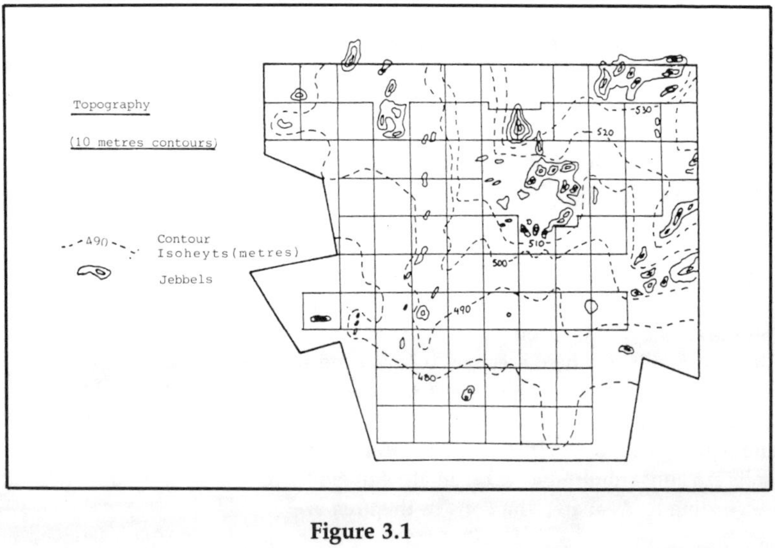

Figure 3.1

Climate and Rainfall Isohyets

Figure 3.2 (a)

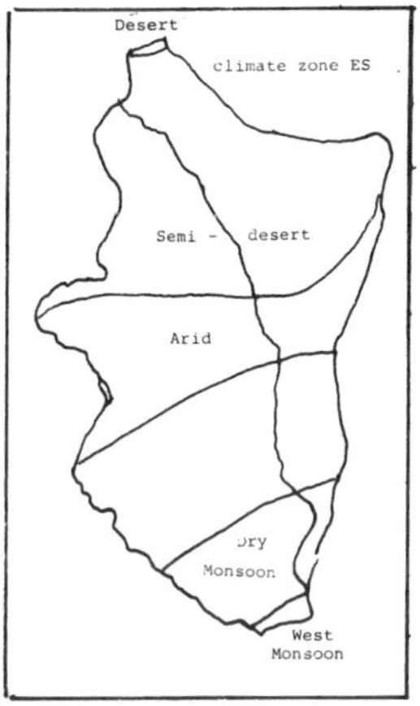

Figure 3.2 (c)

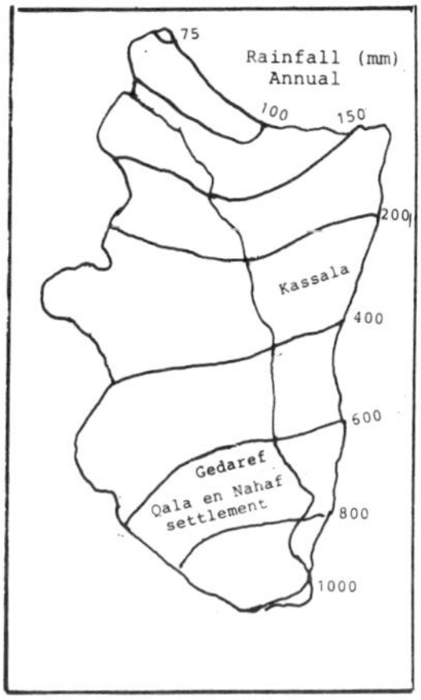

Figure 3.2 (b)

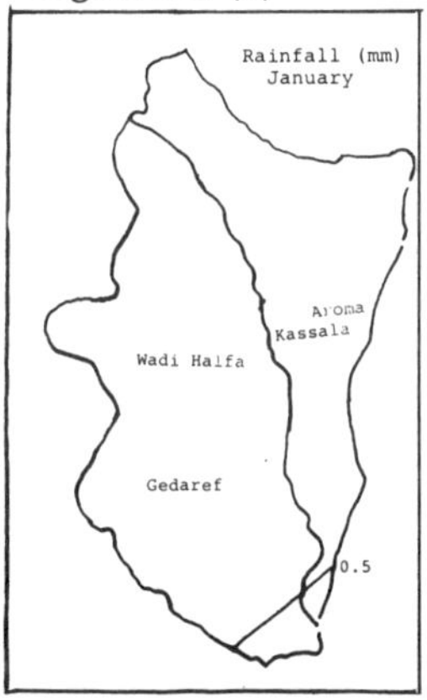

Figure 3.2 (d)

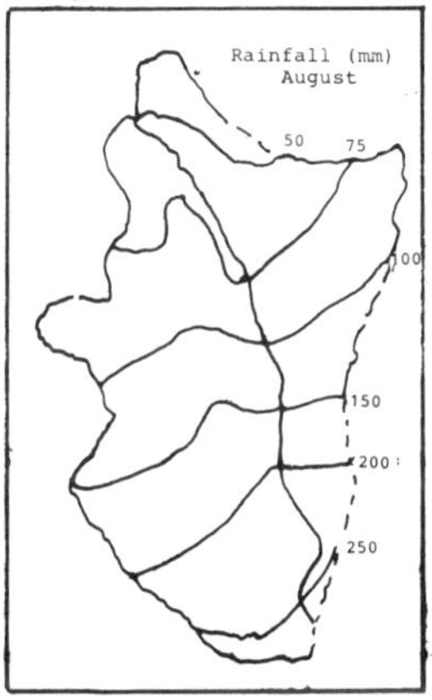

Source: W. Van Der Kevie and Ibrahim M. Buraymah, Exploratory soil survey of Kassala province. Soil Survey Administration, Wad Medani, 1976.

Rainfall occurs during summer, mainly from June to September with some showers in May and October. The annual rainfall in Qala en Nahal ranges from 195.5 mm to 893 mm. In Mufaza, about 40 km from the settlements of Aburakham and Wad Awad, the annual average has ranged from 234 mm to 814.5 mm over twenty years. After the opening of the Rahad irrigation scheme, the Ministry of Irrigation has started recording the amount of rainfall in Aburakham. As can be seen from Table 3.1, the amount of rainfall in 1980 and 1982 was below the minimum necessary for sorghum growth, and there was crop failure in both the seasons. According to the refugee farmers in Aburakham and Wad Awad, late arrival of rains and badly distributed and insufficient rains are some of the major constraints on agricultural production. In most seasons in Qala en Nahal, the amount of rainfall was sufficient to support sorghum and sesame growth. However, even there the variation in rainfall can be great both between and within the seasons. Cropping is restricted mainly by climate to sorghum in Aburakham and Wad Awad and sorghum and sesame in Qala en Nahal. The former is staple food, the latter a cash crop.

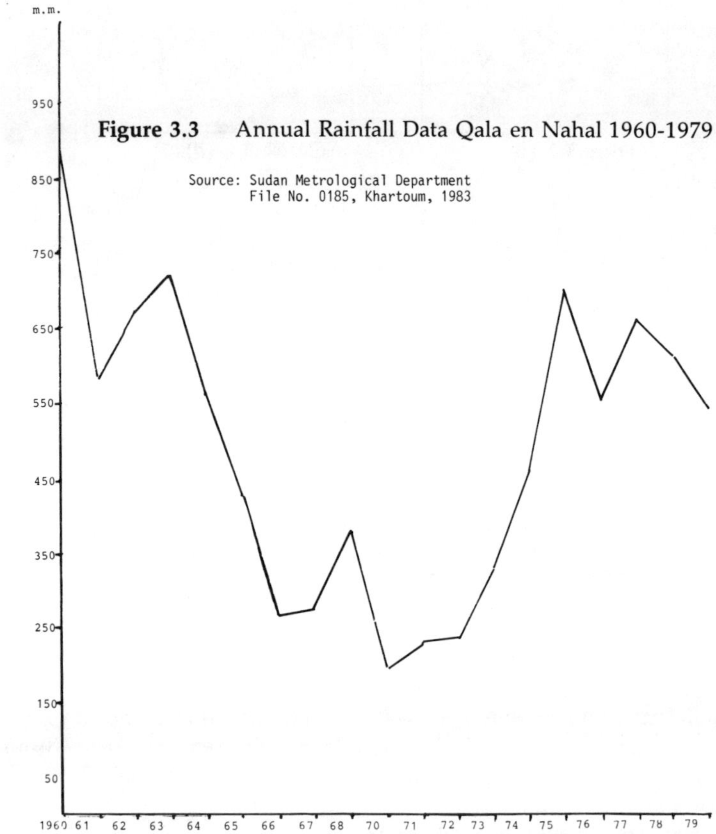

Figure 3.3 Annual Rainfall Data Qala en Nahal 1960-1979

Source: Sudan Metrological Department
File No. 0185, Khartoum, 1983

Figure 3.4 Monthly Rainfall Distribution Qala en Nahal

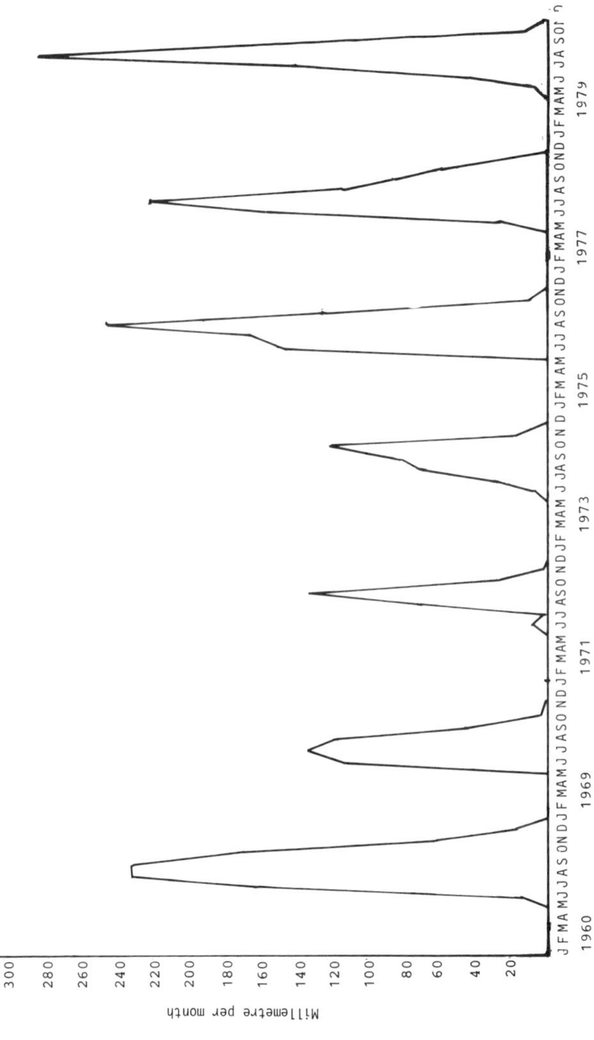

Source: Metrological Department. File No.0185, Khartoum, 1983

Source: Table 2.1

Figure 3.5 Monthly Distribution of Rainfall - Aburakham 1978-82

Source: Ministry of Irrigation, Aburakham, 1983

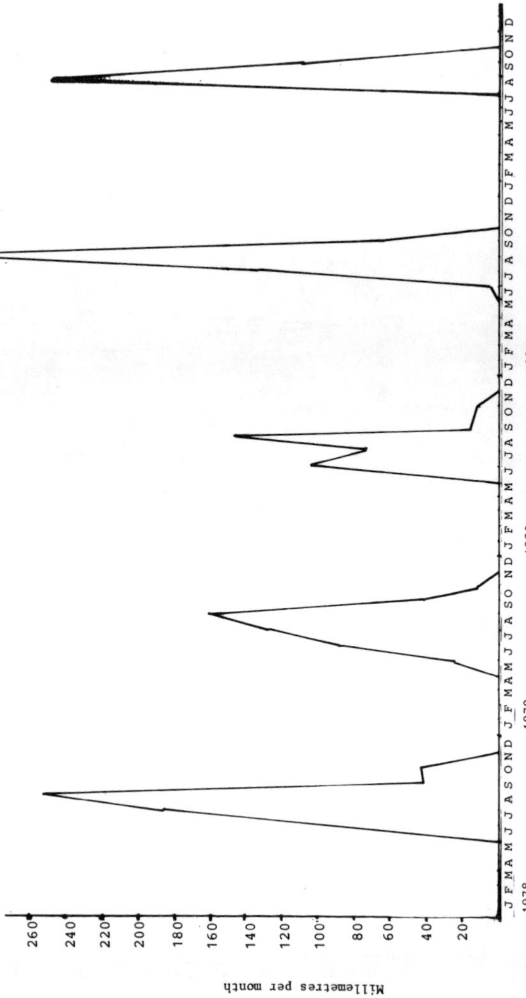

Vegetation
Since the area is one of the most fertile in the rainfed areas of the Sudan, most of the vegetation is cleared for crop production. 'The natural vegetation belongs to the low rainfall woodland savannah of the Acacia Seyal Balanites group.' (Agabawi: op.cit., 74) As a result of this clearing, for crop production does not involve 'great difficulties, bush regeneration in pastures is not a major problem and the climate and soil do not place any great difficulty in the way of mechanization'. (Suliman: op.cit., 25) Sorghum, millet, cotton, groundnuts and sesame are grown. In the Qala en Nahal area, *Acacia seyal, A. senagal, A. campylacantha, A. fistula, Lannea fructicosa* and others are found. (Spooner: op.cit., 25-26) Some of the grasses pose great problems in weeding and cultivation. For example, Spooner notes that 'the tufted grasses of Tuber create a noticeable problem with tractor cultivation and are difficult to remove even with hand pulling. Other troublesome weeds in the vegetation of the cultivated area include the wild sorghum grasses'.

TABLE 3.1. Aburakham Rainfall Data 1978-1982 (mm).

Month	1978	1979	1980	1981	1982
January	0	0	0	0	0
February	0	0	0	0	0
March	0	0	0	0	0
April	0	0	0	0	0
May	0	24	0	0	0
June	0	89	105	5.5	0
July	187	128	75.5	133.6	0
August	253.5	161	147.5	306.0	249.9
September	42.5	42	16.0	63.0	109.0
October	45.0	12	12.3	0	0
November	0	0	0	0	0
December	0	0	0	0	0
Annual	528.0	456	356.3	502.6	358.9

Source: Ministry of Irrigation: Aburakham, 1983.

Water Supplies
As noted earlier, one of the major constraints on the expansion of agriculture production in the Sudan in general and Kassala province in particular is inadequate water supply both for humans and livestock. As a result, the whole Gedaref region, including the town itself, suffers from an acute shortage of domestic water during the dry season. (During our survey,

Figure 3.6 Annual Rainfall Data 1978-1982, Aburakham

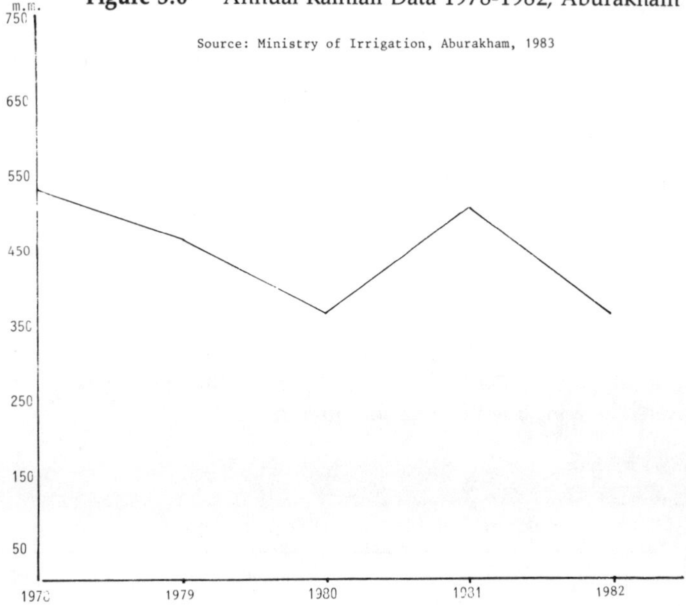

Gedaref town was faced with a very serious shortage.) During the dry season, *hafirs* and shallow wells are the main source of water. To alleviate the problem 'a few deep bores ranging from 540–1000 feet deep have been established in a few isolated areas'. (Agabawi: op.cit., 74) Hafir water is used for human consumption, but it can, if unprotected, be a cause of water-borne diseases. In the absence of better alternatives, however, *hafirs* still remain the major sources of water in most of the region.

Before the establishment of the settlement, there was no water supply system in the Qala en Nahal area. The major source in the season after the rains were shallow wells, which dried up during the period preceding the rainy season. After this happened, the people in the villages either migrated to the Rahad River area or fetched water by camel from the Abu Nahl area, about 34 km from the villages. During the establishment period, water was brought to the settlement by water tanks from the Rahad river. Some years later, water supplies for the settlements and the surrounding Sudanese villages started to be provided from a pump station at Abu Nahl, 34 km away on the river Rahad which supplies the six refugee villages of Zurzur, Umbrush, Dehema, Adingrar, Umsaqata, and Salmin. The Sudanese in the surrounding villages also draw water freely from the refugee villages. As can be seen from Figure 3.7, the system consists of pumped storage on the bank of the Rahad river, at a place called Abu Nahl and a pipeline about 34 km long laid between the storage *hafirs* and the villages. The pipeline from the main *hafirs* feeds four service *hafirs* along the route, and service pipelines provide water to the villages from the service *hafirs*.

When the flow of the water is high enough and free of silt during the rainy season, mainly between July and October, the 24" valves are opened to allow a flow of water into the two storage *hafirs* by gravity. In a fovorable rainy season about 37% of the storage hafirs' capacity can be filled. The rest is filled by pumping.

The water-holding capacity of the two storage *hafirs* is 200,000 m^3 and 150,000 m^3, respectively. (West: 1981, 31) The latter *hafir* leaked and was empty during the survey. It is estimated that about 30% of the water is lost to evaporation, breakage and at the village water points.

From the service *hafirs*, water is pumped through 4" asbestos-insulated cement pipes to storage tanks at the villages. Each village has water points consisting of a storage tank and taps. The water points in the villages are surrounded by a swamp and waterlogged mud mixed with animal droppings, which is often a fertile ground for insect breeding. In Zurzur, Adingrar, Umbrush and Dehema, the waste water from the water points is directed to small plots of vegetable gardens which become good sources of vegetables during the dry season. The plots are very small, about 1/50 feddan in Zurzur, 1/4 feddan in Umbrush, 1/3 feddan in Adingrar and about 1/2 feddan in Dehema. In the villages of Umsaqata and Salmin, where the majority of the inhabitants are former semi-pastoralists, the waste water is left unutilized.

There may be adequate water when both the storage *hafirs* are filled to capacity and when loss of water does not occur due to leakage along the pipeline. However, during the survey between October 1982 and April 1983, both the refugee and the local Sudanese populations were complaining about water shortage, mainly caused by leakages in one of the storage *hafirs* and worn-out engines which had been operating at only 25% of their capacity for the last 12 months. Large quantities of water are also lost due to pipe breakage, often due to damages caused by cattle herders. Between Dehema and Umsaqata, we counted about 34 leakages along the pipeline. It is difficult to estimate the amount of water lost in this manner, but it all adds up to create a critical shortage, especially immediately before the rainy season.

Funds were donated by the Swedish Development Authority (SIDA) to refurbish the water supply system in the Qala en Nahal refugee settlement in 1980, but due to problems of implementation the work was delayed until 1983. The author tried to make a rough estimate of the per capita water consumption in the settlement, and the result was shockingly low. It appears to be about 7 litres per capita a day which is far below the amount required by an average person in a similar climatic condition.

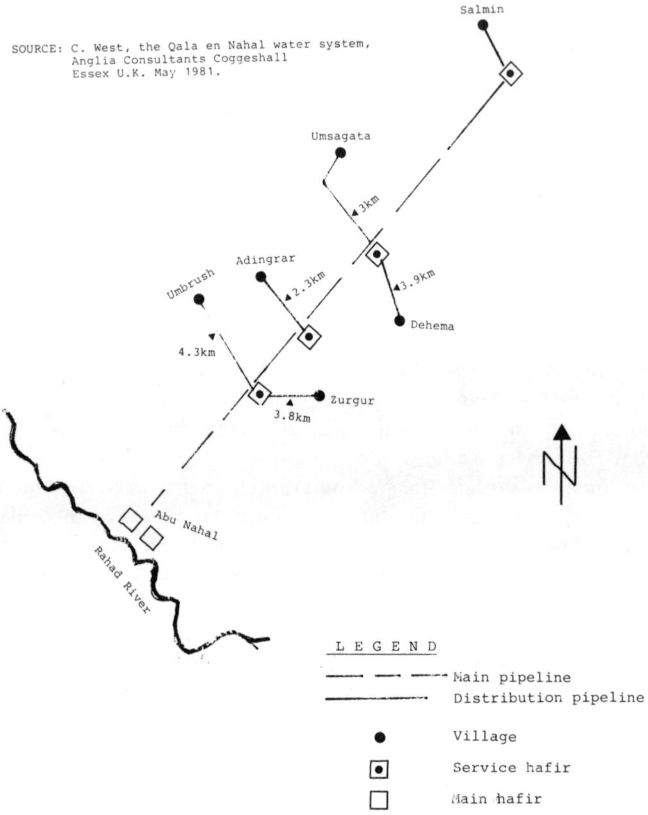

Figure 3.7 Sketch of the Qala en Nahal Water Supply System.

The reasons for such a low water consumption are difficult to understand. The time lost in queuing for water in the often unbearable heat may be one of the factors. Furthermore, charges are collected at the water points and represent considerable costs and therefore a deterrent to the poor refugee households. Most of the refugees' households depend on purchased water. Those who have donkeys fetch water for sale and to compensate for the time spent queuing, they charge high prices; for example, a water bag (one donkey load) costs £0.8. But the main cause of the low consumption is the inability of the water supply system to keep pace with the demand. In order to ease the shortage, cattle are banned from watering in the water points during the dry season.

In the settlements of Aburakham and Wad Awad, there is no shortage of water because a canal passes near the villages, and the refugees draw untreated water from it. There are water taps in the villages, but to avoid the morass surrounding the water points and due to breakdowns, the majority prefer to draw water from the canal.

To determine the quality of the water, the author had long discussions with the medical personnel in each settlement and according to them, the overwhelming majority of the refugees and the Sudanese were suffering from giardia which is believed to be caused by water pollution. In Aburakham, over 80% of the children who visited the clinic in February 1983 had diseases which were water-related. The situation in Qala en Nahal is not qualitatively different from that of Aburakham. There is clearly a great need for a water purification system in the settlements, something which has been neglected so far by the bodies concerned.

BACKGROUND ON THE SUDAN

The Democratic Republic of the Sudan is the largest country in Africa, extending over an area of more than 2.5 million square km. The Sudan is bounded by Egypt in the north, Ethiopia and Eritrea in the east, Zaire, Kenya, and Uganda in the south and Chad, Central African Republic and Libya in the west. According to the latest 1983 census, the population is 21.6 million, out of which 80% live in the rural areas. (Osman *et al.*: 1984, 1) The population density is 8.6 persons per km^2. This low density hides the fact that a great part of the country is unsuitable for agricultural production due to lack of rainfall and irrigation.

The Sudan is among the least developed countries in the world with a per capita GDP of about US$380 in 1981, and most of the population lacks access to some basic amenities, as shown by the following indicators. In 1979, only 46% of the population had access to clean water; 26.4% had access to electricity in 1965; in 1976 adult literacy rate was 20%; primary school enrollment in the same period was 50%. (World Bank Report: 1982) In 1981, the Sudan had 171 hospitals (1.1 per 100,000 persons), 16,596 hospital beds (101 per 100,000 persons), 201 health centers (1 per 100,000 persons), 736 dispensaries (4 per 100,000 persons),1901 dressing stations (10 per 100,000 persons), a physician per 10,300 persons, and 1 medical assistant per 7400 persons. (Ministry of Health and World Health Organization quoted in Saghayroun: 1982) The lack of drugs and other facilities caused by shortage of foreign exchange is very worrying.

The economy of the Sudan is predominantly agricultural. Agricultural represents between 36 and 39% of the GDP. About 90% of the country's foreign exchange earnings come from the agricultural sector, especially cotton.

Agriculture in the Sudan is comprised of three sub-sectors—modern irrigation, mechanized rainfed and traditional rainfed. (For the share of each subsector in area and production, see Table 3.2.) The output in agriculture, except for a few crops, has either declined, increased only slightly, or remained stagnant throughout the 1970s and 1980s. For example, cotton output declined from 671,000 tons in 1973/4 to 287,000 tons in 1970/81. The same was true for all crops except sorghum and groundnuts. There was a recovery for most of the crops in 1981/82, only to be followed by a serious decline in the 1982/83 season. Drought is one of the most important recent causes of the decline in agriculture output.

The decline has led to decreased export earnings, a decreased food supply and, consequently, to balance of payment problems. After 1973 there was a sharp increase of imports and a sharp lag of export earnings. For example, the trade balance for 1980 shows a large deficit, with imports accounting for about 290% of exports. All available evidence indicates that the country is in the grip of a serious economic crisis—and a country plagued by many unresolved problems cannot alleviate the plight of refugees on its own.

TABLE 3.2. Relative Share of Irrigated, Mechanized Rainfed and Traditional Rainfed Crop Sector in Crop Area and Output, 1977/78 Season.

	Per cent of total	
Sub-sector	Area	Production
Irrigated	16	55
Mechanized rainfed	22	10
Traditional rainfed	62	35
	100	100

Source: Recent Performance of the Agricultural Sector: An Analysis of Agricultural Production Trends and Policies in the Sudan. Ministry of National Planning Agricultural Section, Khartoum, December, 1979.

The only exception to the downward trend in agriculture found in cotton, which increased from 387,000 tons in 1981-82 to 465,000 tons in 1982-83. The 1982-83 season was one of the worst seasons for agricultural output. For example, sorghum output declined from 3,256,000 tons in 1981-82 to 1,938,000 tons in 1982-83.

REFUGEES IN THE SUDAN

The problem of refugees in the Sudan dates back to the middle of the 1950s when southern Sudanese crossed the borders of the neighboring countries to seek asylum from political instability, which later became armed conflict. By 1970, there were about 173,000 southern Sudanese refugees in the neighboring countries: in Uganda (74,000), Central African Republic (23,000), The Democratic Republic of the Congo (55,000), and Ethiopia (21,000).

In March 1965 about 7,000 Congolese refugees entered Equatoria Province in the southern Sudan. (NCAR: Documentation for the June 20-23 Conference, Vol. 1, 1980, 1) The same source states that during the years 1966-1970, some 4,000 refugees repatriated voluntarily and the rest remained mostly in Eastern Equatoria. The number of the Congolese refugees remained about 5,000 between 1967 and 1984 (see Table 3.3).

The first influx of the Eritrean refugees occurred in March 1967 when 28,600 refugees crossed into the Sudan following an attack launched by the Ethiopian army against the areas where the Eritrean Liberation Front was operating. The number of the Eritrean refugees has continued to grow since then. After 1974 many refugees from Ethiopia also came to the Sudan and joined the Eritreans. The number of the Ethiopian and Eritrean refugees increased from 28,600 in 1967 to 465,000 in 1984, an increase of about 16-fold. (Table 3.3)

In 1976, about 500 Ugandans sought asylum in the Sudan. However, since 1980 there has been a dramatic increase of the Ugandan refugees. In that year, 69,000 refugees sought asylum in the south and their number has since then continued to grow unabated. In 1984 there were about 200,000 Ugandan refugees in the southern Sudan. The Sudan also received a new wave of refugees in 1980, when about 16,000 refugees from Chad sought asylum in the western provinces.

These statistics are rough estimates rather than precise figures based on census. Refugee statistics throughout Africa tend to be based on 'educated guesses' as countries of asylum find it difficult to register the refugees within their territories. Since about 80% of the Ethiopian and Eritrean refugees are 'spontaneously' settled, it is impossible for the UNHCR and GOS to know their precise number.

Following the Eritrean influx, the GOS appealed to the UNHCR for assistance and the latter allocated $150,000 from the Emergency Fund

> . . . for the refugees from Ethiopia . . . residing near the town of Kassala . . . to cover the local purchase of food commodities and the distribution pending the arrival of World Food Program supplies.
>
> (Official Records of the Gen. Ass., Twenty-third Session, Supplement No. 11 A)

Under the 1968 program the UNHCR allocated $300,000 to facilitate rural settlement of the refugees. The refugees were held in transit camps south of the Kassala town along the Gash seasonal river. (Karadawi & Ibrahim: 1981) When the repatriation of the Eritrean refugees became less feasible, the UNHCR insisted on relocating the refugees to 'permanent' settlements, partly for security reasons and partly to create the conditions for self-reliance. The $150,000 from the Emergency Fund was allocated, while

> pending the elaboration of a long-term solution to the Eritrean refugee problem, the Government shall remove temporarily the refugees from their present location.

TABLE 3.3. Total Number of Refugees in the Sudan 1967-1984 by Country of Origin.

Year	Ethiopia	Congo (Zaire)	Uganda	Chad	Total
1967	28,600	4,700	–	–	33,300
1968	31,000	7,300	–	–	38,300
1969	31,000	7,300	–	–	38,300
1970	55,000	6,000	–	–	61,000
1971	54,500	5,000	–	–	59,500
1972	52,500	4,500	–	–	57,000
1973	46,000	5,000	–	–	51,000
1974	49,000	4,500	–	–	53,500
1975	85,500	5,000	–	–	90,000
1976	105,000	4,500	500	–	110,000
1977	145,000	4,500	500	–	150,000
1978	270,000	3,500	500	–	274,000
1979	346,000	3,500	500	–	350,000
1980	390,000	5,000	69,000	16,000	480,000
1981	419,000	5,000	110,000	16,000	550,000
1982	419,000	5,000	130,000	16,000	570,000
1983	460,000	5,000	184,000	–	649,000
1984	465,000	5,000	200,000	1,000	671,000

Source: Reports of the UNHCR, Gen. Ass. Official Records, 23rd-37th session.
1. UNHCR Information-Sudan August 1982, No. 4 Branch Office Khartoum.
2. UNHCR REfugees, Dec. 1983.
3. Osman *et al.* The outcome of ICARA, 1984.

Historically, the Sudan has been affected by refugees due to internal political instabilities and international conflicts. Before the settlement of the conflict in the south in 1972, the Sudan was one of the major refugee producing countries in Africa. After the Addis Ababa peace agreement of March 1972 between the Sudanese Government and the Southern Sudanese Liberation movement, about 200,000 southern Sudanese returned home. (Adepoju: 1984, 1) If we include the return of those who were internally displaced, this figure increases to 500,000. (See Nobel: 1982, 6) In its attempt to rehabilitate and reintegrate the returnees, the GOS gained invaluable experience. This experience enabled the Government to cope with the influx of hundreds of thousands of refugees who have sought sanctuary from the neighboring countries of Zaire, Eritrea, Ethiopia, Uganda and Chad. The Sudan has also learned to cooperate effectively and to maintain close ties with the specialized agencies of the UN such as the UNHCR and the World Food Program (WFP) and the voluntary non-governmental agencies (NGOs).

In 1972 the GOS acceded to the international and regional instruments concerning refugees, namely the 1951 UN Convention relating to the Status of Refugees, the 1967 Protocol, and the 1969 OAU Convention. However, it must be noted that the Sudan was already pursuing an 'open door' policy for refugees even before its accedence to these agreements. The COR was created in 1967, for instance, five years before Sudan became a party to these instruments. Treatment of refugees was based upon the general principles of international conventions, mainly:

1) that asylum is a peaceful and humanitarian act;
2) that voluntary repatriation is the ideal solution to refugee problems;
3) in the absence of any foreseeable repatriation refugees are to be settled away from border areas with the aim of helping them to become self-supporting.

(Documentation: op.cit., 5)

The Sudan has enacted its own national refugee law known as the Regulations of Asylum Act. This Act is based on the same principles as the other international instruments on refugees and the definition of the term 'refugee' incorporates the same elements that are included in the UN and OAU Convention, although the Sudanese definition is slightly more exhaustive: the term 'refugee' is extended to include children who are not accompanied by adults, or who are war orphans, or whose guardians have disappeared and are outside the countries of their nationalities. (Art. 2 of the Asylum Act)

The Act spells out the rights and duties of the refugees, how refugee status is to be determined, and the authorities that are entrusted with the power to grant asylum and to administer refugee matters. There are certain restrictions imposed on refugees; for example, refugees are not allowed to own land or immovables in the Sudan and cannot leave their place of residence unless they have a travel permit (which is not always easy to acquire).

How is the status of a refugee determined in the Sudan? This is always a tricky question. The procedures in the international instruments on refugees are based on individual eligibility: the recipient country scrutinizes each individual case to determine his or her status. The Sudan has been receiving large-scale influxes of refugees since the mid-1960s and the scrutiny of individual asylum seekers for eligibility has proved to be impracticable. Thus in practice, mass determination of refugeehood is preferred to individual eligibility. Although the Sudanese legislation does not explicitly provide for the determination of refugee status in large-scale influxes of groups of asylum seekers, one of the tasks of the COR, as spelled out in 1967, is 'To determine the status of groups and individuals seeking asylum in the country . . .'. (Quoted in NCAR Documentation for the June 20-23 Conf.: 1980, 6) This is a unique and imaginative approach which has opened a new perspective on the determination of refugee status for large-scale influxes of refugees. However, the Regulation of Asylum Act, which was passed in 1974, neither repealed nor adopted this procedure.

Whenever there is inconsistency between a legislation and a regulation, normally the former prevails. However, since in this case the regulation that empowered the COR existed before the Act was passed, the drafter of the latter would have explicitly repealed the regulation if he had such an intention in mind. As noted earlier, since determination of refugeehood on an individual basis in large-scale influxes of asylum seekers is impossible, the regulation that authorized the COR to determine the refugee status of groups still seems to be the standard procedure.

The reasons that preclude individual eligibility for asylum in mass influxes or make it superfluous are many. First, for rural refugees, the causes of flight are often common to the whole community. Second, most African refugees are self-settled because it is often impossible to reach the refugee areas due to the lack of infrastructure. Third, because of the size of the border areas and the resource contraints in most African countries, it is difficult to control border areas, and refugees can easily avoid detection by the border police. (Refugees take several routes when they cross the Sudanese frontier: through the Red Sea Province, through the rural areas in Kassala, such as Hamdait, Wad Hileu, through the Blue Nile and the Upper Nile provinces, etc.) Fourth, the lack of administrative machinery does not permit the government to screen each individual case.

The Government of Sudan knows that there are disturbances in the neighboring countries and this is often the basis for the decision to allow mass asylum seekers to stay. The subjective fear of the individual asylum seeker is rarely taken into account. This has led to a high proportion of the asylum seekers and at times even 'illegal immigrants' being allowed to stay without their refugee status being formally determined. When a large-scale influx occurs, the GOS is more concerned with meeting the urgent basic necessities of the refugees rather than with determination of individual eligibility. In practice, all persons who cross the Sudanese frontiers from neighboring countries where there are events that disturb public order and who allege that they have left their native country due to these disturbances are regarded as refugees.

Despite the massive influx of asylum seekers and the pressing economic problems, the Sudan maintains an open door policy to refugees. This is one of the most liberal asylum policies in the world. The provision of sanctuary includes legal protection, emergency relief, such as clothing, shelter, medical care and water and, whenever voluntary repatriation is not foreseeable, Sudan collaborates with the UNHCR, WFP and other voluntary agencies to settle the refugees in areas away from the border as stipulated by the OAU Convention.

Settling the Refugees

The Sudan, in keeping with the international community, considers voluntary repatriation as the most durable solution to the problem of African refugees. However, because it has failed to materialize, especially for the Ethiopian, Eritrean and Ugandan refugees, Sudan has developed Africa's most ambitious settlement programs. These aim to enable the refugees to become self-supporting and productive members of the host community. Ultimately, these could also ease the financial and management burden imposed on the Sudan and the international community and, moreover, create a favorable situation whereby the refugees can contribute to the efforts of regional and national development.

Whether these objectives will be achieved is among other things a function of the nature of the host government's policy and subsequently its settlement programs. The National Committee for Aid to Refugees (NCAR) in its documentation for the 1980 June Conference, stated that 'the Government policy for the settlement program sets forth six elementary principles'. We shall only touch upon those policies that can directly or indirectly obstruct full integration of the refugees.

- A settlement should not provide the refugees with more resources or care than is extended to nationals in the area, or *than they used to have access to in their own country*.
- Settlements will be set up so as not to dispossess nationals in the area of land or opportunity. Services provided to the refugees must be open to the local population.
- Settlements must be attractive enough to retain a population of aliens without any initial sense of belonging there, *while at the same time not attracting a further influx*. (Emphasis added.)

The Sudan's generous settlement policy has made large areas of agricultural land available to the refugees. By March 1984, the Sudan was hosting about 671,000 refugees from Ethiopia, Eritrea, Zaire, Uganda and Chad. (See Osman *et al.*: 1984, 3) Although the refugees are scattered throughout the country, the Kassala Province in the eastern region and Equatoria Province in the south have the highest concentrations. The refugees are also found both in the rural and the urban areas. Out of the 671,000 refugees, 165,000 have settled spontaneously in the urban areas, 265,000 are in the organized settlements and the rest have presumably settled spontaneously in the rural areas and in the other small towns. (See Table 3.4)

TABLE 3.4. Distribution of the Refugees in the Urban Areas.

City	Number
Kassala	45,000
Gedaref	30,000
Port Sudan	50,000
Khartoum	40,000
Total	165,000

Source: Osman, Karadawi and Siddik, *The Outcome of the International Conference on Assistance to Refugees in Africa* ICARA I: Sudan Experience: 1984.

The self-settled refugees do not directly receive international aid except in few cases. Thus, they put great strain on the already inadequate social services of the Sudan.

Out of the 465,000 Ethiopian refugees (the majority are Eritreans but the source does not distinguish between Eritreans and Ethiopians), 78.5% are self-settled and only 21.5% are accommodated in the organized settlements. Out of the 200,000 Ugandan refugees, 82.5% are accommodated in 38 settlements and only 17.5% remain self-settled. Even though the overwhelming majority of the refugees are still outside the organized settlements, the GOS is opposed to the idea of spontaneous settlement. In the 1980 Conference in Khartoum, the GOS officially decided to phase out spontaneous settlement: it announced its decision to settle all of the refugees and presented Africa's most ambitious and comprehensive settlement program. Despite this, spontaneous settlement is not only still going strong but is expanding.

TABLE 3.5. Estimated Totals of the Refugees as of March 1984 by Country of Origin.

Country of Origin	Number
Ethiopia	465,000
Zaire	5,000
Uganda	200,000
Chad	1,000
Total	671,000

Source: Osman *et al.* op. cit.

At the opening session of the Khartoum Refugee Conference, the chairman of the National Committee for Aid to Refugees (NCAR), then the country's Vice President, stated that

> the vast majority had settled spontaneously, putting a strain on the inadequate resources and services available, causing competition between refugees and nationals over jobs, and making the refugees' situation more vulnerable since they were unable to attain economic viability. The gravity of this problem coincided with economic difficulties the country had to face. *The Government had therefore decided to phase out spontaneous settlement and to search for new and imaginative solutions to these problems.* (Emphasis added.)
>
> (Quoted in Kibreab, 1985)

Osman *et al.* also argue that 'The unorganized settlement (whatever examples of its success may be cited) is bound to be unwelcome. Its advantages as seen by the outsiders are irrelevant to the affected host community'. (Osman *et al.*: op.cit., 17)

By December 1983, there were a total of 23 organized settlements accommodating about 90,000 refugees in the eastern region. The UNHCR report at the end of 1982 estimated the total number of the refugees in the organized settlements in the east at 101,200. A recent report also estimated the total number of the settled refugees in the east at 100,000 (see Osman *et al.*, op.cit., 3). Out of the 23 organized settlements in the east, eight were established in 1980 and after.

Out of the 24 settlements in the east (the 24th is a transit camp), 6 are wage earning rural settlements, whereby the settlements are located at the boundaries of modern irrigated agricultural schemes, and the refugees are expected to become self-supporting by working for Sudanese tenants who are resettled in these agricultural schemes. One of the settlements is semi-urban, situated about 7 km from Gedaref, and the refugees are expected to work in the town of Gedaref and in the surrounding rainfed mechanized areas. One of the settlements is also a transit camp, wherein the new arrivals are kept until they are transferred to settlements. The rest are land settlements in which the refugees are provided with plots of land for cultivation. The latter type of settlement is the concern of this study.

THE ADMINISTRATIVE STRUCTURES

By 1967 when the influx of the Eritreans began, the GOS had already formulated a policy based on its experience with Sudanese refugees in neighboring countries and the Congolese refugees which had sought refuge in the Equatoria province from 1965 onwards. As the flow of the Congolese and Eritrean refugees increased, the need for the creation of a specialized agency was felt and in 1967 it was decided to appoint, under the auspices of the Ministry of Interior, a Commissioner for Refugees with a separate office and personnel.

The Office of the Commissioner was assigned the following tasks:

1. The administration of refugee matters in cooperation with the Commissioners of the provinces and other related Government Ministries and Departments.
2. To determine the status of groups and individuals seeking asylum in the country and to recommend policies for the ministry concerned.
3. To seek outside assistance for refugees and to coordinate government efforts with those of UN agencies and voluntary organizations.

(Documentation . . . op.cit., Vol. 1, 6)

The head office of the Commissioner for Refugees is in Khartoum with branch offices in Gedaref, Kassala and Juba headed by assistant Commissioners. The Commissioner's office has also a general manager's office in Shewak, which coordinates operations in all the settlements with *modirs* and local authorities in the eastern region. The Office of the Commissioner has also sub-branch offices in every group of settlements headed by *modirs* (scheme managers).

> All settlements are administered with UNHCR support by Sudanese Government personnel based on site and in regional headquarters at Shewak and Port Sudan. (Report on UNHCR Assistance Activities in 1982-83 . . . 1983, 11 D)

The report also states that in 1982 'UNHCR's assistance to these settlements in 1982 involved obligations totalling $US10,318,264 . . .'

Each settlement has its own village committees known as *Legina*. In some of the settlements the *Legina* are traditional leaders while in others they are elected. Their main duty is to execute orders issued by the *modirs,* to settle disputes arising among the refugees and to forward grievances, appeals or demands to the *modir*. In some of the settlements the *Legina* are very powerful. In the studied areas the relationship between the *modirs* and the refugees was very harmonious. Compared to the camp commanders in other parts of Africa, the office of the *modirs* in the Sudan are service-oriented and are rather close to the refugees within the available resource constraints.

The office of the *modirs* is open daily to receive individuals or groups of refugees. However, the relationship between the *modirs* and refugees can vary depending on the character of the individual *modir*.

The Commissioner's Office for Refugees (COR) is the 'implementing agency for all settlement projects and programs relating to refugees'. (Karadawi and Ibrahim: 1981, 5) In other refugee-hosting countries such as Zambia, Tanzania and Zaire, a neutral third party is recruited as an operational agency in a tripartite agreement with the representative government and the UNHCR. The tasks of the operational agency may vary with the nature of the terms of the agreement but often include provision of technical know-how and administration of funds provided by the UNHCR and other organizations mainly during settlement phases. Unlike these countries, the GOS has been reluctant to assign the task of implementation to a neutral third party agency. The reason for this is probably political—in light of the massive refugee influxes, especially in the east, the Government may fear that the refugees can be a source of political instability.

The COR has throughout remained the sole operational partner of the UNHCR in the eastern region. However, in southern Sudan, the GOS has allowed other neutral third party agencies to implement settlement programs, and in the east, following the 1980 Khartoum Conference, Euro-Action Acord was allowed to implement a tractor hire program in Qala in Nahal. In the fields of health, income-generating activities, community development and education, refugee-based organizations and NGOs are implementing various programs under the auspices of the COR or the peoples' local government.

The major partner of the GOS, in meeting the immediate needs of the refugees and in seeking durable solutions to the problem of refugees, has from the outset been the UNHCR. It opened a branch office in Khartoum in 1968. Since its first involvement, the UNHCR's role has been to provide legal protection against expulsion, to safeguard the refugees' right to education, employment, freedom of movement, etc., to assist the GOS in meeting the need for emergency relief by stimulating and coordinating material assistance and to seek with the GOS long-term solutions. Whenever voluntary repatriation fails to materialize, the long-term solutions include: meeting the costs of feasibility studies, the establishment of settlements with clean water, housing, schools, and clinics, the transfer of the refugees from the border areas to the settlement sites, and the initial agricultural inputs such as tractors and seeds. The objective of these undertakings is to enable the refugees to become self-supporting. The World Food Program (WFP) also supplies the refugees with free food during the first two years after the establishment of the settlement, by which time the refugees are expected to have attained a level of self-reliance. Following the Khartoum Conference in 1980, the WFP also agreed to provide food for the vulnerable refugees for a period of three years. (The vulnerable groups comprise families or individuals who due to age, physical handicap or sickness are unable to engage in the 'normal' income-generating activities. These include old people, handicapped, orphans and women-headed households.

Voluntary agencies also play an important role not only in emergency relief but also in other important development undertakings. During our survey of the settlements, there were various voluntary agencies involved in health, agriculture, community development, social work, education and some income-generating activities. These agencies were the Sudan Council of Churches/Eastern Sudan Relief Program (SCC/ESRP), which is involved in the fields of health (particularly mother and child health and the treatment of tuberculosis), community development and social work. Its clinic in Umsaqata treats referral cases from the Government dispensary in Umsaqata. Other agencies that were operating in the east included Islamic African Relief Agency, Sudan Aid, Euro-Action Acord, International Rescue Committee, Lalmba and Red Cross Societies.

Of all these voluntary agencies, the SCC/ESRP program is the most extensive. Not only does the SCC/ESRP provide social services to the refugees, but it is also a major employer of refugees with various skills. In December 1983 there were 457 refugees working for SCC/ESRP in Gedaref and in various settlements in the East. There were about 20 expatriate staff members working for SCC/ESRP during this period. Within their means all voluntary agencies are trying to make the best use of the human and technical resources that exist among the refugees.

LAND SETTLEMENTS IN EASTERN SUDAN

As we saw in Chapter 2, the first Eritrean influx—almost all from the western lowlands—occurred between February and March 1967. Many of the refugees were women and children. In the beginning both refugees and the local adminstration of Kassala province hoped that the political and military disturbance that led to the refugees' flight would cease and that the refugees would return home. But this hope was not to materialize at least within the foreseeable future, and the GOS and the UNHCR deemed it necessary to transfer the refugees to an area where they could settle 'permanently' until they voluntarily returned to their country of origin. The arguments for settlement are, first, as experience has incontestably shown, that to live on handouts in transit camps without having the possibility to take part in social production is physically stifling and psychologically dehumanizing. Experience has also shown that prolonged life in transit camps generates a 'refugee mentality' or state of dependence, which in the future may constitute a major block to achieving self-perpetuating socioeconomic structures. Second, the administrative and financial burdens imposed on the international community and the GOS could only be eased if the refugees became self-supporting. Third, both the transit camp and the area where the refugees were spontaneously settling were close to the border, which is inconsistent with the OAU Convention.

> At the beginning of 1968, in consultation with UNHCR, UNDP, and FAO, the Sudanese Government selected a site at Abu-Sabeka, about 100 miles from the Kassala region, for the rural settlement of the 28,000 refugees from Ethiopia. (Off. Rec. of the Gen. Ass. Twenty-third Session, Supp. No. 11 A)

The site was later abandoned because the territory was found to be unsuitable and a decision was instead taken to settle the refugees in the area around Umsaqata in the Qala en Nahal district.

In December 1968, an agreement was reached between the UNHCR and GOS for the settlement of 23,000 refugees over the 1969-72 period in the Qala en Nahal area 225 km south of Kassala town. Although this decision was not preceded by a feasibility study, the main reasons for selecting the area were 'low existing population and adequate reserves of suitable uncultivated land'. (Hunting: 1976, 10)

The Government also wanted to 'bring a tract of largely unused, yet potentially productive land into the Sudanese rural economy'. (Rogge: 1975 139) But due to the lack of water for human consumption and animal husbandry and the prevalence of biting flies, the area failed to attract settlers despite its suitability for agriculture.

> Mostly wooded, with an absence of permanent water other than a few locations such as Qala en Nahal and Balos and with a prevalence of biting flies, the area did not, in spite of fertile soils, attract any substantial settlement in the past. Even the Shukriya tribesmen, in their seasonal search for pasture, tended to avoid this region and seldom crossed the railway into what is now the scheme area.
>
> (K.M. Barbour quoted in Rogge: op.cit., 136)

Barbour further notes that:

> The few local inhabitants prior to the scheme were Furs or other Western Sudanese who had migrated to the area—They lived in abject poverty, were totally uneducated and appeared generally uninterested in economic advancement. Their villages had a recurrent tendency to spring up and die away as they decided to try their luck elsewhere.

The future of the area depended upon using water from the Rahad River to the southwest. This required heavy investments, which was for obvious reasons beyond the reach of the GOS. When the UNHCR agreed to meet the establishment costs of the settlement, including the basic infrastructures and the water supply system from the Rahad River, it was aware of the costs involved. According to the High Commissioner's Report, it was stated that

> while the provision of water will be a costly operation, it will benefit the whole region, as will the health and education measures to be taken in the settlement. (Official Rec. of the Gen. Ass., 24th Session, supp. No. 12 A)

Since the provision of water was considered a precondition for the successful establishment of the Qala en Nahal refugee settlement, a considerable proportion of the $950,000 was used for this purpose. (including $600,000 under the 1969 program and $350,000 remaining from 1968. An additional $450,000 was again allocated to be used for the construction of water supply in early 1970 from the trust funds.

The first pilot group of 250 refugees was transferred from the Kassala area in June 1969 to the Qala en Nahal. However, the transfer was interrupted by the rainy season and had to be resumed at the beginning of 1970—at which time 9,500 refugees were transferred to join the pilot group. Further transfer was precluded by setbacks in the water supply system in the settlement.

About $420,000 was allocated to facilitate the settlement of the refugees under the 1970 program. An additional 8,000 refugees were again transferred from the Kassala area to the Qala en Nahal settlement in 1971, bringing the total number of the settlers up to 17,750 by the end of the year; $287,000 was granted by the UNHCR under the 1971 program for the construction of primary schools. In 1972 about 3,000 refugees were transferred from a transit village of simple, temporary shelters at Wad Abu Nahal near the Rahad River to Dehema in Qala en Nahal. The total number of the refugees that were originally settled in the Qala en Nahal was in the range of 22,000, although some reports say there were less: a report published by the UNHCR in 1972 estimated the total population in Qala en Nahal to be 18,000 when the last village (Dehema) was completed (UNHCR, Report—Water Road—. . . 1972, 11), and according to Hunting, then UNHCR consultant, the original population of Qala en Nahal settlement was 18,278. (Hunting: 1976, 13) These discrepancies show the level of imprecision that surrounds refugee statistics in Africa. If exact figures for refugees in a newly established settlement are difficult to ascertain, it is easy to see how difficult it is to know the number of refugees in old and spontaneous settlements where there are in-and-out migrations.

Between 1969 and 1972 the six villages of Umsaqata, Umbrush, Dehema, Adingrar, Salmin, and Zurzur were established, totally accommodating about 22,000 refugees. Except the two villages of Zurzur and Adingrar, the other four villages had corresponding Sudanese villages with a total population of 1,691 in 1973. Since then the Sudanese population has increased drastically.

The refugees had no role to play either in the selection of the site or in the decision to establish the settlement. Rogge also states that

> the refugees were given no choice but to participate in the scheme, nor were there any consultations with the settlers regarding the selection of sites for re/settlement. Moreover, in developing the villages, there was little settler participation in such activities as hut construction due to their generally weak physical conditions. . . .
>
> (Rogge: op.cit., 140)

In fact, the refugees were strongly opposed to being transferred to 'permanent' settlements because they thought that this was incompatible with their perception of refuge and their strong desire to return home. As Karadawi puts it,

> . . . the refugees believe that their resettlement in the Sudan was a conspiracy comparable to the Palestinian question as it was also plotted by the UN and the Ethiopian Government in collaboration with the Sudanese authorities.
>
> (Quoted in Kibreab, 1983, 63)

The economic foundation of the Qala en Nahal settlement is agriculture based on a system of family farms, each family being allocated, in theory at least, 10 feddans of cultivable land. Agricultural production is based on a partially mechanized system whereby the settlement management is responsible for the provision and maintenance of tractor services, for which the settlers were eventually expected to meet the running costs. During the establishment period the refugees were exempted from all taxes, and tractor service charges were also waived. The machinery pool consists of 21 tractors and 20 wide-level drills, based at the village of Umsaqata and distributed to the various villages according to their needs during the cultivation period. This was provided by the UNHCR, to be centrally managed by the settlement manager appointed by the COR.

Land is provided by the GOS, and most of the initial costs such as health services, elementary school education, clean water supply, costs incurred in the transfer of the refugees, housing and machinery capital costs wre borne by the UNHCR. The WFP supplied food rations in the establishment period. Various voluntary organizations were also involved in the creation of the basic necessary infrastructure. The Swedish Red Cross financed the dispensary at Umsaqata, and other organizations such as the Refugee Council of Denmark, Finland, Iceland and Norway, the British Council of Churches, and Christian Aid made donations to the UNHCR to finance a school building program, which was begun in 1972 under the direction of the Ministry of Education and the Interior. Of all the undertakings, the water supply system proved the most prohibitively expensive and was not completed until 1973, which necessitated supply through tanker trucks. This was a very expensive and unreliable means of supply given the condition of roads and maintenance facilities and the supply of spare parts and fuel.

By 1972, most of the land was under cultivation, the construction of the primary schools was also completed and some progress had been made in installing the water supply system.

The total cost of the scheme in the establishment period (between 1968 and 1972) was in the range of $3,057,000. This only refers to the amount which was spent on durable solutions, such as the construction of huts, roads, health services, primary schools, water supply system, seeds and tractors, and does not include the costs incurred by the WFP. (Out of this sum $450,000 was

Organised refugee settlements in Kassala and Blue Nile Province

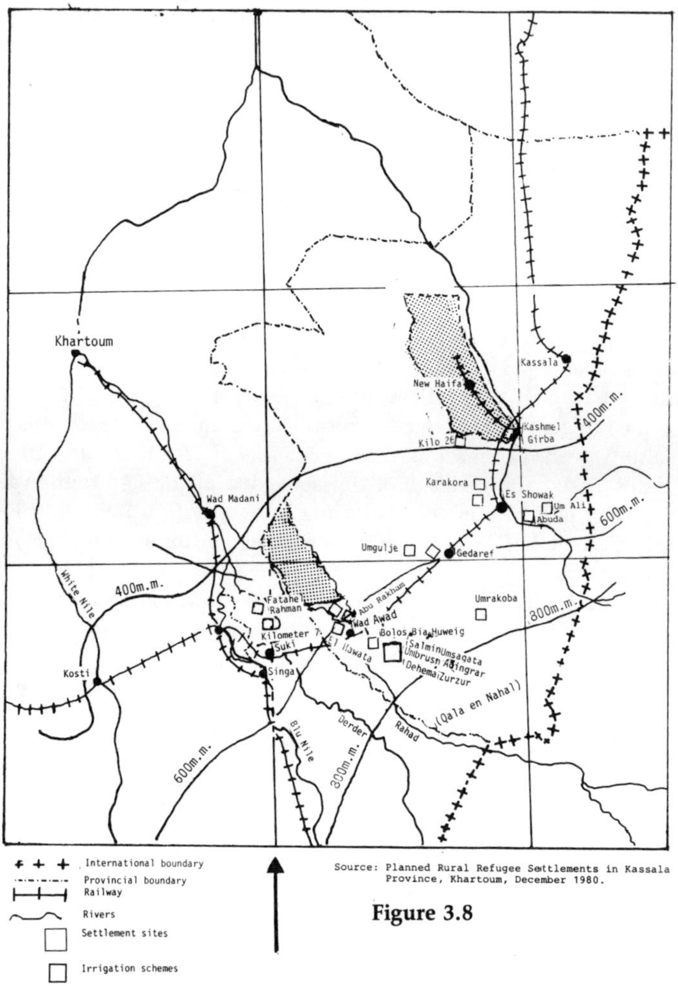

Source: Planned Rural Refugee Settlements in Kassala Province, Khartoum, December 1980.

Figure 3.8

contributed by the Swedish and Danish Governments and from proceeds obtained from the sale of the record "World Star Festival" to meet part of the cost of the water supply system.)

In 1978, 5,500 Eritrean refugees were transferred from the transit camp of Wad Hileu near the border to the permanent settlements of Qala en Nahal,

Umgurgur and Es Suki in accordance with the plan drawn in 1976 to relocate the refugees from the border areas to permanent settlements. Of the 18,000 refugees in the transit camp of Wad Hileu, some 12,000 were transferred to the land settlements of Aburakham, Umgurgur, Karakora, Qala en Nahal and Es Suki in 1979. New wage-earning settlements were also established during the same year, accommodating about 6,000 refugees in Kashmel Girba and Kilometer 26. By the end of 1979, the total number of refugees in rural settlements in Kassala province reached about 42,000.

CHAPTER 4

The Refugee Households

Literature dealing with African refugees often states that African rural refugees consist of mainly women, children, old men and old women. But it appears from our study that when flight involves whole communities (villages), there are no remarkable differences in age and sex structures between refugee communities and non-displaced rural communities. In this chapter we present the demographic and occupation structures of the refugee households and whenever possible compare them with the rural population of the area. Demographic data and data on past and present occupation structures are crucial for the planning of income generating activities and for the provision of infrastructural services to the refugee communities.

THE POPULATION

During the survey there were 16 land settlements accommodating about 100,000 Ethiopian and Eritrean refugees in the East. However, this figure varies according to different sources, and to date there are no accurate data on the actual number of refugees either in the settlements or in the Sudan in general. Table 4.1 gives an estimation of the total population in the settlements according to various sources.

According to the official statistics, the total number of settlers in the six villages of Qala en Nahal was over 18,000 in 1970 and their number declined drastically up to 1976. According to the same source, the number of settlers again increased considerably in 1980. However, despite the fact that the official records in Umsaqata showed a population of slightly over 22,000, the Documentation for the June 20-23 Conference in the same year noted that

> Today, the settlement accommodates 30,000 in the villages of Umsaqata, Salmin, Umbrush, Adingrar, Zurzur, and Dehema.
>
> (Conference Documentation Vol. 1: 1980, 8)

TABLE 4.1. Population Distribution by Village according to Various Sources 1970-83.

Village	1970	1976	1980	1981	1983
Salmin	4,091	3,471	4,400	4,610	6,367
Umsaqata	3,629	3,276	4,606	3,910	4,526
Dehema	1,213	1,270	3,222	1,750	3,276
Adingrar	2,513	2,087	3,696	2,940	3,217
Umbrush	2,832	1,745	3,780	2,840	4,136
Zurzur	4,000	1,438	2,696	2,000	2,918
Total	18,278	13,287	22,156	18,050	24,440

Source:
1-3: Scheme Administration Records Agricultural File M/A/L/2/A/1, Umsaqata, 1970-1980.
4: Euro Action-Accord Survey 1981.
5: Questionnaire Survey plus SCC/ESRP TB Campaign Records.

However, a careful calculation shows that the total number of persons accommodated in the six villages in Qala en Nahal in 1983 was about 24,000.

The total population in Aburakham and Wad Awad are 2,664 and 2,112, respectively. The refugees in the settlements came to the Sudan over a period of about 15 years. (See Table 4.2)

As can be seen from Tables 4.2 and 4.3, out of the total sample households in Qala en Nahal, about 66% of the households crossed into the Sudan between 1967 and 1973 and about 65% of the sample were transferred to Qala en Nahal between 1969 and 1973. The rest came to the Sudan in the following years with the largest influx in 1975. After the major transfers that occurred during the establishment period (1969-72) in Qala en Nahal, about 25% of the settlers in Umbrush, Dehema and Adingrar were transferred in 1978 and 1979, while the overwhelming majority of the refugees in Aburakham and Wad Awad came to the Sudan after 1974.

The number of families in Umsaqata, Umbrush, Dehema, Adingrar, Aburakham, and Wad Awad in late 1982 and early 1983 were 742, 701, 546, 585, 600, and 320, respectively. In Salmin and Zurzur (Qala en Nahal) the total families were 1,117 and 512 respectively.

THE FAMILIES

Size

The distribution of the sample households according to the size of the family is given in Table 4.4.

TABLE 4.2. Percentage Distribution of the Household Heads by Year of Arrival in the Sudan.

Year	Umsaqata	Umbrush	Dehema	Adingrar	Aburakham	Wad Awad	Total
1961-66*	1.7	2.2	–	–	4.7	–	1.0
67	83.3	40.0	19.1	20.0	3.4	3.1	29.7
68	3.3	–	2.1	–	–	–	1.0
69	3.3	–	–	–	–	–	1.0
70	–	6.7	17.0	28.0	–	3.1	9.0
71	–	–	10.6	14.0	–	–	4.1
72	–	2.2	2.1	4.0	1.7	3.1	2.1
73	–	–	2.1	–	1.7	3.1	1.0
74	–	13.3	4.3	10.0	3.4	–	5.2
75	1.7	22.2	27.7	14.0	37.3	15.6	20.0
76	3.3	2.2	8.5	–	16.9	9.4	6.9
77	–	–	–	6.0	5.1	9.4	3.1
78	3.3	6.7	2.1	4.0	20.3	37.5	11.0
79	–	4.4	2.1	–	5.1	15.6	3.8
80	–	–	–	–	1.7	–	0.3
81	–	–	2.1	–	–	–	0.3
82	–	–	–	–	1.7	–	0.3
Total	99.9	99.9	99.8	100.0	100.0	99.9	99.8

*These are people who risked persecution individually in the period preceding the escalation of the war.

TABLE 4.3. Percentage Distribution of the Refugee Households by Year of Arrival in the Settlement.

Year	Umsaqata	Umbrush	Dehema	Adingrar	Aburakham	Wad Awad	Total
1969	8.8	4.4	–	6.0	–	–	4.1
1970	70.2	37.8	–	18.0	–	–	25.2
1971	7.0	2.2	–	24.0	–	–	8.6
1972	3.5	–	24.0	18.0	–	–	4.8
1973	–	2.2	10.6	–	–	–	2.1
1974	–	2.2	8.6	–	–	–	0.3
1975	–	2.2	–	–	–	–	0.3
1976	–	–	2.1	–	–	–	0.3
1977	–	–	–	–	–	–	–
1978	7.0	31.4	16.4	14.0	–	–	9.6
1979	1.7	4.4	31.9	18.0	79.7	–	25.7
1980	–	6.7	–	–	13.6	84.4	13.0
1981	1.7	6.7	6.4	2.0	5.1	15.6	5.5
1982	–	–	–	–	1.7	–	0.3
Total	99.9	99.9	100.0	100.0	100.1	100.0	99.8

TABLE 4.4. Percentage Distribution of the Sample Households by Family Size.

Number of members	Umsaqata	Umbrush	Dehema	Adingrar	Aburakham	Wad Awad	Total
1-2	15.2	20.0	12.8	6.0	28.8	15.6	16.8
3-4	30.5	17.8	29.8	42.0	22.0	12.5	26.7
5-6	32.2	31.1	27.6	28.0	35.6	34.4	31.5
7-8	16.9	31.1	19.1	18.0	8.5	18.7	18.2
9-10	5.1	–	10.6	4.0	5.1	18.7	6.5
over 10	–	–	–	2.0	–	–	0.3
Total	99.9	100.0	99.9	100.0	100.0	99.9	100.0

About 43% of the families have one to four individuals each. About 50% have between 5 to 8 individuals, while only about 7% have over 8 individuals each. The sample households' sizes varied considerably among the villages. Out of the six villages studied, Aburakham has the lowest average family size—4.4 persons. This is because of the relatively high proportion of households headed by females (about 36% of the sample) and the high proportion of single men and women. (See Table 4.7.) Wad Awad has the largest average family size among the refugee villages—6.6 persons. (See Table 4.5)

Even though the extended family system is not totally absent in the refugee communities, the nuclear family is the basic unit of production. The family is usually composed of husband, wife and children (who are often unmarried or newly married) and a few dependents who are under the direct responsibility of the household heads.

The average family size in northern rural Sudan is 6.7; it is 7.0 in Kassala Province. (See Rural Labor Study... Table 19: 1983) In the New Halfa irrigated agricultural scheme, the average size of the household is 8 persons. (Khalil: 1980, 5) For the Gezira irrigated agricultural scheme, the average family size is 8.5 persons. (Hamid quoted in Khalil: 1980) The difference in average family size between the refugee households and rural Sudanese households is difficult to explain. However, the extended family system is weakened in the settlements, and this may partly explain the difference.

According to our findings over 72% of the sample families consisted solely of the nuclear family. Where the extended family system did exist, it was relatively more prevalent in the two settlements of Umsaqata and Umbrush, among the Beni Amer ethnic group.

The phenomenon of monogamy has also become a dominant form of marriage even among Moslem communities. (See Table 4.6)

A considerable number of the older refugees claim to have divorced their wives after arrival in the Sudan. As given in Table 4.6, about 92% of the total sample of male household heads are monogamous. The causes that weakened

TABLE 4.5. Average Size of the Sample Households.

Settlement	Nuclear	Extended
Umsaqata	5.0	6.1
Umbrush	5.1	5.9
Dehema	5.2	6.0
Adingrar	5.2	5.5
Aburakham	4.2	4.4
Wad Awad	6.0	6.6
Average for total	5.0	5.7

TABLE 4.6. Distribution of the Sample Household Heads by Number of Wives (Per cent).

Number of wives	Umsaqata	Umbrush	Dehema	Adingrar	Aburakham	Wad Awad	Total
1	96.0	89.7	92.5	88.6	97.4	82.7	91.7
2	4.0	7.7	7.5	11.4	2.6	14.0	7.4
3	–	2.6	–	–	–	3.4	0.8
Total	100.0	100.0	100.0	100.0	100.0	100.1	99.9

the traditional extended family structure and polygamous practices among the refugee communities are not easy to understand. It is by no means a result of the refugee women's fight for equality because practically nothing is done to bring them out of their seclusion and to diminish the economic and cultural domination of the refugee males. According to the refugees, monogamy is a reflection of the level of impoverishment in the settlements. They claim it is difficult to maintain two women and their children.

During the establishment of the settlements, cultivable land and huts for shelter were distributed at random without the individual refugees being able to choose the location within the village, and members of the extended families could no longer live in the same compound. Another factor which may also have weakened the system is that after the refugees crossed into the Sudan, the head of the extended family lost his power gradually as he lost the means to sustain the members of his family; his place was taken by the *sheikhs* (clan heads) who were distributing all rations and other facilities from donor organizations.

Age, Sex Structure and Marital Status

The distribution of the sample household heads according to their sex is given in Table 4.7. About 85% of the total sample households are headed by men and 15% are headed by females. However, the total average hides the fact that about 36% of the sample household heads in Aburakham are headed by females.

How does this compare with the situation in northern rural Sudan? In northern rural Sudan 3.3% of families are headed by females. The refugee communities clearly have more families that are headed by females, and the situation in Aburakham is yet again different from the rest of the refugee settlements. However, this does not mean that, as is often claimed, these families have fled their areas of origin leaving their male household heads behind. The majority of the refugees in Aburakham are originally from the border towns of Humera and Um Hajer, where prostitution and brewing were widely prevalent. Hence, those communities were from the outset characterized by the presence of more female-headed households, and thus it is not surprising that there are many more households which are headed by females in this village than in the other villages.

As Table 4.8 shows, there is no major difference between the marital status of the refugee communities and the rural population in northern Sudan, except that there are about 13% more single individuals among the Sudanese than among the refugees. However, the difference is probably due to the fact that the data on the Sudanese rural population is based on total population and the data on the refugees is based on sample household heads. The latter does not include those persons who have attained marriage age, but are still residing with their parents. The data on the rural Sudanese is based on marriage age rather than on household heads, i.e., those individuals who have attained

TABLE 4.7. Sex Distribution of the Heads of Households in the Sample (Per cent).

Sex	Umsaqata	Umbrush	Dehema	Adingrar	Aburakham	Wad Awad	All villages
Male	83.6	86.7	89.4	94.0	64.4	100	84.7
Female	16.4	13.3	10.6	6.0	35.6	–	15.3
Total	100.0	100.0	100.0	100.0	100.0	100	100.0

TABLE 4.8. Marital Status of the Heads of the Households (Per cent).

Marital status	Umsaqata	Umbrush	Dehema	Adingrar	Aburakham	Wad Awad	Total	Northern[1] Rural Sudan
Married	83.6	86.7	87.2	88.0	66.4	87.5	82.3	72.6
Single	3.3	4.4	2.1	4.0	6.8	9.4	4.8	18.2
Sep./Divorced	–	2.2	2.1	2.0	10.2	–	3.1	2.0
Widow/Widower	10.0	6.7	6.4	6.0	15.2	–	8.2	6.9
Grass Widow	3.3	–	2.1	–	1.7	3.1	1.7	–
Total	100.2	100.0	99.9	100.0	100.3	100.0	100.1	99.8

[1]Source: Ministry of Finance and Economic Planning (Planning), *Rural Labor Study in Northern Sudan.* 1983.

marriage age were classified as single even when they were still living with their parents. The distribution of the sample household heads according to their age is given in Table 4.9. About 49% of the household heads are between 21 and 60 years of age. Only about 11% are over 60 years of age and this does not seem to differ remarkably from what is prevalent in non-displaced communities in rural Africa.

The distributions of the sample households according to age and sex structures are given in Table 4.10: about 36.5% of the refugee population in the settlements are children below 10 years; about 27% are between 11 and 20 years; about 34% are between 21 and 60 years; and only about 3 per cent are over 60 years.

In all the villages the sex ratio is similar, except in Dehema, Aburakham, and Wad Awad where females outnumber males. In Umsaqata and Umbrush, males slightly outnumber females. The overall average sex ratio in the six villages is 48.7% males and 51.3% females.

How does the age structure compare with the age structure of the population in northern rural Sudan in general and Kassala Province in particular?

As can be seen from Table 4.11, there is no significant difference in the age structure between on the one hand, the refugee communities and on the other, the rural population in northern Sudan, in Kassala Province and in the eight peasant associations in Ethiopia. The number of children below the age of 10 years and the number of old people in the refugee communities is not more than among the non-displaced rural communities. The sex ratio in northern rural Sudan is also the same as in the refugee sample households—48.7% males and 51.3% females. In Kassala Province the sex ratio is 46.7% males and 53.0% females.

It can be concluded here that the widely upheld view that rural African refugees often consist of old men, women and children is without empirical support in the case of the Eritrean rural refugees in eastern Sudan. The only remarkable difference observed among the refugee communities is that the number of families headed by females is higher among the refugees than among the rural Sudanese population.

THEIR WORK

The occupational distribution of the household heads when they were in their country of origin is given in Table 4.12. About 25% of the sample households in Unsaqata and Umbrush were nomads in their country of origin, while in the four villages in Qala en Nahal about 20% were nomads before their arrival in the Sudan. Out of the total sample, only 47% gave farming as their occupation. The majority of those who reported farming as representing their occupation, especially in the settlements of Qala en Nahal, were agro-pastoralists, i.e., they

TABLE 4.9. Age Distribution of the Heads of the Sample Households (Per cent).

Age group (years)	Umsaqata	Umbrush	Dehema	Adingrar	Aburakham	Wad Awad	All villages
0-20	–	–	–	2.0	–	–	0.3
21-30	18.0	15.6	17.0	18.0	13.6	21.9	17.0
31-40	32.8	13.3	19.2	16.0	37.2	21.9	24.5
41-50	23.0	28.9	31.9	32.0	28.8	28.1	28.6
51-60	18.0	20.0	19.0	22.0	11.9	25.0	18.7
Over 60	8.2	22.2	12.8	10.0	8.5	3.1	10.9
Total	100.0	100.0	99.9	100.0	100.0	100.0	100.0

TABLE 4.10. Age and Sex Structure of the Sample Households (Per cent).

Age group (years)	Umsaqata		Umbrush		Dehema		Adingrar		Aburakham		Wad Awad		Total
	M	F	M	F	M	F	M	F	M	F	M	F	%
less than 10	19.0	15.7	17.1	14.9	18.9	20.0	19.8	15.3	19.1	21.9	17.5	20.8	36.5
10-20	13.7	12.0	16.0	13.6	12.4	14.8	13.3	15.6	11.8	9.3	11.8	17.5	26.9
21-30	4.0	7.3	3.1	3.9	2.0	4.4	1.9	4.6	0.8	5.3	3.1	5.1	7.7
31-40	6.3	5.7	2.2	5.3	3.6	4.8	3.8	4.2	6.5	8.5	3.6	5.1	10.0
41-50	3.7	4.7	5.7	4.4	4.8	5.2	5.0	7.2	5.3	4.9	5.1	4.6	10.0
51-60	2.7	3.0	3.5	4.8	3.2	2.8	4.2	2.3	2.0	2.0	4.1	1.0	5.9
over 60	1.3	1.0	3.5	1.7	2.0	0.8	1.9	0.8	0.8	1.6	0.5	0.5	2.8
Total	50.7	49.4	51.1	48.6	46.9	52.8	50.0	50.0	46.3	53.5	45.7	53.8	99.9

TABLE 4.11. Age Distribution of the Population in the Refugee Settlements, Northern Rural Sudan, Kassala Province, and in Eight Peasant Associations in Ada District in Shoa Province - Ethiopia.

Age group (years)	Refugee settlements[1]	Northern Rural Sudan[2]	Kassala Province[2]	Ada District[3]
less than 10	36.5	34.9	36.2	34.9
10-20	26.9	23.8	21.5	20.5
21-60	33.6	35.4	36.3	36.0
over 60	2.8	5.9	5.7	7.7

Source: [1]Questionnaire Survey
[2]Rural Labour Study in Northern Suday, 1983.
[3]Fassil Gebre-Kiros, "Agricultural land fragmentation: A Problem of Land Distribution Observed in Some Ethiopian Peasant Associations", in *Ethiopian Journal of Development Research.* Oct. 1980, Addis Ababa.

combined crop production with pastoralism, with the latter taking more of their time. According to the village elders, some of those heads of households who called themselves farmers were mainly cattle herders and they said that pastoralism rather than crop production was the dominant means of subsistence before their flight. This is only true of the refugees in Qala en Nahal and not in Aburakham and Wad Awad. Even though agriculture (crop and livestock production) constituted the main source of livelihood, the data in Table 4.12 also show that there was some kind of diversification. About 25% of the sample household heads were engaged in off-farm income-generating activities. Trade, for example, was the third dominant occupation among the household heads.

How does this compare with the present occupational structure of the household heads? Has any kind of tranformation taken place? Their present occupational status in the settlements is given on Table 4.13. The most interesting change is that pastoralism has disappeared both as a basic occupation and as a way of life, i.e., a process of denomadization has taken place, and a sedentary way of life has now become the dominant form. The Qala en Nahal settlement has been in existence for about 15 years, and it can be said that the former pastoralists and agro-pastoralists have demonstrated a remarkable ability to adjust themselves to sedentary life which for the majority was a drastic change from their previous way of life. Out of the total sample, only two households still considered themselves as pastoralists.

Another interesting observation is the fact that despite farming (crop production) being expected to represent the basic occupation of the household heads, only about 52% considered it as their basic occupation. In northern rural Sudan approximately 72% of the total rural labor force is engaged in

TABLE 4.12. Percentage Distribution of Previous Occupation of the Sample Household Heads - in Their Country of Origin.

Occupation	Umsaqata	Umbrush	Dehema	Adingrar	Aburkham	Wad Awad	All villages
Farmer	50.0	36.7	58.3	62.7	33.9	43.2	47.2
Pastoralist	21.7	26.5	10.4	15.7	–	–	12.8
Farm laborer	5.0	2.0	4.2	2.0	6.8	2.7	3.9
Skilled laborer	1.7	–	2.1	2.0	6.8	8.1	3.3
Craftsman	–	–	2.1	–	3.4	10.8	2.3
Trader	3.3	14.3	4.2	2.0	13.6	10.8	7.9
Charcoal producer	–	2.0	4.2	3.9	3.4	8.1	3.3
Unemployed	–	–	–	–	1.7	–	0.3
Student	3.3	–	2.1	3.9	1.7	8.1	3.3
Housewife	15.0	12.2	10.4	5.9	11.7	–	10.5
Soldier	–	2.0	2.1	2.0	5.1	5.4	2.6
Domestic servant	–	–	–	–	3.4	–	–
Commercial farmer	–	–	–	–	1.7	2.7	0.6
Teacher	–	4.1	–	–	5.1	–	1.6
Freedom fighter	–	–	–	–	1.7	–	–
Total	100.0	99.8	100.1	100.1	100.0	99.9	99.6

TABLE 4.13. Percentage Distribution of Occupations of the Sample Household Heads in the Six Villages.

Occupation	Umsaqata	Umbrush	Dehema	Adingrar	Aburakham	Wad Awad	All villages
Farmer	52.2	57.7	56.6	57.9	35.8	60.5	52.4
Pastoralist[1]	–	1.9	1.9	–	–	–	0.6
Farm laborer[2]	16.4	11.5	11.3	15.8	19.4	7.9	14.4
Skilled laborer[3]	6.0	1.9	1.9	5.3	3.0	5.3	3.9
Guard	–	1.9	–	1.7	–	2.6	0.9
Craftsman[4]	–	–	–	1.7	4.5	–	1.2
Charcoal producer[5]	3.0	1.9	5.7	1.7	3.0	–	2.7
Trader[6]	7.5	9.6	9.4	5.3	6.0	5.3	7.2
Firewood and water collector[5]	7.5	5.8	5.7	5.3	3.0	5.3	5.4
Teacher	1.5	1.9	1.9	–	3.0	2.6	1.8
Disabled/Old[7]	3.0	5.7	5.7	5.3	16.4	5.3	7.2
Domestic servant	–	–	–	–	3.0	–	0.6
Sanitary worker	3.0	–	–	–	3.0	5.3	1.8
Total	100.1	9.8	100.1	100.0	100.1	100.1	100.1

1. Pastoralists refers to those who live on pastoralism without taking part in farming. It does not include those who combine farming and livestock herding.
2. Farm labor refers to those whose main source of maintenance is wage labor. They are mainly landless persons or are persons who for some reason do not cultivate their plots if they have any.
3. Skilled labor—refers to mechanics, welders, drivers, masons, brick layers, in short to those who possess skill acquired through experience or formal education.
4. Craftsman—refers to blacksmith, carving, basketry, matmaking, pottery, weaving and embroidery, shoe repair and making, radio repair, watch repair, tannery, etc.
5. Charcoal production, firewood collection and water fetching—refers to those who are engaged in these activities throughout the year. It doe not include those refugees who sell firewood, water and charcoal on a part-time basis or during the slack season.
6. Trader refers to shopkeepers, taylors and owners of cafés, restaurants, camel oilpresses and trucks, etc.
7. Disabled/old—refers to those persons who either due to old age or physical handicap cannot take part in farm labor. This is by no means an occupation. It is included in the table in order to show the presence of the vulnerable group among the household heads.

agriculture. (For our purpose even farm wage labor is considered as off-farm income generating activity. Farm activity here refers to an agricultural activity in one's own land. This land may be allocated, rented, received as gift, cultivated on a share cropping basis, etc.)

In Table 4.12 we see that only 25% considered non-farm activity as representing their basic occupation, while in the settlement over 40% consider off-farm income-generating activities constituting their basic occupation. A comparison of Tables 4.12 and 4.13 also shows that the number of wage laborers has considerably increased in the settlement. Before their flight only 7% of the household heads gave wage labor as their basic occupation while in the settlements this has increased by more than 150%. These facts clearly show that settlement for many household heads has brought with it a new way of life which is radically different from the way they used to live.

The high proportion of the vulnerable groups in Aburakham is mainly due to the fact that some of the female heads of the households considered themselves unable to carry out agricultural operations and consequently considered themselves disabled. If we exclude Aburakham, the prevalence of the disabled persons (either due to old age or physical handicap) is slightly more among the refugees than among the rural population in northern Sudan. In the latter only 3% are disabled or too old to work.

As we saw above, the refugee communities are engaged in diverse economic activities by making their own adjustments, and agricultural production is only one of the many income-generating activities carried out by the refugee households.

CHAPTER 5

Land in the Settlements

When the Eritrean refugees could not be repatriated due to the escalation of the war, the UNHCR and the GOS knew that they would need to remain in the Sudan for a considerable period. It was therefore thought desirable that they should become self-sufficient in the production of food crops and be able to earn enough cash to buy goods and services which they themselves did not produce. Initial production inputs and services were therefore provided by the GOS and the UNHCR to enable the refugees to develop agriculture systems, and land was donated by the GOS. The fundamental objective was to create viable agricultural economic systems capable of providing the refugee households with levels of material consumption equivalent to those of the surrounding Sudanese communities.

The viability of the agricultural settlements is critically dependent on their resource base, and one of the most crucial resources is land. Therefore, the land available to each family must be big enough for the refugee families to achieve self-sufficiency. Furthermore, since the refugees will remain in the Sudan for sometime, the available land needs to be adequate not only for the immediate future but for the whole period that the refugees might be expected to remain in the *settlements,* i.e., the available land must be adequate to enable the families to meet the customary expenditure on consumption and the current farm expenses and to allow them practice fallowing so as not to deplete the fertility of the soil from continuous cultivation. The cultivable land available must also be adequate to accommodate future land demands arising from natural population growth.

To enable the refugees to achieve the above goal, the GOS decided to allocate each family in the Qala en Nahal settlement 10 feddans of cultivable land. While in the relatively new settlements of Aburakham and Wad Awad, it was decided to allocate each family five feddans of cultivable land. (Qala en Nahal is a collective name for the six refugee villages of Umsaqata, Umbrush, Dehema, Adingrar, Zurzur, and Salmin. There are also Sudanese villages adjacent to the refugee villages: Salmin, Dehema, Umbrush, Umsaqata,

Huweig, Bolos, Bia, and Utash. In Wad Awad it was decided later to allocate the households with seven or more family members/10 feddans.)

The aim of this chapter is therefore first to examine the availability of cultivable land vis-à-vis population density and to see whether or not adequate land planning has been practiced during and after the establishment periods. Second, this chapter looks at the allocation and present distribution of cultivable land among the refugee families to see if any changes have taken place in regard to land distribution. If such changes have occurred, the mechanisms of change will also be examined. Third, since the productive capacity of the cultivable land in the future is related to its present and past utilization, the possibility of the families to practice fallowing in the light of their land resource will also be examined.

LAND IN THE QALA EN NAHAL SETTLEMENT

The six refugee villages in the Qala en Nahal area lie about 40 km south of the small town of Qala en Nahal which is located about 60 km south-west of Gedaref. This site was selected in accordance with the settlement policy of the GOS which states that

> the settlements should not operate in a way so as to dispossess nationals in the area from land or opportunity . . .
>
> (Khartoum Refugee Conference Documentation: 1980)

This area was inhabited by a relatively small number of migrants from Western Sudan, Nigeria and Chad from the beginning of the 1940s, but there is still abundant land that could accomodate the new influx.

According to the agreement entered between the GOS and the UNHCR in 1968, the former agreed to provide 'an area of 103,000 feddans for the occupation and provision of land for cultivation'. (Khartoum Conference Documentation, Vol. 1: 1980, 7) In return, the UNHCR 'provided funds for the building of the infrastructure; mainly water supply, roads, village establishment, education and the expenses of administration'. (Ibid.)

However, not only is the exact total amount of land demarcated for the refugees difficult to estimate exactly, but the land itself is not exclusively allocated to the refugees. There are seven Sudanese villages that use land in the scheme. The land distribution among the the refugee and Sudanese villages as it stood in 1980 is given in Table 5.1 and 5.2, respectively.

To estimate the total amount of cultivable land available in the Qala en Nahal refugee settlement, we use two different sources. These are the administration land records in Umsaqata and Euro Action-Acord (EA-A) 1980 Field Survey. The scheme administration land records do not contain complete information about the land used by the Sudanese villages in the surrounding region. Thus, they cannot be used to estimate the total amount of cultivable land within the scheme.

TABLE 5.1. Land Available by Villages and by Category in Feddans (Estimate) Refugees only.[1]

Type of land	Umsaqata	Dehema	Adingrar	Umbrush	Zurzur	Total
Total area	10,800	4,600	6,900	8,050	9,050	39,400
Uncultivable	3,050	100	400	950	250	4,750
Flood risk	1,600	900	1,150	200	1,450	5,300
Wood land	500	500	1,050	1,000	2,350	5,400
Uncultivated	2,550	1,500	1,850	3,650	2,450	12,000
Cultivated	3,100	1,600	2,450	2,250	2,550	11,950
Net cultivable[2]	5,650	3,100	4,300	5,900	5,000	23,950

1. Since the survey does not distinguish between Sudanese and refugee land in the village of Salmin, it is not possible to include the land belonging to the refugees in Salmin.
2. This is the total of uncultivated and cultivated land.

Source: Calculated from EA-A Field Survey, 1980.

As can be seen from Table 5.1, the total amount of land available to the refugee villages (excluding the land in Salmin) is about 39,400 feddans. Out of this 4,750 feddans are uncultivable, and 10,700 feddans are woodland and land subject to flood risk. The latter is classified as potentially cultivable but according to the EA-A field survey part of it is unsuitable for cultivation. A total of 23,950 feddans are cultivable, but this includes marginal and grazing land. Bringing the land which is subject to flood risk under cultivation would, for instance, require drainage which may in return require the provision of an effective extension service which is certainly not presently available.

If we include the woodland and the land subject to flood risk in the net cultivable land, the total amount of land (cultivated and potentially cultivable) which is available to the refugees is in the range of 34,650 feddans. (Table 5.1) As noted earlier, the Sudanese villages in the surrounding areas are also using land in the scheme. (See Table 5.2)

Out of the total land available within the scheme, 38,730 feddans are used by the Sudanese farmers; 21,730 of this is cultivable, while 9,050 feddans is woodland and land subject to flood risk. This brings the total potentially cultivable area which belongs to the Sudanese to about 30,780 feddans.

Thus the total net cultivable land within the scheme (belonging to Sudanese and refugees) is about 45,680 feddans, out of which about 52% belongs to the refugees. If we include the woodland and the land subject to flood risk, the amount available is 65,430 feddans, and about 53% belongs to the refugees.

In order to countercheck the EA-A 1980 Field Survey data, we examined the administration land records in great detail. According to the scheme administration records in Umsaqata, the total amount of land which is distributed between the five refugee villages in Qala en Nahal, excluding the land allocated to Salmin, is about 3,492 hawasha or 34,920 feddans. (The reason for excluding Salmin is in order to make the data comparable to the data in Table 5.1, in which Salmin is not included; 1 hawasha in the Qala en Nahal = 10 feddans.)

The results are very interesting because there is no significant difference between the 1980 EA-A Field Survey and the data obtained from the administration land records. The difference between the two sources with regard to land belonging to the refugees is only 270 feddans. However, the administration land records do not divide the quality of the land into various categories.

Now we shall look at the total amount of land available in the settlements of Aburakham and Wad Awad.

LAND IN THE ABURAKHAM AND WAD AWAD SETTLEMENTS

Aburakham and Wad Awad agricultural settlements were established in 1979 and 1980, respectively. Both are located about 130 km south-west of Gedaref

TABLE 5.2. Land Belonging to Sudanese Farmers within the Scheme in Feddans (Estimate).

Type of land	Umsaqata	Dehema	Utash	Umbrush	Bolos	Total
Total area	6,650	5,530	8,700	4,500	13,350	38,730
Uncultivable	2,200	500	1,250	150	3,850	7,950
Flood risk	100	100	650	350	700	1,900
Woodland	1,700	400	650	550	3,850	7,150
Uncultivated	450	1,500	650	2,150	1,600	6,350
Cultivated	2,200	3,030	5,500	1,300	3,350	15,380
Net cultivable	2,650	4,530	6,150	3,450	4,950	21,730

Source: Calculated from EA-A Field Survey, 1980.

town. The refugees in Aburakham are mainly people from the border areas who fled their places of origin between 1975 and 1979. (See Table 4.2 in Chapter 4) Between 1975 and 1979 they stayed in the transit camp of Wad Hileu near the eastern border and the majority were transferred to Aburakham in 1979. (See Table 4.3 in Chapter 4.)

The majority of the settlers in Wad Awad arrived in the Sudan between 1975 and 1979 and especially in 1978, following the re-capture of the Eritrean cities in the western lowlands by the Ethiopian troops in 1978. Many of them stayed in Kassala until their transfer to the present settlement in 1980.

The total area of cultivable land in the schemes according to the administration land records are 6,000 feddans in Aburakham and 3,000 feddans in Wad Awad. According to the same source, each family is allocated five feddans of cultivable land. In Wad Awad those families with seven or more family members receive 10 feddans of cultivable land. Since both settlements are administered by the same office, it is not clear why different policies are pursued in regard to land allocation. According to the agricultural officer, there is shortage of cultivable land in Aburakham while in Wad Awad the shortage of land is mitigated by the fact that many families have left the settlement and migrated to the cities illegally. The abandoned land is re-allocated to the large families. The families who emigrated from the settlement were mainly former urban settlers who considered village life as incompatible with their former way of life.

Owing to lack of other dependable sources, we have relied on information from the scheme administration in estimating the total amount of cultivable land in both settlements. Unfortunately, there are some inconsistencies which we could not overcome. For instance, according to the records, each of the 600 families in Aburakham has received five feddans of cultivable land within the scheme and this was verified by referring to the sketch representing the total amount of land allocated to the refugees. The same record gives the total amount of land cultivated in 1982 as 5,640 feddans.

Since the total amount of land allocated to the refugees is only 3,000 feddans, and since it is not likely that all the families had cultivated all their holdings in the 1982 season, the total amount of land cultivated in that season was probably less than 3,000. Recultivation of holdings is carried out in cases of failure of seed germination, but it is hard to believe that about 88% of the total holdings were recultivated. According to the scheme land records, out of the 6,000 feddans of cultivable land, only 3,000 feddans are allocated. Another 31 feddans were also allocated for horticulture and vegetables, and citrus trees such as lemon, orange and grapefruit are grown in the village garden.

According to the administration land records in Aburakham, the total amount of cultivable land in Wad Awad is about 3,000 feddans, out of which 2,500 feddans were under cultivation in the 1982 season. Another 300 feddans were also allocated to the village cooperative.

LAND POTENTIAL AND POPULATION

Land is a critical factor of production and a key variable to the success of the rural land refugee settlements, therefore it will be the aim of this section to examine the cultivable land versus population densities. At this stage we shall only discuss it at the village level without going into individual holdings, which cannot be ascertained from the scheme administration land records. The total net amount of cultivable land and family/man ratios are given in Table 5.3.

TABLE 5.3. Net Cultivable Land/Man Ratio and Land/Family Ratio per Village.

Village	Total Net Cultivable Land	Land/Man Ratio	Land/Family Ratio
Umsaqata	5,650	1.2	7.6
Dehema	3,100	0.9	5.7
Adingrar	4,300	1.3	7.3
Umbrush	5,900	1.4	8.4
Aburakham	3,000	1.1	5.0
Wad Awad	2,500	1.2	7.8
	24,450	1.2	7.0

As can be observed from Table 5.3, the land/man ratio in the six settlements is 1.2:1 and the land family ratio is 7.0:1, i.e., under equitable land distribution the average holding per family would be 7.0 feddans. If we exclude the settlements of Aburakham and Wad Awad the land/family ratio in the four villages of Qala en Nahal would be 7.4:1. If we include the woodland and the land subject to flood risk the land/man ratio in Umsaqata, Dehema, Adingrar, and Umbrush would be 1.7, 1.4, 2.0, and 1.7, respectively. While the land/family ratio would be 10.4, 8.2, 11.1, and 10.2, respectively. Despite the ecological marginality of the land in the Aburakham settlement, the available cultivable land/family ratio is only 5:1.

According to the economic conditions prevailing at the end of the 1960s, the UNHCR and the GOS considered 10 feddans of land enough to allow each refugee family to become self-sufficient. However, 14 years after the establishment of the Qala en Nahal refugee settlements, our findings show that the total amount of cultivable land in relation to the population density is insufficient to enable all the families to receive 10 feddans of cultivable land even under the most equitable land distribution. As pointed out earlier, the net cultivable land/family ratio in the Qala en Nahal is 7.4:1. If we were to include the woodland and the land subject to flood risk, the land/family ratio in Qala en Nahal would be 10:1. However, a greater part of the latter land is not suitable for cultivation.

These facts clearly show that there was inadequate land planning during the establishment of the settlement and that no corrective measures were taken to increase the availability of the total cultivable land within the schemes. The planners had not considered the need for additional unallocated land which would be required as a result of natural population growth. Owing to legal restrictions, the refugees cannot cultivate new land outside the designated area, i.e., the total cultivable land within the refugee settlements is held constant while the number of the settlers is constantly increasing as a result of natural population growth and immigration. This has created great pressure on the land resource.

After the massive refugee influx that occurred in 1975 in the border areas of Kassala Province, the GOS decided to remove the refugees from the border to other areas where they could gradually become self-supporting. In 1976, the UNHCR assigned the consultants, Hunting Technical Services, Ltd., to identify suitable settlement sites for the refugees. One of the sites studied was the Qala en Nahal refugee settlement. The consultants identified about 13,000 feddans of unallocated cultivable land within the scheme and this was considered available for allocation to new arrivals. (See Hunting: 1976)

Accordingly, new refugees were transferred to the villages of Umbrush, Dehema, and Adingrar in 1978 and 1979 and all of the remaining unallocated land was distributed among them.

The arrival of new waves of refugees to the Sudan indisputably indicated that the refugees would remain in the settlements for a considerable period. Clearly their demand for new cultivable land would increase as a result of natural population growth and as a result of the need to practice fallowing so as to regenerate soil fertility. Therefore, it is difficult to understand why the remaining land was allocated to new settlers. It seems that the decision-makers were mainly concerned with solving the immediate problem temporarily and at the lowest possible cost. Transferring new settlers to existing settlements with already built-up infrastructures is cost-effective, but only if there is a sufficient resource base to enable both the old and the new settlers to become self-supporting, not only in the short-run but in the whole period that they might remain in the settlements.

ALLOCATING THE LAND

In the region where the refugee land settlements are located, land belongs to the state. The Unregistered Land Act 1970 states that

> all lands of any kind whatsoever, whether waste, forest, occupied or unoccupied which is not registered before the commencement be the property of the government and shall be deemed to have registered as such as if the provisions of the Land Settlement and Registration Ordinance have been duly complied with.
>
> (quoted in El Mahdi: 1979)

Since the 1940s the Central Plains in the Gedaref rainfed region have constituted the major supplier of food crops in Sudan. Land tenure in the area is regulated by the Land Settlement and Registration Ordinance of 1925. As the demand for cultivable land increased in the area, the Ministry of Interior passed a regulation governing its distribution. This was known as the 'Scheme for Disposal of Rainlands, 1959'. In accordance with the regulation, a Land Allotment Board was created to allocate land to private tractor-owners on lease basis. The Government always retained the right of ownership. Allocations were made in 1,000 feddan units to private tractor-owners while cooperative societies could be allocated up to 5,000 feddans and enterprises and registered companies could receive 5,000 or more feddans. To qualify for such land allocation, the applicant must be Sudanese, must be able to procure the necessary agricultural machinery, must have sufficient capital to meet the recurrent costs and new investments, and must have agricultural knowledge, experience, managerial ability, and time. (Agabawi: 1968, 78)

Even though the refugee land settlements are all located in the central rainlands in the Gedaref region, they are not regulated by the same laws for the simple reason that the refugees are not Sudanese. Hence a special arrangement is made for the establishment of the land settlements. The refugees tenural right is regulated by the Regulation of the Asylum Act, 1974, which explicitly states that 'no refugee shall own lands or immovables in the Sudan'. (Section Nine of the Asylum Act) In a draft implementation to the Regulation of the Asylum Act, 1974, we find the following policy formulations about the refugees' right to land:

> The Minister shall allocate agricultural land within the settlement area for individual refugees during their stay in the country and according to the Government's investment system. *Such land may not be inherited, or prescribed but may be transferred to family members. The refugee should not dispose of land in the way of rent or in any other way for the benefit of another person except with the permission of the authorities.*
>
> (Quoted in Nobel: 1983, 25) (Emphasis added.)

It is not clear which authorities are competent to issue such a permit. Is it the *modir* (scheme manager)? The people's local government? Or the Office of the Commissioner for Refugees (COR)? The conditions under which such a permission could be issued are not spelled out either.

Despite these legal restrictions, all societies, including refugee communities, involve continuous and uninterrupted movements. This is reflected by the fact that some families have lost their holdings while others retain them in fragmented forms; there are yet others who manage to accumulate more land than was originally allocated to them. These shifts in land holding have rendered the scheme's administration land records, in which the original land allocations among the refugee families are kept, out of date. However, as we saw earlier, the records of land allocation were very important in estimating the total amount of cultivable land available within the scheme.

According to a survey carried out in 1970, the Qala en Nahal scheme was divided into regular square blocks of land measuring 2,000 by 2,000 meters. The square blocks are separated by numbered concrete posts placed at the corners of each block. Each block consists of 1,000 feddans called *meshrua,* and each meshrua is further divided into 100 family units known as *hawasha,* consisting of 10 feddans each.

When a family was originally allocated land, a certificate of possession was issued, noting the head of the household's name, the number of the *meshrua* and the *hawasha* allocated to it. After this the head of the family is shown the exact location and the boundary of his *hawasha.* The *hawasha* are not numbered but are separated from each other by standing trees or by uncultivated strips of land.

We now go on to look at the land hunger as it was apparent in 1982 and 1983 with regard to the distribution of land among the farm households and the implications of this distribution for economic self-reliance. Before we discuss the present distribution of land, however, we shall first look at the original allocation of land among the households. Since the refugees came to the settlements at different periods, original allocation means the land distributed to the households upon their arrival.

TABLE 5.4. Percentage Distribution of the Households with and without Original Land Allocation.

Village	With Original Allotment	Without Original Allotment	Total
Umsaqata	81.7	18.3	100.0
Umbrush	75.5	24.4	99.9
Dehema	78.7	21.3	100.0
Adingrar	80.0	20.0	100.0
Aburakham	83.0	16.9	99.0
Wad Awad	100.0	–	100.0

As can be seen from Table 5.4, out of the total sample about 18% claimed that they never received any allotment. The households without an original allotment in Qala en Nahal amount to about 21%.

Despite the fact that transfer of land for the benefit of a third party is legally prohibited, the refugee communities, like any other dynamic community, in the short period of their existence in the settlements (a decade and a half), have undergone continuous changes and developments: some of the households with original allotments have now become landless, some of them have holdings that are fragmented below economic levels and others have managed to accumulate several holdings at the cost of the poor section of the population. This indicates that social changes cannot be arrested by legal prescriptions. Table 5.5 shows the changes that have occurred with regard to land possession as they appeared in 1982/83.

As can be seen from Table 5.5, about 21 per cent of the sample households with original land allocations now have more cultivable land at their disposal than was allocated to them. It is interesting to note that this phenomenon is insignificant in the relatively new settlements of Aburakham and Wad Awad.

In Qala en Nahal about 37% of the sample households with an original land allocation now have less cultivable land than was originally allocated to them. Again, this is hardly seen in the villages of Aburakham and Wad Awad. Out of the sample with original land allotments in Qala en Nahal, only about 36% possess the same amount as their original allocation; in Aburakham and Wad Awad no major changes have taken place. In Qala en Nahal, about 6% of the sample with an original allocation have completely lost their holdings. In Aburakham about 8% of those who have received land have now become landless. The latter are mainly female-headed households without able-bodied family members, who due to lack of labor have abandoned their holdings.

As a result of the changes that have occurred in the last decade and a half, the present distribution of holdings among the households cannot be ascertained from the scheme's land records, and classification of the households according to the records is misleading. As the disposition of land for the benefit of a third party is prohibited by law, the purchase, sale, renting, sharecropping, usufructuary mortgaging and fragmentation of the holdings are carried out 'off the record', by avoiding the formal legal prohibitions. Thus the records do not show the households that for various reasons abandon, or lease out part or all of their holdings, or the rich households that rent, buy or take over abandoned land or acquire land on the basis of sharecropping. The apparent egalitarian picture in the land records hides the real differentiation of the households with regard to land holding.

To understand the present land distribution of the households, we asked the sample households to state the size of their holding; the results are given in Table 5.6. Out of the total sample, about 23% are landless, about 36% have between one and five feddans, about 31% have between five and 10 feddans,

TABLE 5.5. Percentage Distribution of Present Holdings among the Sample Households as Compared to their Original Allocation.

Present holdings vis-à-vis original allocation	Umsaqata	Umbrush	Dehema	Adingrar	Aburakham	Wad Awad	Total
More	25	17.6	21.6	17.5	2.1	6.2	15.1
Less	39.6	44.1	32.4	32.5	4.2	6.2	26.3
Same	25.0	35.3	37.8	47.5	83.3	87.5	52.3
None	10.4	2.9	8.1	2.5	10.4	=	6.3
Total	100.0	99.9	99.9	100.0	100.0	99.9	100.0

TABLE 5.6. Percentage Distribution of the Sample Households by Size of Present Holding 1982-83.

Size of holdings (feddans)	Umsaqata	Umbrush	Dehema	Adingrar	Aburakham	Wad Awad	Total
Landless	26.7	26.7	27.6	22.0	25.4	–	22.9
1-3	3.3	13.3	–	4.0	–	6.2	4.1
3-5	3.3	6.6	23.4	22.0	72.9	71.9	31.7
5-8	–	6.6	–	6.0	1.7	9.4	3.4
8-10	50.0	33.3	31.9	32.0	–	12.5	27.3
Over 10	16.7	13.3	17.0	14.0	–	–	10.6
Total	100.0	99.8	99.9	100.0	100.0	100.0	100.0

while about 11% have over 10 feddans. If we only consider the four villages in Qala en Nahal, about 26% of the sample are landless, 21% have between one and eight feddans, about 38% have between eight and 10 feddans, while about 15% have over 10 feddans of cultivable land. In Aburakham almost all of the households with land holdings have five feddans. Table 5.7 clearly shows that despite the initial intention of the GOS to provide each household with 10 feddans of cultivable land in Qala en Nahal, many of the households with holdings have less than 10 feddans, and about one-fourth of the sample households are landless.

Contrary to these facts, the documents that were presented at the 1980 Khartoum Conference stated that

> Today, the settlement /Qala en Nahal/ accommodates 30,000 refugees in the villages of Umsaqata, Salmin, Umbrush, Adingrar, Zurzur, and Dehema. *Each family is allocated 10 feddans for cultivation of dura (sorghum)* and sesame.
> (National Committee for Aid to Refugees: Documentation for the June 20-23 Conference, Khartoum: Vol. 2, B)

But Table 5.6 shows that there is no empirical support for such a claim.

LANDLESSNESS

About 26% of the sample households in Qala en Nahal are landless. Since extensive discussions with the key informants revealed that the number of landless households is probably higher than the results of the questionnaire survey suggested, we decided to supplement our data with information obtained from other sources—the *Legina* (resident committees), the *sheikhs* (clan leaders) and the administration records. However, it is important to note here that *the land question is the most sensitive issue in the Qala en Nahal refugee settlement.*

In 1982 a list of landless families was drawn by the *Legina* and was submitted to the *modir* (scheme manager) for action.

According to Table 5.7 the number of landless households varied from 27 to 14% of the total households with the highest in Umsaqata and the lowest in Umbrush. On the author's second visit to the settlements, it became clear that even the list submitted to the *modir* was not exhaustive. The *Legina* had deliberately excluded the landless illegal residents in order to protect them against eviction. According to the regulations, no family is allowed to immigrate without being authorized by the authorities concerned, but there are many that do so. They risk eviction if brought to the notice of the *modir.*

This also indicated to us that there may be families that reside with relatives without having their own residence, and that they would not be represented in

TABLE 5.7 Distribution of Landless Refugees according to the List Submitted to the Settlement Manager by Village.

Village	Total No. of Families	Landless	(Per cent)
Umsaqata	742	205	27
Salmin	1,117	242	21
Zurzur	512	90	18
Adingrar	585	70	15
Dehema	546	42	18
Umbrush	701	97	14
Total	4,203	745	17.7

our sample. To overcome this bias, the author discussed this on several occasions with the *Legina* and the *sheikhs* in the villages and received the following enumeration of landless families: there were 120, 300, 90, and 250 landless families in Adingrar, Umbrush, Dehema, and Umsaqata, respectively, i.e., among the total households about 21%, 42%, 17%, and 34% were landless in Adingrar, Umbrush, Dehema, and Umsaqata, respectively.

All of the three sources show that a large proportion of the refugee households in the land settlements are without land.

Who are the landless households? To determine their characteristics, we examined them in great detail.

Physical Absence

The families that were not physically present during the distribution of land were not allocated cultivable land. As we saw in Chapter 2, most of the families that crossed into the Sudan at the end of the 1960s were pastoralists and agro-pastoralists with no or little experience in farming, and some of them were not interested in receiving holdings. This lack of interest was also partly due to a negative attitude to settlement. At the initial stage, the refugees were unenthusiastic about settlement programs in the Sudan because they thought they would return home after the cessation of the cause of their flight. Thus some of the families that did not understand the value of cultivable land, as well as those who were staunchly opposed to being settled, did not take part in land allocation. Table 5.7 shows that the number of landless families is highest in Umsaqata and Salmin, where the majority of the settlers are former pastoralists—the Beni Amer and the Maria. (See Table 6.5 in Chapter Six)

Newly Established Families

During the establishment of the settlements in 1969-72, land was allocated only to families. Unmarried refugees were excluded from land allocation and did not receive land. There has been no land redistribution since the establishment of the settlements, except in the case of the refugees who were transferred to Qala en Nahal in 1978 and 1979 from the border areas. Therefore those who were married after 1970 received no land, and this group constitutes the majority of the landless in Qala en Nahal. Among the refugees without original land allocation are women-headed households who, due to lack of family labor and previous experience in farming, have shown no interest in land. Aburakham was established in 1979 and the problem of newly established families is not yet felt.

Immigrants

People who came to join their families, relatives, and friends from the cities and other settlements such as Kashim el Girba, Es Suki, Kilo 26 and Eritrea after the land had already been distributed received no land. Welfare is much better in the Qala en Nahal refugee settlements than in the wage-earning settlements of Kilo 26 and Es Suki where conditions are desperate. The refugees in the Qala en Nahal settlement claim that the welfare there or the perception of it 'pulls' refugees from different areas in the Sudan. This has added to the creation of landless refugees. The size of this group is very difficult to estimate because, as mentioned earlier, refugees who immigrate into the settlements on their own without being formally transferred by the settlement authorities risk eviction if they are found out. Maintenance of a low profile seems to be the survival strategy of the 'illegal' immigrants.

Divorced Women

When spouses separate, the woman becomes landless. In almost all cases, the husband takes the land and the female divorcee joins the ranks of the landless. Her position of landlessness can only be changed by getting remarried to a man who has land. Land is registered in the name of the husband and the woman's access to land is secured through him. The only exception to this rule are families that were female-headed during the time of the establishment of the settlements.

Abandoned Land

Following land allocation, recipients were required to clear it of trees and shrubs or else they would not receive the cultivation service. Some of the families without sufficient family labor as well as those who were opposed to being settled failed to clear their *hawasha* and many, according to our key informants, left the settlements in search of livelihood elsewhere, while others remained in the settlements as landless families. Those who did not clear their land of trees and shrubs gradually lost their holdings.

Owing to land shortage, no fallowing is practiced among the majority of the households. Subsequently, the return from the land deteriorates to below economic levels. Following continuous cultivation, some families abandon their holdings when they are severely affected by weed infestation, especially by a special parasitic type of weed known as *Striga hermontheca* (Latin), buda (Arabic), hawi-ainu (Tigrinya) or kololehat (Tigre).

Some of the families whose plots are located within the vicinity of the villages have had their crops destroyed by animals, and have abandoned their land, claiming that their appeals for replacement were of no avail.

Causes of Land Alienation

As we say in Table 5.5, 37% of the sample households with original land allocation in Qala en Nahal reported that they now have less than their original allotment, whereas 6% have lost their original allotment altogether. The causes of land alienation among the households who reported that they had lost some or all of their original holding are given in Table 5.8. This table shows that legal probition notwithstanding, there is a continuous shift of land holding among the refugees. Land has become a commodity which can be sold, can be rented out, can be held as collateral to secure loans and can be transferred to family members, as if the prohibitions did not exist. Out of those who reported having lost part or all of their holding, 38% claimed to have sold, rented out or mortgaged their usufructuary right to secure a loan; about 46% claimed to have given part of their holding to their married sons who lacked land of their own. In the settlements of Qala en Nahal about 49% of those families who possess less land than originally claimed to have shared their holdings with their landless married sons. Apart from land abandonment mainly caused by lack of liquidity and family labor, there is no significant shift of holdings in the settlements of Aburakham and Wad Awad.

Land fragmentation is a major problem in the old land settlements. Those families which arrived after the establishment of the settlements did not receive land from the GOS. They have either become agricultural laborers or have received part of their parents' holdings. The latter has led to an overfragmentation of holdings. The level of fragmentation among some families is so serious that a number of holdings are reduced to uneconomic levels. For instance, if family A had four unmarried male children aged 18, 15, 13, and 10 years in 1970 when the settlements were established, by 1983 four of them will have their own families and have to either share their parents' holding or join the ranks of the agricultural laborers. According to the refugees, men get married at about the age of 23 years on the average. This means that most of the children who were seven years old during the establishment period are now married and have their own families. Even though there is no legal prohibition against temporary alienation of land to family members, in economic terms the land allocated according to farm budget calculations made in the late 1960s is the minimum amount sufficient to secure a reaonable income to an average family, and thus its fragmentation contradicts the fundamental principle underlying the agriculturally-based settlements.

TABLE 5.8. Causes of Alienation of Allotment (per cent).

Cause	Umsa-qata	Umb-rush	Deh-ema	Adin-grar	Abura-kham	Wad Awad	Total
Sale	11.5	–	12.5	–	–	–	6.6
Renting out	7.7	–	18.7	21.4	12.5	–	11.8
Usufructuary mortgage	23.1	5.2	43.7	14.3	12.5	–	19.7
Abandoned	3.8	26.3	6.2	7.1	75.0	–	15.8
Partly given to married son/s	50.0	68.4	18.7	57.1	–	–	44.7
Taken away by government	3.8	–	–	–	–	–	1.3
Total	99.9	99.9	99.8	99.9	100.0	–	99.9

ACQUIRING MORE LAND

The existence of landlessness implies that there will be a certain degree of land concentration. Since refugees are not legally allowed to possess more land than was officially allocated to them, many of the rich refugees were very reluctant to reveal the actual size of their holdings. However, since some of them were convinced that the author had no connection with the authorities, they were willing to admit that they now possess more *hawasha* than was officially allotted to them. This came as a surprise to the author, but in fact it was well known to the scheme administration. Furthermore, not only is possession of several *hawasha* by some of the rich households known to the management, but anomalously enough some of the holdings were registered in their own names. Our impression was that the level of land concentration was more than was revealed to us and than is shown in Table 5.9.

As we saw in Table 5.5, out of the total sample households with original land allocations, 21% reported that they now have more land than their original allocation. The methods of acquiring additional lands, according to them, were through purchasing, renting and sharecropping and the taking over of abandoned land.

Clearly the refugee communities in Qala en Nahal are not, as is widely believed, an undifferentiated and homogeneous whole but rather a socially and economically differentiated group of people. This differentiation did not begin with the establishment of the settlements. The refugees in Qala en Nahal, especially the Beni Amer and the Maria in Umsaqata, Umbrush and Salmin were highly stratified long before the advent of Italian colonialism in Eritrea. (Paul: 1950; Seligman: 1912; Nadel: 1945; Trevaskis: 1960) A considerable concentration of land exists in Umsaqata, Salmin and Umbrush, where the Beni Amer and the Maria represent the majority of the refugees. The conditions of existence that prevailed in the transit camps before the refugees' transfer to the present settlements and the conditions now in the settlements tend to maintain and reproduce the old relations that were operative in their country of origin.

As can be seen from Tables 5.9 and 5.1, about 4% of the total number of the households in Umsaqata, Umbrush, Dehema, and Adingrar control over 12% of the total cultivable land; in Umsaqata 5% of the households control about 20% of the cultivable land; in Umbrush 6% of the families control about 27% of the cultivable land; in Dehema 3% of the families control 10% of the land, and in Adingrar 5% of the cultivable land is controlled by 2% of the families.

According to well-informed sources in the settlement of Qala en Nahal, the level of land concentration on the one hand and dispossession on the other is greater than what we have been able to show. This is because land is legally prohibited from being transferred for the benefit of a third party. Those involved in such 'illegal' transactions act in secrecy, lest they risk being brought to the notice of the management of the scheme which may declare the transactions null and void.

TABLE 5.9. Frequency Distribution of the Refugee Households Possessing More than 10 Feddans - Qala en Nahal.

Size of Holding (Feddans)	Umsaqata	Umbrush	Dehema	Zurzur	Adingrar	Salmin
20	26	26	15	10	10	30
30	4	8	–	13	–	5
40	5	6	–	–	–	6
50	4	5	–	–	–	7
60	–	1	–	–	–	2
70	–	–	–	–	–	1
90	1	–	–	–	–	–
Total No. of families	40	46	15	23	10	51

A closer investigation of the households in Qala en Nahal shows that out of the very poor households about 58% are landless, out of the poor households about 19%, out of the middle-income households about 5%, and among the rich only 3% are landless. Among the very poor households who have cultivable land, none has more and 64% have less than their original allocation. Only 36% have the same amount of land as was originally allocated to them. Among the land-possessing poor households, 8% have more, 39% have less and 53% have the same amount of land as their original allocation. Among the middle-income households, 20% have more, 41% have less and 39% have the same land as their original allocation. The picture is totally different among rich households, where 70% have more, 10% have the same and 20% have less than their original allocation. These findings show that the shift of holdings that has taken place seems to have been detrimental to the very poor, poor, and to the majority of the middle income households, while the overwhelming majority of the rich households have benefitted from it.

WORKING THE LAND

It was stated earlier that the land available to the farm households must be adequate not only to enable them to meet their customary expenditure on consumption and current farm expenses but also to enable them to practice fallowing so as to maintain soil fertility. But due to land shortage and, to some extent, to lack of tenural security, the majority of the households do not practice fallowing, and consequently the probability of soil depletion is very high.

Due to land shortage the majority of the households crop their holdings continuously. In the Central Plains, where the refugee land settlements are located, this leads to drastic crop yield decline. (See Simpson & Khalifa: 1976(a), 1976(b); Agabawi: 1969; Document of the World Bank: 1978; O'Brien: 1983; Agrisystems: 1981; Tuttas: 1976) Shifting cultivation is the major cultural practice undertaken by the local farmers to counter the soil depletion caused by continuous cropping. In areas where land availability is not a constraint on agricultural production, the smallholder can at will abandon his old holding after some years when it seems to him that its fertility is being depleted by successive cropping. Soil fertility is then

> ... improved by the natural regrowth of vegetation that springs up when cultivation shifts to new patch.
>
> (Ny & Greenland: 1960)

According to Balamoan

> ... the average subsistence farmer anywhere in savanna Sudan works so-called virgin bush for four years before breaking new ground.
> (Balamoan: 1981, 250)

Owing to loss of soil fertility and to weed infestation, the farmer in the rainfed areas of the Sudan rarely uses his cleared land for more than six years. (Tuttas: 1976, 4)

When new land is brought under cultivation, high crop yields are obtained during the first two or three seasons. By the 7th or 8th season, yields decline below economic levels, and the farmers abandon their farms and cultivate new areas. O'Brien also notes that a mechanized scheme is abandoned after five or seven years due to declining yields. (O'Brien: 1983, 18). In their empirical study of the Central Rainlands, where the refugee land settlements are located, Simpson and Khalifa found that crop yields decline below '... economic levels in about 9 to 10 years after initial cultivation. Farmers then applied for new land...." (Simpson & Khalifa: 1976(a), 99) The soils in the rainfed agricultural areas are characterized by a low nitrogen content, and continuous cropping, especially of exhaustive crops, leads to nitrogen deficiency. (Agabawi: 1968, 71; IBRD quoted in Agrisystems: 1981, 4)

In the central rain lands where land is allocated in 1,000 feddan units to private tractor owners, a system of shifting cultivation is operated:

> An eight-course rotation of four years cropping and four years bush has been enforced by the Ministry of Agriculture since the mid-1950s.
> (Agabawi: 1969, 107)

A study conducted by the ILO also notes that '... there is an obligation to keep the land fallow'. (ILO: 1976, 267)

If the practice of an eight-course rotation of four years cropping and four years resting has been prescribed by the Ministry of Agriculture since the mid-fifties and since this is necessitated by the specific characteristics of the soil in the region, why did the GOS not allocate enough land to the refugee settlements to allow the households to leave part of their holdings fallow?

In the following we shall see how widespread the practice of fallowing is among the refugee households, their reasons for not practicing fallowing and the methods used to maintain fertility.

As can be seen from Table 5.10, out of the total land-possessing households, about 90% had no land lying fallow in the 1981-82 agricultural season, and only 11% of the land-holding families reported leaving between 1/4 and 1/2 of the holding fallow.

Since the data is based upon one year's experience, it is difficult to generalize for other years. We therefore asked the village leaders and Euro-Action Acord personnel if there were any reason to believe that the 1981-82 season was any different from the other seasons. In their opinion the 1981-82

TABLE 5.10. Percentage Distribution of the Sample Households by Amount of Land that was Lying Fallow in the 1981-82 Season.

Amount of land	Umsaqata	Umbrush	Dehema	Adingrar	All villages
None	84.4	88.9	87.9	94.9	88.9
All of the holding	–	–	–	–	–
¼ of the holding	2.2	2.8	6.1	2.6	3.3
⅓ of the holding	–	–	–	–	–
½ of the holding	11.1	8.3	6.1	2.6	7.2
⅔ of the holding	2.2	–	–	–	0.6
¾ of the holding	–	–	–	–	–
Total	99.9	100.0	100.1	100.1	100.0

season was the same as the others, and they saw no reason to believe that the farmers practiced fallowing more in the other seasons than they did in 1981-82. None of the refugee farmers in the settlements of Aburakham and Wad Awad had any land in fallow during this season. This was because climatic factors prevented crop rotation, with possible serious consequences for soil fertility. The settlements in Qala en Nahal have been in existence for about 15 years and most of the refugees have been cultivating their holdings continuously without practicing adequate fallowing.

The distribution of the land-possessing households, according to the reason for not practicing fallowing, is given in Table 5.11. The data in the table clearly indicate that the refugees are acquainted with fallowing. Out of the total, there were only 4% who stated that fallowing was not necessary. About 88% of the total sample gave land shortage as the reason for not practicing fallowing, while in Qala en Nahal about 12% of the sample gave insecurity over tenure as the reason. For small farmers, a minimum amount of land possession is necessary if fallowing is to be practiced . . . an amount that allows both fallowing and cropping without threatening the subsistence security of the household. If the land is below this minimum amount the households are forced to crop even when the level of fertility depletion is highly critical. The long-term consequence of such practice is no doubt incompatible with the achievement of self-reliance which is the fundamental aim of the settlements. As long as the land bank remains constant an ever increasing population will lead to continuous cropping and overfragmentation, the deterioration of soil fertility and consequently yield decline. This could threaten the foundation on which the agricultural settlements are based.

The households in Qala en Nahal alternate sorghum with sesame, and this may help to retain soil fertility, but it is important to note that soil fertility cannot be maintained indefinitely with this method. The eight-course rotation is recommended in the region despite the fact that sorghum is alternated with sesame, indicating that there is need for holdings to rest a certan number of years, even when rotation is practiced. The refugee and Sudanese farmers with long experience in the area say that alternating sorghum with sesame rejuvenates the soil, but that when this practice is prolonged it tends to lose its effect; and the soil fails to support healthy crop plants and becomes a good breeding ground for weeds. They say that when the fertility of the soil is depleted, certain species of weeds emerge, indicating the need to abandon the holding and to clear new land.

Many of the refugee farmers say that the return from their holdings is declining and that soil depletion from continuous cropping is one of the most important factors to account for the decline.

Neither the refugees nor the Sudanese commercial farmers in the area use organic or inorganic fertilizers. They say that animal droppings contain weed seeds which can infest holdings. The refugee farmers are particularly afraid of a particular species known as 'adar', sometimes called false sorghum or

TABLE 5.11. Percentage Distribution of the Sample Households by Reason for not Practicing Fallowing.

Reason	Umsaqata	Umbrush	Dehema	Adingrar	Aburakahm	Wad Awad	All villages
Not necessary	–	6.9	3.6	5.7	4.5	3.2	3.9
Shortage of land	86.1	89.7	64.3	91.7	95.4	96.8	88.2
Fear of losing possession	13.9	3.4	32.1	2.8	–	–	7.8
Total	100.0	100.0	100.0	100.2	99.9	100.0	99.9

Sudangrass, which is very difficult to distinguish from *dura* plants before maturity and can easily escape weeding. The author saw some holdings that were totally taken over by "adar" in the 1982-83 agricultural season. The use of organic fertilizer is not only unpracticed in the region, but according to Simpson and Khalifa, most large-scale Sudanese farmers

> . . . regarded the introduction of animals to their land with horror—because of the danger of weed seeds being introduced through animal droppings.
>
> (Simpson and Khalifa: 1976, 15)

However, the attitude of the refugee farmers towards application of manure could be changed if an effective extension service were to be provided. The use of inorganic fertilizer requires capital and research which is beyond the financial and educational level of the refugees. It is not even certain if the soil in the area is responsive to chemical fertilizer application.

Thus in summary, the overriding reason for not practicing fallowing in the settlements is the shortage of land, which is exacerbated by the inequitable distribution of what land there is. Our findings show that no sound land planning based upon long-term needs of the settlers was practiced at the initial period, nor were any measures taken to rectify the error committed during planning. In fact, it does not even seem that there is an awareness on the part of policy-makers of the urgent need to solve the problem of land shortage.

LAND TENURE AND THE REFUGEES

What are the refugees' legal rights of tenure? As we saw before, the refugees can neither own land or immovable property nor can they dispose of their right of usufruct. Their usufructuary right is not inheritable. The only exception is that the right of usufruct can be transferred to family members, although not in a form of inheritance. If land (the right of usufruct) can be transferred to family members, why is it not inheritable?

What can be bequeathed is still not the ownership of land, for the refugees cannot own land, but the right of usufruct. The intention of the GOS is probably to avoid complications after repatriation of the refugees. By limiting the transfer of the right of use to the refugee family members, the right will automatically revert to the government following the refugees' repatriation. If such a provision did not exist, the refugees could dispose of their usufructuary right to their neighbors or friends among the Sudanese population when they returned home. Although theoretically the government can evict any occupant of land that was not registered at the commencement of the unregistered Land Act 1970, in practice such a decision may entail some political problems.

In the following we shall look into how the question of land tenure is perceived by the households and how this tenural insecurity affects the refugees' long-term commitment to improve their holdings.

Our findings indicate that there is a total lack of information about their rights and duties as well as about the legal remedies that could regulate disputes over land. When land is allocated to a certain household, it is kept in the register of the scheme management in the name of the household head, which is invariably a man except in the female-headed households. Most of the refugees are given a certificate of possession with all the particulars about their respective holdings. Over 90% of the sample households in Qala en Nahal had such certificates during the survey. In the overwhelming majority of cases, there are no third party claims made on the households' land.

To assess how informed the households are about their tenural rights, we asked them whether they thought they could bequeath their holdings. About 90% of the sample households in Qala en Nahal said that they are legally entitled to do so. However, the refugees in Aburakham and Wad Awad said that they could not bequeath what they did not own. The distinction between right of ownership and possession of usufructuary right seemed too abstract to be grasped by the refugee farmers in Qala en Nahal.

We also asked the sample households whether lack of land ownership affected their decision to improve their holdings; 76% of the sample households in Qala en Nahal said it did, i.e, that if they could own the land they cultivate, about 76% would make improvements to it. In the settlements of Aburakham and Wad Awad, 9 and 19%, respectively, said that they would improve their holdings if they had the right of ownership. Although the household heads' answers may reflect the level of confusion and the state of tenural insecurity that exists among them, it is not clear what kind of improvements they would make if they owned land, given the existing constraints and opportunities in the area.

In conclusion, it can be stated that land is one of the major constraints on agricultural production. The sample households were asked to state three factors which, in their opinion, imposed a constraint on production. The results show that the majority among all the income groups, except among the medium-income group, consider land to be one of the three chief scarce factors. Out of the total land-possessing very poor households in Qala en Nahal, about 54% gave shortage of land as one of the three major constraints; among the poor, middle and rich land-holding households, about 68%, 44%, and 70%, respectively, cited land as one of the chief constraints on production. This result excludes the landless households who, due to lack of land, cannot produce any crop at all. Thus, if we include the landless households with those who cited land as one of the three major constraints on agricultural production, about 80%, 75%, 47%, and 68% of the very poor, poor, middle and rich households, respectively, considered land as one of the major constraints on agricultural production in Qala en Nahal. In Aburkham, on the other hand, except those which had become landless, all households in all the income groups cited land as a major constraint, and in Wad Awad, all households, except one from the very low income group, cited it as a major constraint.

Our results clearly show that even the rich households' efforts to expand are curtailed by land shortage. However, the impact of land shortage on the various income groups varies. Land shortage may constrain the rich households' efforts to produce marketable surplus. Among the other income groups, however, land shortage may threaten their subsistence security and consequently shake the foundation of the agriculturally-based settlements.

CHAPTER 6

Labor in the Settlements

The major constraints on labor in the refugee households are determined by demographic factors—the size of the household, the age and sex composition of the household and the cyclical process of family development. Since demographic factors are not static, there are shifts in the age and sex structure as the family develops. A second important factor determining labor availability is the social norms and values which regulate the participation of the different segments of the population in farm and other income-generating activities. These values and norms are deeply entrenched in the social fabric of the refugee communities, so it is assumed that no considerable change will occur in the short-run. However, since the refugee communities are not culturally homogeneous, norms and values do vary with different national and ethnic groups. In some exceptional cases, participation in work may also vary with the households' socioeconomic status, ethnic origin notwithstanding.

Within the availability constraint, the extent to which a household uses its own and its family labor for productive employment is a function of the net utility derived from the benefits of employment and the disutility of employment. These in turn are functions of the household's personal values, production possibilities and market relations. Whether a household transforms a certain amount of leisure into work, and its satisfaction from the goods and services accruing from that work, are affected by its personal values which in turn are determined by the prevailing value structures and income levels. Since both leisure and goods and services are subject to declining marginal utility, the utility derived from an addition of leisure or goods and services differs not only from individual to individual but even for the same individual from time to time as leisure and income vary. (Mellor: 1966).

Within the given availability constraint operative in the refugee households, labor supply for the different activities competing for the same labor time is determined by economic factors, i.e., if the reward for labor in a given activity increases relative to the rewards in other activities, the supply of labor to that activity increases. If there is no involuntary unemployment or underemployment, i.e., if the supply of labor has reached the socio-demographic maximum, the supply for other activities will be decreased in the short-run. However, in the long-run the rewards to labor may generally tend to rise considerably and may induce increased participation of the segments which are at present marginal to the labor force.

It is important to note that since most economic activities in the region are related to agriculture and, since agricultural production is seasonal, periods of unemployment and underemployment usually alternate with short periods of full employment of the available labor force.

FAMILIES AND LABOR

How does the age structure of the household members affect labor availability? It is only after a certain age that children take part in economic activities, and their contribution is proportional to their age; children are not as strong as adults and are often said to be less resistant to hardship. Depending upon the labor indices used to estimate family labor availability, a child's full contribution to work is only achieved after a certain age. (See Table 6.1) (Often it is very difficult to estimate the exact labor unit equivalent except when one has measured the exact labor inputs by different age and sex groups in different agricultural tasks, for the nature of the task can also influence the level of contribution by different groups. FAO's, Memento d'Agronome's and Norman's tables of labor indices are for West Africa, yet their variation is very considerable, especially Norman's where male children above the age of 15 contribute the same amount of labor units. These variations are to a certain extent a reflection of the imprecision involved. Division of tasks among men, women and children is often culturally mediated and standardization is often misleading. Tony Barnett's labor indices are for the Gezira tenants where cotton production is the major crop. Children's participation in cotton picking starts at an early age and his findings are obviously influenced by the specificity of the dominant task in his area of study. According to him, children above the age of 12 contribute the same amount of labor units as adult males. He also does not distinguish between male and female labor. Although we are not certain about the degree of women's participation in Gezira, it is often agreed by extension workers in rural development that due to domestic chores, women's over-all contribution to farm activity is less than that of male adults. We found it necessary to use our own indices because none of the above suited the reality in the refugee settlements. Using the FAO and Memento d'Agronome indices would lead to underestimation, while Norman's and Barnett's would lead to overestimation. Hence, to overcome the problem the author has constructed his own labor indices with the refugee farmers. But since our construct is not based upon actual records of labor inputs, it must be taken as indicative of relative work levels rather than measurement of actual labor inputs. We shall use these indices to estimate the amount of labor available in the settlements.)

How does sex structure affect labor availability? Assuming that there is no social barrier to female participation in farm and other income-generating activities, there is no reason to believe that sexual distribution of family members significantly affects labor availability. However, when a girl's contribution begins to equal an adult male's labor unit, often she marries and moves to her husband's house. There, because of other competing demands for her labor—childbirth, domestic chores such as preparing and cooking food, washing clothes and utensils, cleaning huts and compounds, attending to children, and sometimes collecting firewood and fetching of water—her contribution to farm work and other economic activities cannot often be full. (See Table 6.1.) Females also get married earlier than males. Therefore, the households with more females have less units of potential labor than the households which have more male members. All these are determined by chance factors.

We attempted to calculate the potential total labor units available to the sample households in every village according to age and sex, and the results are given in Table 6.2. The average family labor units in the sample households by sex are also given in Table 6.3. The average family units of labor varied from 3.1 in Wad Awad, 2.7 in Umsaqata, Umbrush and Adingrar to 2.0 in Aburakham. The reason for such a low unit of labor available in Aburakham is because Aburakham has the lowest average family size. (See Table 4.5 in Chapter 4) On the other hand, as can be seen from Table 6.3, the sample households in Wad Awad have the largest average units of labor per household. This clearly indicates that large households have greater units of labor available to them, while smaller families have less access to family labor. This enables the large families to diversify their activities both within agriculture—such as working on subsistence and cash crops simultaneously—and in off-farm income-generating activities which are crucial to supplement farm income and to spread risks among different economic activities.

If we exclude female units of labor, the average male units of labor are 1.5 for the four villages of Umsaqata, Umbrush, Adingrar, and Wad Awad. The lowest averge is in Aburakham—1.0.

Family Development

How does the family's development cycle affect labor availability? A newly established household, as Barnett notes,

> . . . has only two units of labor available; a 'mature' household has two adults together with their teenage children; and an elderly household may once again be reduced to two adults, although they are now elderly and unable to undertake a heavy workload.
>
> (Barnett: 1983, 290)

TABLE 6.1. Labor Indices by Sex and Age.

Sex	Age	Index[1]	Category	Index[2]	Sex	Age	Index[3]	Age	Index[4]	Sex	Age	Index[5]
M or F	11-15	0.25	Children		M or F	0-6	0.00	<6	0.00	M or F	0-5	0.00
M or F	15-20	0.50	Children		M or F	7-14	0.50	6<12	0.60	M or F	6-10	0.25
M	20-60	1	M Adult	1	M	15-64	1.00	12<64	1.00	M or F	11-15	0.50
F	20-60	0.67	F Adult	0.5-1.0	F	15-64	0.75	64-70	0.60	M or F	16-18	0.75
M or F	over 60	0.50	Old people	0.3-0.7	M or F	over 65	0.50	>70	0	M	19-60	1.00
										F	19-60	0.70
										M	over 60	0.50[6]
										F	over 60	0.00

Sources:

1. FAO Notions d'Economic Generale et d'Economic Rurales 1973 quoted in Murphy & Sprey, 1981.
2. Memento de l'Agronome quoted in Murphy & Sprey, 1981.
3. Norman, 1973.
4. Barnett, 1983.
5. Author's estimation based upon thorough discussions with refugee elders in the settlements.
6. It may sound unreasonable to assume that the potential units of labor of a male of 61 and 90 years of age are the same. However, in the particular situation of the refugees, people over 70 years do not often take part in farm or in other income-generating activities.

TABLE 6.2. Total Family Labor Units Available in the Sample Households by Age and Sex.

	Umsaqata			Umbrush			Dehema		
Age Group	M	F	M&F	M	F	M&F	M	F	M&F
6-10	13.0	7.75	20.75	7.00	7.0	14.00	7.5	7.00	14.50
11-15	12.0	10.00	22.00	11.50	8.5	20.00	10.0	10.50	20.50
16-18	10.5	11.25	21.75	6.75	6.0	12.75	4.5	6.75	11.25
19-60	55.0	43.40	98.40	37.00	32.9	69.90	40.0	30.10	70.10
Over 60	2.5	–	2.50	4.50	–	4.50	2.5	–	2.50
Total	93.0	72.40	165.40	66.75	54.4	121.15	64.5	54.35	118.85

(continued)

	Adingrar			Aburakham			Wad Awad			All villages		
Age Group	M	F	M&F	M	F	M&F	M	F	M&F	M	F	M&F
6-10	6.00	7.5	13.50	5.00	5.25	10.25	5.00	3.75	8.75	43.5	38.25	81.75
11-15	9.50	16.5	26.00	6.50	7.50	14.00	3.50	9.00	12.50	53.0	62.00	115.00
16-18	6.75	3.0	9.75	8.25	3.00	11.25	3.75	8.25	12.00	40.5	38.25	78.75
19-60	50.00	35.0	8.50	41.00	39.20	80.20	37.00	30.70	67.70	26.0	211.30	471.30
Over 60	2.5	–	2.5	1.00	–	1.00	0.50	–	0.50	13.5	–	13.50
Total	74.75	62.0	136.75	61.75	54.80	116.70	49.75	51.70	101.45	410.3	349.80	760.30

TABLE 6.3. Average Family Labor Units in the Sample Households by Sex (this includes the heads of households).

Umsaqata			Umbrush			Dehema			Adingrar			Aburakham			Wad Awad			All villages		
M	F	M&F	M	F	M&F	M	F	M&F	M	F	M&F	M	F	M&F	M	F	M&F	M	F	M&F
1.5	1.2	2.7	1.5	1.2	2.7	1.4	1.1	2.5	1.5	1.2	2.7	1.0	0.9	2.0	1.5	1.6	3.1	1.4	1.2	2.6

Khalil, in his socioeconomic survey of the New Halfa tenants, also notes that,

> A family can reckon to have adequate labor supply only at a certain point in its life cycle.
>
> (Khalil: 1980, 44)

Each family has a particular development cycle which usually begins with marriage, continues with the arrival of children and ends with death. In the early stage of their development cycle, children are mainly consumers without being able to contribute to farm and other economic activities. At the teenage level, children represent unpaid family labor until their marriage or even until a few years after their marriage.

A few years after their marriage they establish their own families and enter into their own development cycle. If such is the case there must be a particular stage when the household head's access to unpaid family labor is at the optimum level. To test this hypothesis, we correlated the ages of the household heads with the amount of labor units available to each age group, and the results are unmistakenly positive. In Table 6.4 we have calculated the amount of labor units available in each age group without including the head of the household and his wife. The results show that household heads in the age group 41-50 years have the highest access to family labor.

The youngest families, with heads below the age of 21, have no access to family labor except that of the husband and wife. Even the households with heads in the age group 20-30 years have insignificant access to childrens labor. When the household head is between 40 and 50 years, his access to family labor is optimal. After he enters the 50-60 age group, his access declines relatively because his children are by now married and work on their own. The situation declines further in the age group over 60 years.

TABLE 6.4. Total Labor Units in the Sample Families by Age Groups of Household Heads in the Six Villages Excluding the Households Heads and Their Wives.

Age group (years)	Male	Female	Total
0-20	0.00	0.00	0.00
21-30	5.00	5.00	10.00
31-40	24.75	28.25	53.00
41-50	95.75	87.75	183.50
51-60	49.25	39.75	89.00
Over 60	19.50	11.00	30.50

Table 6.4 does not show the real picture because of the unequal age distribution of the household heads. As can be seen from Table 4.8 in Chapter 4, the age group 41-50 years occurs most often and can influence the results in Table 6.4. But as can be seen from Table 6.5 and Figure 6.1, the average family labor units available to each family per age group of household head are still optimum in the families whose heads are between 41 and 50 years.

TABLE 6.5. Average Family Labor-Units per Age of Household Head Excluding the Husband and Wife.

Age group (years)	Male	Female	Both
0-20	–	–	–
21-30	0.1	0.1	0.2
31-40	0.3	0.4	0.7
41-40	1.1	1.0	2.2
51-60	0.9	0.7	1.6
Over 60	0.6	0.3	0.7

Source: Questionnaire survey.

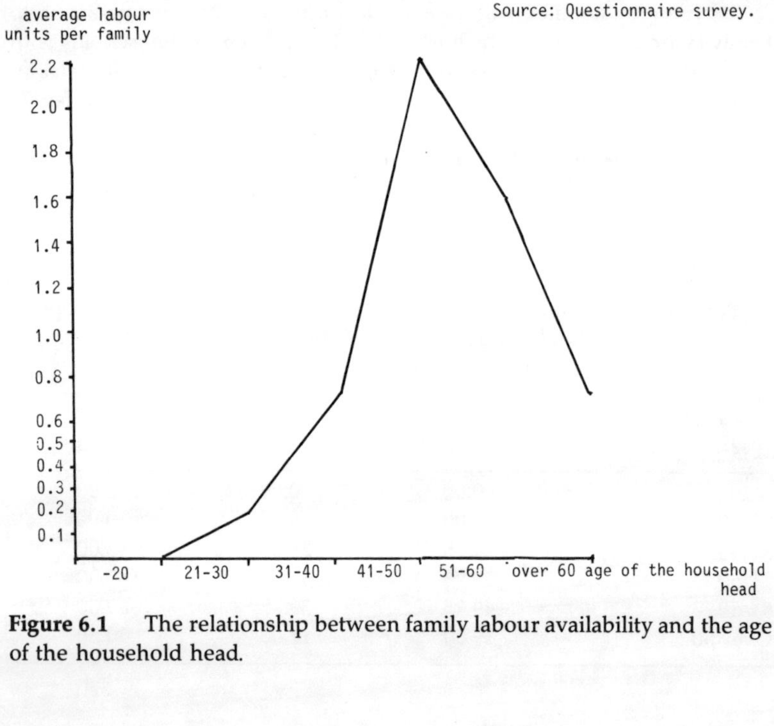

Figure 6.1 The relationship between family labour availability and the age of the household head.

Table 6.5 shows that the households whose head is in the 41-50 age group have 2.2 family labor units accruing to them from their children. The younger families have no doubt an unfavorable ratio between those who consume and those who produce, but this will be alleviated in the later phase of the family's cycle. The situation of the elderly familes is different because their disadvantage is twofold. The older they grow, the more the effectiveness of their labor declines. Furthermore, their children also leave them to have their own families. However, after a certain age, parents become dependent mostly on their sons, who are socially obliged to take care of or to help them.

TRADITIONAL DIVISION OF LABOR

In traditional societies one of the basic determinants of labor availability is the division of labor among men, women and children. Often the division of labor is strongly influenced by the social norms and cultural values that govern the participation of the different segments of the population. Tradition, like any other historical phenomenon, is subject to change and development. These changes occur as a result of structural factors and conscious human action. Sometimes old traditions may prevail, even though they impose a critical constraint on the progress of a community. This is often because certain forces benefit from maintaining such traditions. In general the dominant social norms will persist over long periods of time, and no considerable change will take place in the short run.

Shortage of labor is a major constraint on agricultural production in the settlements, but the participation of females in production is still nonexistent or very marginal. The traditional division of labor in farm work continues to exist in the settlements. Furthermore, even refugee females from the national groups with a very long history of female participation in farm work and in other economic activities are tending to abstain more and more from field work, with very serious consequences for labor availability. As we saw in a previous chapter, females constitute about 51.3% of the sample refugee population (Table 4.9 in Chapter 4). The communities will not easily overcome the labor availability constraint without the involvement and active participation of over 50% of their members, not only in farm and non-farm income-generating activities but in all aspects of the communities' social life.

Women's lack of participation not only causes a shortage of labor, but it also curtails women's access and control over the means of production and other household economic resources. Their exclusion from economic activities has resulted in their marginalization in all kinds of village affairs. Females do not take part in village meetings, nor are they represented in any kind of leadership. (Their participation in production per se does not guarantee equal access to and control over the means of production and other resources but there is no doubt that their awareness of the need to fight for their rights to be treated and accepted as equal members of society is a product of their participation in social production. Domestic drudgery is physically tedious and mentally stifling, and as long as women remain limited to kitchen work it is unlikely that they would be the motive force for their own emancipation. But this must not be construed to indicate that women's participation in social production automatically leads to emancipation. Despite their participation in agricultural production in the Eritrean highlands, women have never participated in the main social affairs of their communities.)

We tried to identify how tasks are allocated among men, women and children in the settlements. According to our results the following tasks are allocated to men: seed-bed preparation (including land clearing), sowing of crops, plowing, weeding, harvesting, threshing path preparation, threshing, sack filling, transporting, livestock herding, milking, cutting of trees, construction works and charcoal production.

Food processing (grain cleaning, flour grinding, wet pounding and cooking), washing clothes and utensils, house and compound cleaning, child care and other related domestic chores are exclusively the responsibility of women. Who fetched water varied among the settlements. In Salmin, Umbrush and Umsaqata, where the Maria and the Beni Amer are well represented, married women do not take part in water-fetching. In the other settlements, especially in Dehema, Adingrar and Zurzur, where the Saho national group is dominant, married women do fetch water. The distribution of the refugee households according to ethnic and national groups is given in Table 6.6. Often water-fetching and firewood collection are assigned to children. The former mainly falls on small children between the ages of six and ten of both sexes, while the latter is mainly performed by boys between the ages of 10 and 16. Parents are reluctant to send their female children to distant places to collect firewood, so the task is allocated to boys only. Both firewood and water for domestic use and for sale are mainly carried by donkeys and sometimes by camels. Children also participate in weeding, harvesting, threshing, filling, transporting of crops, and fetching thatch grass. The participation of children is limited by school attendance (between October and May).

To find out whether there are some activities that are exclusively reserved for a single category, we asked the respondents to state which activities they consider to belong exclusively to men, women or children. For some activities the line of demarcation was fluid, but for others there was a strong taboo that prevented men from doing women's work and vice versa. The results show that 98% of the respondents considered plowing to be the exclusive task for men, 81% considered weeding as the major task of men and 72% considered harvesting as the task of men; 98% and 99% of the respondents considered child care and food preparation, respectively, as exclusively the domain of married women. The tasks allocated to male children are determined by the physical inability of children to perform the same work as male adults, rather

TABLE 6.6. Percentage Distribution of the Households by Ethnic or National Group Origin.

Ethnic or National group origin	Umsaqata	Salmin	Dehema	Adingrar	Umbrush	Zurzur
Beni Amer	12	67	4	5	45	27
Maria	35	7	–	–	7	1
Baria	14	20	–	–	7	2
Saho	32	2	83	84	11	66
Tigrinya	–	–	10	–	5	–
Others	7	4	3	11	25	4
Total	100	100	100	100	100	100

Source: EA-A Survey, 1981.

than by tradition. According to our results, 77% of the respondents stated that children take part in weeding; 78% said that water-fetching is done by the children; and 86% said that firewood collection is children's work.

As was noted in Chapter 2, Eritrean society does not consist of a single national group, and is therefore not characterized by a single tradition and religion. The roles of males and females also vary accordingly and, because of this, it is difficult to generalize about the role of women in Eritrean society. In the Eritrean highlands, where small sedentary farmers have always constituted the bulk of the population and where Christianity is the dominant religion, women have always taken part in farm and other income-generating activities. Even though the women were excluded from land ownership, their participation in economic activity was recognized; their participation in farm labor was indispensable for household food self-sufficiency. This is succinctly put in popular Tigrinya proverbs such as, 'If you don't have business, don't travel; if you don't have a wife, don't farm'. (Quoted in Liberation: 1977, 14)

In the Eritrean lowlands, on the other hand, except among the Baria and Kunama, where sedentarized farming is the dominant mode of existence (see Chapter 2)

> . . . most of the people are nomadic herdsmen who seasonally migrate in search of grazing grounds for their cattle . . . women are totally excluded from ownership of property and participation in social production and are relegated to domestic work. Among some of the nomadic population, women are confined to the inner parts of the houses so as not to be seen by men and are thus even deprived of the sunshine.
>
> (Liberation: 1977, 14-15)

In the settlements, even though women participate very little in economic activities, they are no longer confined to 'the inner parts of the houses'. In fact, none of the traditional women tried to hide from us when we came to interview their husbands or themselves. In this respect it can be said that some social changes have occurred. However, what struck the author most was that even those women in settlements who were originally from the Eritrean highlands (Tigrinya) or who had historical links with the highlands seem to be participating less in farm work and in other income-generating activities. This has tremendously affected the households' labor availability.

According to the Economic Commission for Africa, in African societies women

> . . . account for about 60-80 per cent of the agricultural labor force.
>
> (Economic Commission for Africa quoted in Tobisson: 1980, 1)

Tobisson also notes that studies conducted in Tanzania '. . . show that the work load on women is excessive relative to men'.

However, data from other parts of Africa show that the participation of women in economic activity is either non-existent or marginal. For example, according to the Agricultural Census of 1964-65, the rate of female participation in agricultural labor in Kassala Province is only 6%. In Northern Nigeria, Norman found that the participation of females in farm labor was insignificant due to '. . . partial or complete seclusion of Moslem wives'. (Norman: 1976, 12) These facts clearly indicate that the participation of the different segments of the rural population in Africa is governed by social norms and cultural values, especially religion.

In the refugee settlements, even though we could not measure exactly the participation of women, it was generally either non-existent or very marginal. The dominant religion in Kassala Province is Islam, which relegates women to domestic chores and keeps them partly or completely secluded. These cultural practices in the country of asylum have reinforced the archaic traditional division of labor that existed among the refugees from the Eritrean lowlands and have discouraged the other refugee women from other parts of Eritrea from emancipating themselves from the drudgeries of domestic work and have indirectly forced them to conform to decadent practices. This is reflected in the fact that even the Tigrinya and Baria women, with a long tradition of participation, are not only increasingly relegated to domestic chores but are even directly or indirectly pressurized to wear the veil, which was never part of their culture in Eritrea.

Furthermore, the socioeconomic set-up of the settlements does not give any incentive to women to participate. For instance, except in the case of female-headed households, land is always given to the man as head of the household. In the case of divorce, the woman becomes landless and often homeless. This tends to strengthen the old relations.

It is noteworthy here to state that our findings indicate two exceptions—given below. These occur in exceptional cases and where the socioeconomic status of the household is a critical factor which could influence the division of labor within the household.

First, there is evidence which suggests that when the subsistence security of the household is imminently threatened by an acute shortage of food supply, women tend to participate in farm work and other income-generating activities. A typical case is that of households headed by females and of even very poor households headed by males. This can to some extent be seen in the data in Table 6.7.

According to Table 6.7, about 12% of the family women reported having worked for wages. During the dry season most of the very poor families in Adingrar, Dehema, Zurzur and some in Umsaqata and Umbrush migrate to Semsem, a rainfed state farm not very far from the Qala en Nahal settlement, to pick cotton. They are given a very low wage, so it would seem that the refugees are mainly attracted by the ration distributed by the employer as part of their wage. Since for many households the opportunity cost of their labor during

TABLE 6.7. Percentage Distribution of the Family Women Who had been Engaged in Wage Labor in 1981-82 Season.

Umsaqata	Umbrush	Dehema	Adingrar	Aburakham	Wad Awad	Total
6.5	6.7	12.8	36.0	5.1	3.1	11.9

the slack season is almost zero, they migrate so that they can at least save their food at home for the hungry season. Some of the female-headed households and very poor households also admit that their women take part in farm work and in other income-generating activities.

The second factor which tends to weaken the traditional sexual division of family labor is the urgency of an agricultural operation. When the household lacks cash to hire wage labor and cannot resort to any other sources of labor and if the operation requires urgent execution, the women in such households are sometimes forced to take part in farm work. For example, sesame harvesting is highly labor intensive. If sesame is not harvested a few days after maturity, the crop is lost due to shattering. Sesame commands a very high producer price and its loss would constitute a great financial blow which no family can easily afford.

Within these exceptions, the traditional division of labor seems to be intact among the households and it seems that it will persist over a long period of time. Therefore, women's non-participation in farm and non-farm income-generating activities is one of the factors that limits labor availability in the settlements.

AGRICULTURAL LABOR

The viability of the agriculturally-based settlements is critically dependent on their resource base. One of these crucial resource bases is labor. In the refugee land settlements the family or the household is the basic unit of production. Despite the relative entrenchment of market relations, the household or the family still provides the social basis of subsistence production and the organizational framework for the allocation and division of labor.

We now investigate the various sources of labor to see whether labor represents a constraint on agricultural production. We also look at the factors that affect utilization of the potentially available labor on the households' farm, at the labor strategy adopted by the farm households in allocating their labor among the various activities, and, finally, briefly at the market orientation of the households.

Sources of Agricultural Labor

In subsistence economies, in which the household fends for its basic requirements, the major source of agricultural labor is the farm household itself. However, relatives and mutual help or labor exchange among neighbors or friends is also widely practiced. Depending on the level of exchange of goods and services that exists in such economies, casual hired labor may also be used to supplement the family's labor resource during peak seasons. Some of the households may hire labor in order to provide the material basis for their existence while others may use hired labor to produce marketable surplus. This also presupposes the presence of households who are willing to sell their labor power in order to meet their subsistence need or who are compelled to earn cash in addition to subsistence production.

The more market relations (for example, conversion of labor into commodity) entrench themselves, the more developed is the social division of labor. By the same token, the traditional sources of farm labor, namely communal labor, even among relatives and labor exchange among the members of the community, tend to disappear gradually and give way to commercialization of labor. This process often leads to the complete or partial separation of some members of the community from their means of production and consequently part or all of their basis of material existence has to originate from proceeds obtained from the sale of labor power. The degree to which labor has become a commodity is a reflection of the relative dominance of market relations and is also evidence of the phenomenon of social and economic differentiation that exists in the community concerned.

In the refugee land settlements, even though a full scale commercialization of labor relations has not yet taken place, there are many households whose basis of material existence fully depends on income obtained from the sale of labor power. There are also a considerable number of households, marginal farmers, who work for wages to supplement their subsistence need, to buy essential manufactured and other commodities and to meet their social and other obligations. There are also a considerable number of the households which hire casual labor to overcome peak labor requirements. There are again others who depend solely on hired casual agricultural labor while they themselves engage in more profitable non-farm income-generating activities.

The distribution of the sample households according to their source of agricultural labor is given in Table 6.8. Out of the total sample of land-holding households, about 45% depend only on family labor, while about 26% combine family and hired labor to work their farms. However, it must be noted that the average for all the settlements conceals the real differences that exist among the villages with regard to hired labor. In the four villages of Qala en Nahal about 33% of the sample households hired labor in addition to their family labor. The average amount of labor units available per household, excluding female labor units, is about 1.5, whereas if we include female labor, the average labor units available per household is about 2.6. However, even though some females among some ethnic groups participate in farm labor, their overall participation in farm work is very marginal and the household can only count on its male labor.

As can be seen from Table 6.8, about 13% of the land-holding households rely fully on hired labor, i.e., while the household head engages in more profitable non-farm income-generating activities, casual labor is hired for agricultural operations. It is very interesting to note that in Aburakham where the size of the allotment is the smallest and the location of the settlement is ecologically very marginal, about 20% of the land-possessing sample households engaged in non-farm activities while they hired wage laborers for farm work.

TABLE 6.8. Percentage Distribution of the Sample Farm Households by Sources of Labor.

Sources of Labor	Umsa-qata	Umb-rush	Deh-ema	Adin-grar	Abura-kham	Wad Awad	Total
Family	31.8	39.4	47.0	45.0	56.8	53.1	45.4
Relatives	4.5	–	–	2.5	2.3	–	1.8
Labor Exchange	2.3	–	–	–	6.8	6.2	2.6
Hired Labor	18.2	6.1	11.8	7.5	20.4	15.6	13.6
Family & Relatives	6.8	6.1	14.7	10.0	4.5	3.1	7.5
Family & Mutual Help	2.3	3.0	2.9	2.5	–	3.1	2.2
Family & Hired Labor	34.1	45.4	23.5	30.0	9.1	18.7	26.4
Relatives & Mutual Help	–	–	–	2.5	–	–	0.4
Relatives & Hired Labor	–	–	–	–	–	–	–
Total	100.0	100.0	99.9	100.0	99.9	99.8	99.9

This suggests that owing to the size of the allotment and due to unreliability of rainfall, a considerable proportion of the households consider non-farm activities as more profitable than farm activities.

Table 6.8 clearly shows that the traditional practices of communal labor such as among kinship group and labor exchange (*wofera* in Tigrinya) among the community members is gradually vanishing except in a few cases. Of all the sample households only about 6% relied on relatives and on labor exchange while about 7% reported having received help from their relatives. Those who fully relied on labor contributed by relatives are the vulnerable groups who lack able-bodied male family members and liquidity to hire casual labor.

It is interesting to classify the sample households into different social strata and see which of the income groups combine family labor with hired labor and which income groups depend completely on hired labor.

As can be seen from Table 6.9, out of the total sample households that hire casual labor, about 6% are from the very poor households while about 13% are from the poor households. Out of those who hired wage labor, about 40% are from the middle-income households while the other 40% are from the rich households.

The results become more interesting if we relate the proportion of the households that hire wage labor to their respective income groups. Out of the very poor households, about 5% hire labor, out of which about 60% combine wage labor with family labor while about 40% fully rely on hired casual labor for farm work.

Among the poor households about 18% hire wage labor. It is interesting to note that all those poor households who hired casual labor did so to overcome peak labor requirements. None of them was fully dependent on hired labor. Among the middle-income households,about 45% hire casual labor. Out of those who hired labor, about 75% did so to supplement their family labor, while about 25% reported having fully relied on hired labor. Among the rich households, about 92% of them hire labor, out of which about 48% combine family labor with hired labor while the majority, i.e., about 52% do not directly participate in farm work but fully rely on hired labor.

As can be seen from Table 6.9, not only the medium-income and the rich households but even some of the very poor and poor households also hire casual labor. These are foremost vulnerable households who, due to age, physical handicap or a lack of able-bodied adult male family members, are forced to hire casual farm laborers. Second, some of the households in this category also hire wage labor when the demand during the peak season exceeds the family's labor capacity. Third, there are families whose adult members are hired out for wage in the rainfed areas or within the settlements and hire laborers in their farms. Most of the agricultural operations, especially weeding, in the rainfed areas are carried out on a contractural basis whereby a group of laborers agrees to weed a certain area for a certain amount, and this often requires the continuous presence of the laborer until the contract is fully

TABLE 6.9. Distribution of the Farm Labor Hiring Sample Households by Income Group.

Category	Umsaqata	Umbrush	Dehema	Adingrar	Aburakham	Wad Awad	Total
Very poor	4.3	11.8	8.3	–	7.7	–	5.6
Poor	8.7	17.6	16.7	13.3	7.7	22.2	13.5
Middle	34.8	41.2	33.3	46.7	46.1	44.4	40.4
Rich	52.2	29.4	41.7	40.0	38.5	33.3	40.4
Total	100.0	100.0	100.0	100.0	100.0	99.9	99.9

performed. Timeliness in weeding is crucial, so households hire laborers to weed their farms. This practice is more widespread in Aburakham where, due to shortage of rainfall and the small size of the holdings, some households consider that the return of their labor would be higher in alternative income-generating activities, including wage labor, than working in their own farms. Fourth, in Qala en Nahal there were some very poor and poor households who had received loans in cash or in kind from rich households on condition that they would work for the creditor at the peak period. Labor requirements in their own plots occurs simultaneously with their obligation to work for the creditor and the need to weed their holdings in time necessitates hiring of wage labor.

As noted above, about 52% of the rich households do not themselves take part in farm labor. The reason for this is partly social but mainly economic. Farm work in the climatic and soil conditions in the area is extremely arduous and unpleasant. The rich farmers, in balancing physical effort and the unpleasantness of the operation against expected return, seem to take into account not only economic but social factors as well. In some of the ethnic groups with a long history of social and economic differentiation, especially the Maria and the Beni Amer, the upper stratum has always been reluctant to do manual work. Thus, some of the rich heads of households seem to prefer non-farm activities such as shopkeeping even when the return for their labor is not necessarily higher than in agriculture. It seems that abstention from manual labor is considered socially desirable by some of the well-to-do households. However, this does not imply that those who abstain from manual work are not engaged in alternative activities. They are indeed involved in a wide variety of activities, and many of them admit that their engagement in these is often a prerequisite for the realization of higher farm income.

It is important to state here that even though the conditions of the refugee families' livelihood and the social relations of labor are continuously changing, one must not overstate the case. The proportion of the households that fully or partially depend on wage labor for their material existence and the proportion of the rich households who depend on hired farm labor are presently considerable, but it is not proper to argue that labor relations in the settlements are fully commercialized.

For the majority the household is still the basic unit of production in the sense that it still constitutes the social basis of subsistence production by providing the organizational set-up and conditions for the allocation and reproduction of labor. It is important to note that most of the very poor, poor and even many of the medium-income households that reported having hired wage labor had themselves worked for wages for other farmers. Thus, in many cases, the hiring of wage labor is a reflection of the shortage of family labor and 'subsistence funds' rather than a reflection of the availability of surplus to pay for wages.

LABOR THROUGH THE SEASONS

By virtue of the climate factors in the region, labor use in the refugee land settlements is highly seasonal. Generally, the agricultural calendar extends between the second week of June and the first or second week of December. The sequence of farm activities can be seen in Figure 6.2.

Agricultural activities in the settlements begin with land clearing, which consists of removing weeds, shrubs or other plants or roots that may prevent effective ploughing. This activity is carried out either in the period preceding sowing or after harvest. Cultivation begins in the second week of June, assuming there has been sufficient rain to allow ploughing, and the following six weeks represent the period of optimal cultivation. However, the time of sowing is determined by weather conditions. In Qala en Nahal in the 1981 season cultivation began on 28 June while in the 1982 season cultivation did not begin before the 15 July and continued for 14 and 10 weeks, respectively. (Since sowing and ploughing are carried out in one single operation cultivation, sowing, and ploughing are used interchangeably except when the farm households use alternative traditional methods such as draft animal or digging-stick locally known as seluka.)

Weeding starts two or three weeks after sowing and builds up during July, and the requirement for weeding labor is at its peak in August. However, the period of peak labor requirement is determined by the date of sowing. Depending on their family labor resource or on their access to cash to pay for casual labor, farmers carry out between one and two weeding operations for sorghum and between one and three for sesame. Depending on the time of the first rains, weeding is carried out between July and September.

Sesame is harvested between the end of September and the first two weeks of October, but this is again a function of the date of sowing. The sesame harvest is a critical operation, and timing is crucial if heavy crop losses through shattering of overripe seed pods are to be avoided. This represents the second peak labor requirement.

The sorghum harvest begins usually in November and lasts until December. The sorghum harvest is not a critical operation and can be extended for several months without any risk of grain loss through shedding, but owing to fear of theft and animal trespass, the refugee farmers harvest their crops within a few weeks after maturity of the crop. Some time after harvest, the crop residues are cleared either by burning, or the stubble is collected to be used as livestock feed or thatching material. The rest of the year, i.e., between January and the first two weeks of June, represents the trough or the slack season. During this period, farm labor (with the exception of livestock herding) is essentially inactive.

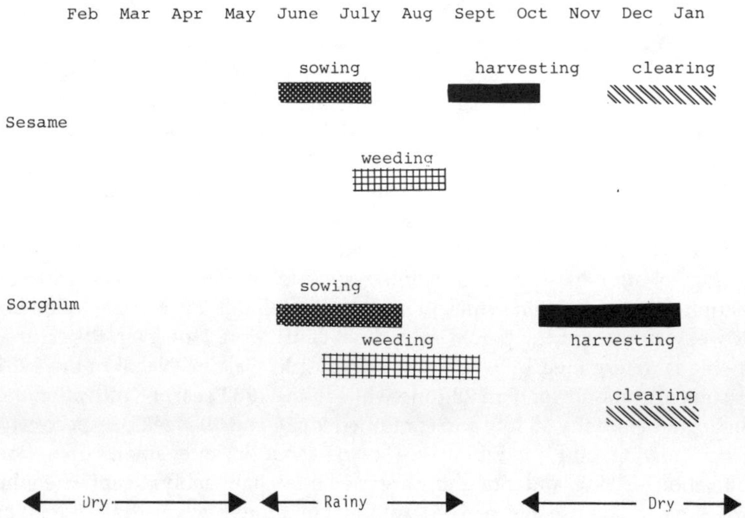

Figure 6.2 Sequence of Labour Activity

Seasonal Labor Requirements

Farming in the refugee land settlements consists of various operations such as initial land clearing, precultivation weeding, ploughing, sowing, thinning and weeding, cutting, thresh-path preparation, threshing, winnowing, filling,stitching, transport, removal of stalks, storage and marketing. The amount of labor required for each operation is determined by various physical and other conditions. Labor requirement for clearing, for example, depends on whether the land is populated by trees, bushes and roots which can be difficult to destump. The labor required for precultivation weeding will also depend on the timing of the ploughing operation and rains. The labor required for cutting will also depend on plant population. The labor requirement per feddan of land, for example, in weeding is determied by many factors, among which the most important are the number of times the land is cultivated before seeding, the number of times and the quality of weeding the farm had received in the previous season, the amount of rainfall in the season, the number of years the farm has been under continuous cultivation, and timing and quality of ploughing. A good quality and timely cultivation can effectively kill weeds and consequently reduce the amount of labor required. The use of a digging stick (*seluka*), for example, does not kill weeds and the labor required for weeding is reported to be higher in the farms sown by the use of *seluka* than those which are cultivated by tractors.

Earlier we discussed the determinants of family labor availability. Here we shall look at how a household's demand for non-household labor is determined. It is very important to distinguish between the amount of labor required by a household's farm and the effective demand for labor by that household. Under some circumstances, farm labor can become an effective constraint despite its abundance. This can happen under three main conditions. First, farm labor can become an effective constraint when, owing to high wages or unfavorable terms of trade for agricultural products or low productivity, the marginal revenue of agricultural output is at such a low level that it does not pay to increase output by hiring more labor. Second, labor shortage can in essence be a reflection of capital shortage when the households, faced with labor shortage, lack financial resources to hire laborers. Third, labor can become an effective constraint, despite its abundance, when real wages are below the subsistence margin or when the perceived return to the worker valued at the opportunity cost of his labor is considered uneconomic.

A household's demand for non-household labor is therefore determined first by the size, quality, and development cycle of the family's labor force, and second by the household's financial resources derived either from its own savings, assets or credit. The problem of labor shortage in the refugee land settlements, especially among the very low, low and medium-income groups, is more than anything else a problem of lack of financial resources rather than a problem of supply, whereby the households are unable to hire laborers or to work on their own farms during the hungry season when the labor requirement is at the peak.

The fact that the amount of labor required for the different farm operations is affected by various cultural practices and by physical conditions suggests that it is difficult if not impossible to standardize the amount of labor requirement per unit of land for the different operations not only at a regional or village level but even at interfarm level. Owing to this variation, estimates of labor requirement per feddan vary from source to source drastically. For example, according to the Rural Labor Study in Northern Sudan (1983) six man/days are required to weed one feddan of sorghum. Cree and Jonsson (1982) estimated the amount of labor required for weeding at the refugee settlements at 8.3 man/days per feddan. While according to the EA-A Survey (1981) a maximum of about 12 man/days are required to weed one feddan of sorghum.

The large differences between the results of the EA-A and the Rural Labor Study may partly be explained by the fact that the second is highly aggregated and is based on data from large mechanized rainfed farms, while the first is based on small holdings at a micro-level which are cultivated by tractors or by the *seluka* (plough stick). The amount of land and other assets that are available to the refugee households are less than that available to the commercial farmers in the region. As a result their allocation of labor per feddan will differ because the refugee farmers may be forced by the need to survive to use labor even when the marginal productivity is near zero. It is also probable that a given quantity of labor has a greater marginal productivity when used on several feddans than when concentrated on a small part of a feddan. In order to meet its subsistence need, the refugee household with small cultivable land will utilize its family labor even when the marginal productivity of labor is negligible to the commercial farmer. These may be the factors that account for the large differences of labor required per feddan in the large mechanized rainfed areas on the one hand and in the refugee land settlements on the other. Therefore, we shall assume that the maximum amount of labor required for the different farm operations in the rural refugee land settlements is as that provided in the EA-A survey. (See Table 6.10) However, it is interesting to note that the trend is the same even though the level of labor deficits during the peak months differ, i.e., periods of severe unemployment or underemployment alternate with periods of full employment and labor shortage.

However, these data are estimates based on case studies and group discussions rather than measurements. Most African rural farmers have no watches or clocks and empirical measurements of labor input requires huge enumerator time. An enumerator has to follow the farmer to his field and record labor input. However, as Spencer notes, an enumerator using this technique cannot cover more than one farmer a day and this is the reason why many measurements of labor input are based on estimates. (Spencer: 1972, 12)

The EA-A survey does not state whether the time given in Table 6.10 includes the time spent walking to and from the farms and time spent resting. Owing to the humid and very hot climate, most of the farmers rest between 12 to 3 p.m. Since the survey assumes 10-hour working day, it seems that it did not take these factors into account. Despite its shortcomings, the estimations on labor requirement as given in Table 6.10 can at least enable us to see the periods in which peak labor requirements occurs and the periods in which agricultural labor is underemployed or unemployed.

To identify the period in which there is shortage of farm labor and the period in which there is an excess of a potentially available labor force, we have compared the monthly man/days required with the monthly man/days available, and we have also tried to estimate the level of labor utilization in every month. The results are given in Table 6.11.

In reading the data in Table 6.11, one must remember the following assumptions. First, the household's potential stock of labor is fully utilized in farm work, i.e., the non-farm activities are for simplicity assumed as non-existent. Second, the household has 10 feddans of holding under crop and no part of the holding is lying fallow. Third, there are no obstacles that reduce the effectiveness or prevent full utilization of the household's potential labor.

TABLE 6.10. Estimations of Labor Requirements of Sorghum and Sesame by Month in Man Days per Feddan (Assuming a 10-Hour Working Day and a Six Day Working Week).

Month	Sorghum	Sesame
January	1.5	–
February	–	–
March	–	–
April	–	–
May	1.0	1.0
June	2.0	2.0
July	3.0	8.5
August	6.0	11.0
September	1.5	–
October	–	8.0
November	8.0	–
December	4.0	–
Total	27.0	30.5

Source: EA-A Survey 1980.

The household's level of labor utilization during the different months shows that there is a great surplus of labor during the dry season and large labor deficits during the peak periods of July and August when sesame and sorghum are weeded and in October and November when sesame and sorghum are harvested, respectively. A study conducted by the World Bank, in southern Darfur in 1976 on farm labor use also reveals the same pattern. (Quoted in Kedeman: 1979, 82) Various studies in the surrounding area and in the refugee land settlements point out that weeding during the months of July and August represents the major constraint on production. (See Kedeman: 1978; ILO: 1976; Agabawi: 1969; Spooner: 1981; Simpson & Kalifa: 1976; Fre: 1981) The second period of peak labor requirement in which our households are faced with labor deficit is in October when sesame is harvested. The sesame harvest is labor intensive, and the farmer has to strike a balance so that no grain would be lost either due to overmaturity or immaturity of the seeds. This suggests that the operation cannot be spread without leading to grain loss by shattering or premature cutting. If it were not for fear of theft and animal trespass, the problem of labor deficit in November could be avoided because the sorghum harvest can be spread over a long period without risk of grain loss.

Seasonal Fluctuations of Labor Use

The distribution of the households by the number of hours worked per week during the different seasons is given in Figure 6.3. Our primary concern here is

TABLE 6.11. Estimated Average Monthly Labor Required, Availability and Level of Utilization per Household per 10 Feddans.

Month	Man-days required[1]	Man-days available			Labor utilization as percentage of availability	
		Male[2]	Female[3]	Both[4]	Male[5]	Female[5]
January	7.5	34	29	63	22.1	0
February	0	34	29	63	0	0
March	0	34	29	63	0	0
April	0	34	29	63	0	0
May	10	34	29	63	29.4	0
June	20	34	29	63	58.8	0
July	57.5	34	29	63	100.0	0
August	85.0	34	29	63	100.0	0
September	7.5	34	29	63	22.1	0
October	40.0	34	29	63	100.0	0
November	40.0	34	29	63	100.0	0
December	20.0	34	29	63	58.8	0

Sources:
1. Calculated according to Table 6.10 and assumes 5 feddans under sorghum and 5 feddans under sesame.
2. The average male labor unit per household is 1.4 (Table 6.3) and it is assumed that the average number of working days (less holy days) per month is 24 days. Column 2 is obtained by multiplying the monthly working days by the average family labor unit. The same procedure is used for columns 3 and 4.
5. For our purpose women do not take part in farm labor. The percentage utilization of the available labor is calculated from the male labor units only.

not to measure the actual labor time spent in farm operation, but rather to show the seasonal fluctuation in farm labor use so as to determine the period in which peak labor requirement occurs and the period in which labor is either underemployed or laid off; the data in Figure 6.3 clearly indicate these phenomena. Work days were, as expected, longest in the cultivation season and shortest in the slack season.

From the end of December, or after harvesting is completed, many of the poor families migrate to pick cotton on the state farm of Semsem and return to the settlements between April and May. Thus, those who reported working for

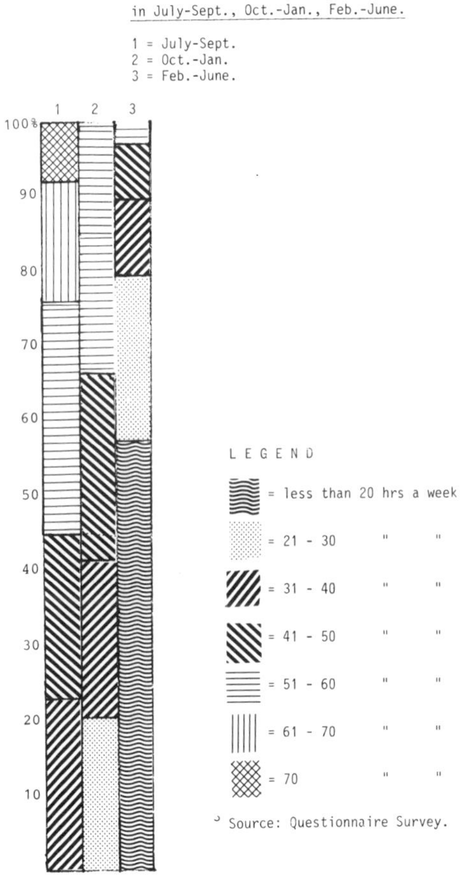

Figure 6.3 Number of hours worked per week

more than 20 hours in the months of February to June are mainly emigrants, cattle herders, merchants, charcoal producers, and fetchers of firewood, water, thatching-grass and animal feed. No agricultural work is done during these months, the only exception being a few days of removing shrubs and weeds in May and June. (See Table 6.11) There may also be some households that plough their holdings manually in June assuming there are early rains. It can be generally concluded that the period between February and June is marked by underemployment or unemployment of farm labor.

CONSTRAINTS ON LABOR

Within the limits imposed by physical conditions, growth in agricultural output in the refugee land settlements can mainly be explained in terms of inputs of land, labor and capital. In African traditional agriculture, where neither mechanical nor draught power is used, land and labor are the only inputs used. However, in the refugee land settlements, cultivation is mechanized and capital input is equally important.

To find out the major constraints on crop production, the respondents were asked to state three factors which they considered as the major constraints on production. The distribution of the sample households that cited labor as one of the three primary constraints is given in Table 6.12.

Out of the total land-possessing sample households about 65% gave shortage of labor as one of the three major constraints on increased agricultural production. One factor which was closely associated with the shortage of labor was shortage of capital (cash) which could be used to hire casual labor during the peak period or to maintain the household members during the cultivation season which is the remotest point in time from the previous harvesting season. It is important to note here that almost all the farmers that cited labor as a constraint also reported that if they had capital (money) they could recruit farm laborers without difficulty. Therefore, the shortage is not actually caused by shortage of labor supply as such. Instead it is the shortage of capital which could enable the households to hire laborers or to intensify their activities on their own holdings instead of hiring themselves out for wages during the peak season.

As can be seen from Table 6.12 out of those who cited labor as one of the three primary constraints, about 27% are from the very low income group. While about 26, 37, and 9% are from the low, medium, and high-income groups, respectively.

Among the land-possessing very low income group, about 76% gave shortage of labor as representing one of the three major constraints on production. Among the low income, medium, and high income groups, 64%, 73%, and 35%, respectively, cited labor as one of the three constraints on production. This suggests that even though about one-third of the rich

TABLE 6.12. Constraint on Crop Production by Percentage Distribution of the Sample Households, Citing Labor as One of the Three Major Constraints.

	Umsaqata	Umbrush	Dehema	Adingrar	Aburakham	Wad Awad	Total
Very poor	20.6	30.4	22.2	14.8	57.1	26.7	27.2
Poor	23.5	17.4	33.3	22.2	28.6	33.3	25.8
Middle	35.3	43.5	37.0	55.5	14.3	33.3	37.4
Rich	20.6	8.7	7.4	7.4	–	6.7	9.5
Total	100.0	100.0	99.9	99.9	100.0	100.0	99.9

households complained about labor shortage, and consequently shortage of capital (money) to hire labor, they are the least affected by such a constraint. However, the results of our survey show that shortage of labor at the peak period is one of effective constraints on production.

However, the consequence of labor shortage on the welfare of each income group is highly variable, i.e., while labor shortage may constrain the well-to-do households' efforts to produce more marketable surplus, for the lowest and low income groups labor shortage may threaten their subsistence security and consequently the reproduction of labor itself.

As noted in Chapter 4, the size of the refugee households as well as the refugees' age and sex structure do not remarkably differ from that of northern rural Sudan in general and Kassala Province in particular. How can we explain the problem of labor shortage which many households are faced with during the cultivation season? As noted earlier, the participation of women in farm labor among most of the ethnic groups is either non-existent or highly marginal, but this alone cannot explain the shortage. Below we shall try to examine some of the factors that may directly or indirectly affect the utilization of the potentially available labor force on the family farm.

THE UTILIZATION OF LABOR

> . . . in many tropical environments the wet season is the most critical time of year especially for the poorest people, women and children. Commonly at that time, malnutrition, morbidity and mortality peak; the costs of sickness to society in lost agricultural production and to families in food and income forgone are at their highest.
>
> Robert Chambers: 1979

In rainfed agriculture, especially in areas where crop production is limited to one season a year and where there are no opportunities for employment in the non-agricultural sector, periods of severe unemployment and underemployment tend to alternate with periods of full employment. However, it will be argued here that the problem of labor in the refugee land settlements is not mainly due to an absolute shortage of labor required for agricultural operations but is also due to other factors.

We will now briefly investigate some of the other factors that reduce the effectiveness of the potentially available family labor force or prevent the intensification of the households' activities on their own farms. Foremost of these is the availability of a food supply that the households require in order to maintain their families during the hungry season when their crops are not yielding revenue. In addition there are conflicting demands on labor time such as working on subsistence and cash crops, school attendance of children and farm distance from the places of residence, and finally, the condition of health and nutritional status of the household members.

Food Availability, Morbidity and Employment

The seasonality of the agricultural calendar affects the seasonal availability of subsistence. Crops are harvested between October and December, and the stock of grain of the poor households runs out when farm activities are at their peak. We argue that in the refugee land settlements the running out of the poor households' stocks of grain, the peak energy requirement of the farm households, the peak period of labor requirements at the households' farms and the effective demand for wage labor within and outside the settlements (excluding demand of labor in the agricultural irrigated schemes for cotton picking) occur simultaneously. Morbidity as noted by Chambers has also a 'seasonal pattern and peak during the wet season'. (Chambers: 1979, 1)

This can be demonstrated in a hypothetical case in Figure 6.4 whereby labor requirement during the agricultural season, i.e., between June and December is relatively very high with the highest peak occurring in July and August. The level of employment opportunities both within the settlements, in the surrounding Sudanese villages and in the large mechanized rainfed areas also reveal the same pattern. The curve representing the level of morbidity also shows the same trend. However, the curve representing subsistence availability shows the opposite trend, i.e., when the labor requirement of the household is at its peak, its 'subsistence fund' declines below the subsistence minimum. When the 'subsistence fund' of the household declines below the minimum

Figure 6.4

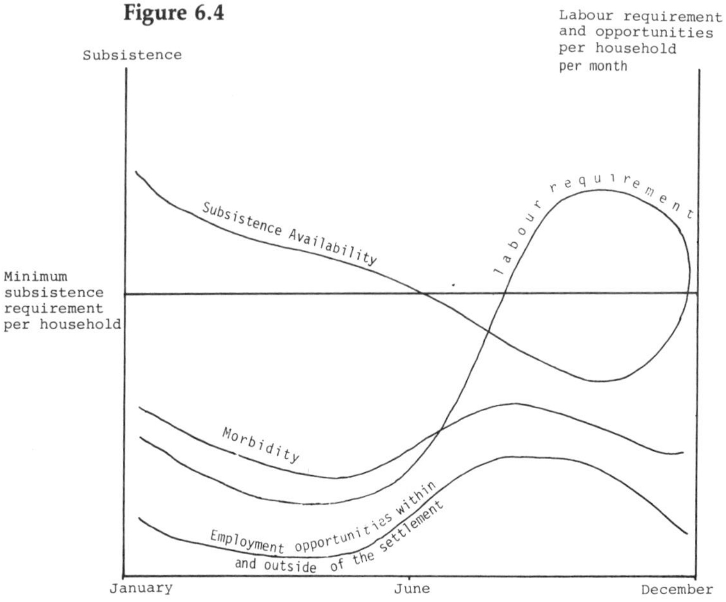

subsistence level, the household has three alternatives. The first of these alternatives is to tighten its belt by cutting its consumption drastically. However, since most of the poor households are often on the verge of the 'subsistence margin', their space of maneuver is extremely limited, i.e., their belt is already very tight and tightening it further may mean starvation. The second alternative is to take *shayl*, i.e., money or consumer goods lent against the future delivery of crops. Crops, especially sesame, are bought during the hungry season against advance payment at a price much lower than the market price. In 1982, merchants extended *shayl* at £S.35 per one sack of sesame while the market price of sesame during the harvesting season was between £S.75 and £S.80. (Credits in the settlements are only available to those who are credit-worthy. The poor section of the refugee farmers have no access to credit facilities.) The third alternative open to the household is to postpone timely weeding of its farm and sell its labor power to others. Delayed weeding leads to increased labor requirements per acre and affects yields negatively. A household which is forced to work for wages at the peak period either weeds its holdings lightly or weeds part of its holding only. This effectively leads to future weed build up. This again reduces the farm produce which will run out at the time when the family's labor is critically needed at the family's own farm. To guarantee the survival of the household members, the head of the household or other members will be forced to work for wages, again postponing work on the household's own farm. In other words, the household enters a vicious circle or an impasse which due to lack of a sufficient resource base cannot be overcome easily.

The employment opportunities within and outside of the settlements are concentrated in the cultivation season. This can be illustrated by the following results. Out of the 108 households that worked for wages in the Qala en Nahal settlement in 1981/82, about 92% worked between July and January. Out of the 55 households that reported having worked for wages in the surrounding Sudanese villages, about 96% worked between July and January. Out of 24 households that worked in the mechanized rainfed areas in Aburakham, about 96% worked between July and January. In Wad Awad about 90% of the nine households that worked in the rainfed areas worked between July and January. The only exception is that out of the 45 households in Qala in Nahal that worked in the mechanized rainfed area, only about 7% worked between July and January., while about 93% worked as cotton pickers in Semsem during the dry season. The irrigated schemes do not provide significant employment opportunities for the refugees despite the fact that cotton is picked when farm labor is almost completely laid off. In Qala en Nahal only 13 out of 202 households reported having worked in the irrigated schemes. In Aburakham only five out of 59 households worked in the Rahad irrigated scheme.

The reason the poor refugees gave for not participating in cotton picking was the very low wages paid by the cotton growers or by the Sudanese tenants in the irrigated schemes. To this must be added that the demand for cotton pickers takes place in the immediate post-harvest period when the household's stock of grain has not yet begun to run out and consequently the households consider that the disutility of the loss of leisure outweighs the net utility derived from the returns obtained from cotton picking. Their response to the demand for cotton picking would probably be different if it were to occur when the poor families' stock of grain had already run out or when there were no other better paying employment opportunities.

All these facts suggest that the exhaustion of the poor households' stock of grain, the requirement for labor in the household's farm and the demand for hired labor within and outside of the settlements occur simultaneously and put the poor households in severe stress.

If the refugee households had sufficient food supply during the hungry season, they would not work for wages before weeding their own farms. In such a case the rich refugees and the Sudanese farmers in the area would suffer a labor shortage or be forced to import laborers from other provinces which would mean higher transport costs. During July and August roads in the area are unserviceable, and this would exacerbate the condition of agricultural labor supply and consequently lead to higher wages. Since the timing of weeding is highly critical, a delay caused by transport difficulties would no doubt increase not only weeding costs, but even yields would decline per unit of land. In this respect the settlements can be viewed as producers of a cheap labor pool not only for the Sudanese farmers but also the few rich refugee farmers. The poverty of some of the households has become a prerequisite for the rich farmers to overcome labor bottlenecks during the periods of peak labor demands. The presence of a class of landless laborers, and the presence of hungry families, land possession notwithstanding, are necessary for the rich farmers' accumulation of wealth.

One of the factors that reduce the effectiveness of full utilization of household farm labor is the population's state of health. An unhealthy work force is less capable of doing hard work and is even more susceptible to infectious diseases which tend to peak at the cultivation season. The condition of health of the population in the settlements is difficult to show for lack of representative data. The available morbidity statistics are only useful to a limited extent, because all medical services except the SCC/ESRP antituberculosis campaign have hitherto been concentrated on curative rather than preventative measures. Hence, the records contain only the number of patients who sought help at the clinics by themselves. It may not be proper to assume that the rest of the population is healthy.

In the tropics and in the semi-arid areas, some diseases have a seasonal pattern, i.e., their prevalence is higher during the period of peak labor requirement. The morbidity statistics from the SCC/ESRP also seem to reveal this seasonal pattern. (See Figure 6.5 and Table 6.13) This evidence may not be conclusive, but it is clear from the data that the number of the patients tends to increase during the summer and autumn when farm labor requirement is at its peak.

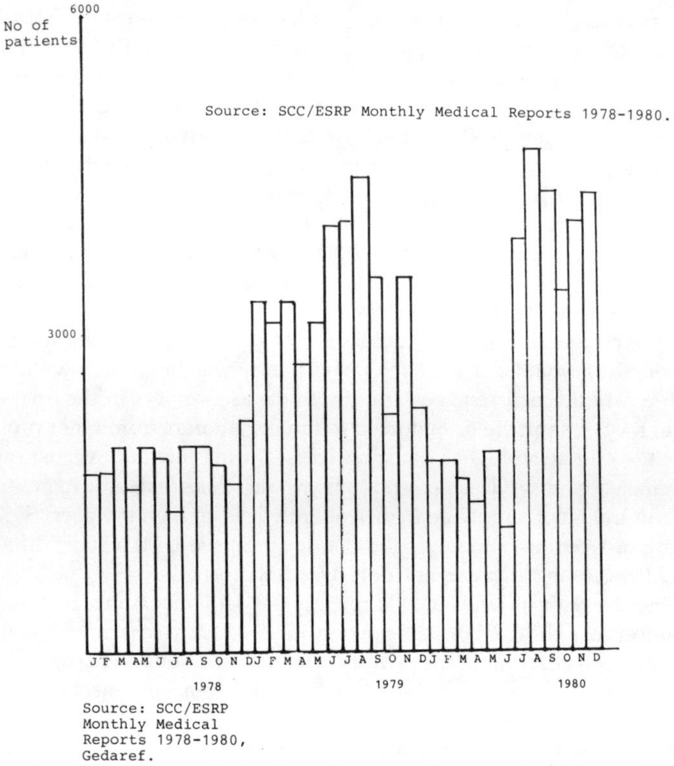

Figure 6.5 Morbidity statistics in refugee settlements in Qala en Nahal 1978-1980.

As can be observed from Figure 6.5, in the years 1979 and 1980 there has been real increase in the number of patients between July and November. Even in 1978 the number of patients was a little more in the months of August and September.

As can be seen from Table 6.13, about 93% of the patients visited the clinics as a result of a complaint of one or another disease while 7% visited the clinics for a general check-up or other undetermined diseases. Out of the 93% about 80% suffered from infections and the remaining 13% suffered from non-infectious diseases. The seasonality of the infectious diseases is unmistakable. Out of the 19 types of diseases given in Table 6.13, 14 or 74% seem to coincide with the period when farm labor requirement is at the peak. In fact, over 50% of the diseases—malaria, eye and ear infections, upper respiratory infection, anemia, non-parasitic gastrointestinal diseases, lower respiratory tract infection, upper tract infection, skin diseases and pertussis are at their peak in August when farm labor requirement is at its peak.

TABLE 6.13. Annual Diagnosis of Diseases in the Qala en Nahal Refugee Settlements, 1980.

Month	Healthy	Protein calorie malnutrition below 60%	Protein calorie malnutrition below 80%	Malaria	Eye infection	Ear infection	Upper respiratory tract infection	Anemia	Non parasitic gastro-intestinal disease	Parasitic gastro-intestinal disease	Lower respiratory tract infection	Urinary tract infection	Skin	Vitamin deficiency	Others	Kalanazar	Pertussis	Dental problems	T.B.C.	Measles
J	186	52	22	423	189	41	211	6	140	76	66	13	97	6	186	8	–	1	469	–
F	140	41	54	241	176	67	265	4	102	116	82	33	68	20	102	12	2	5	16	–
M	142	79	14	479	144	78	216	16	169	70	26	12	171	9	198	8	–	7	5	2
A	157	57	42	412	66	27	135	5	46	126	59	12	29	5	65	3	2	12	12	–
M	231	98	162	450	93	55	239	17	162	152	98	27	40	10	102	–	6	–	11	3
J	71	39	163	308	83	48	340	3	169	194	39	9	36	3	122	2	11	6	3	2
J	79	28	41	831	392	257	536	58	459	484	179	63	50	5	180	81	–	46	7	91
A	146	16	20	923	570	294	560	473	614	83	253	62	17	8	560	3	–	7	13	2
S	304	182	256	1481	403	275	605	86	80	618	337	97	114	319	338	7	154	43	15	2
O	433	186	172	600	344	241	472	54	85	383	184	76	71	143	225	8	–	14	103	196
N	279	140	72	657	321	227	440	16	40	157	89	52	116	138	172	13	–	7	10	16
D	342	295	244	557	298	186	479	21	54	370	174	38	68	218	302	19	–	23	11	25
Total	2510	1213	1262	7362	3079	1794	4498	770	2113	2815	1586	493	877	944	2554	164	175	171	675	341
%	7.1	3.4	3.6	20.8	8.7	5.1	12.7	2.2	6.0	8.0	4.5	1.4	2.5	2.7	7.2	0.5	0.5	0.5	2.0	1.0

Conflicting Demands on Labor Time

In the settlement of Qala en Nahal, sesame and sorghum are grown while in Aburakham only sorghum is grown. Since cultivation is mechanized, the whole holding of a farmer can be sown with sesame and sorghum in the same day. How does sowing the farmer's holding in one day or sowing sesame and sorghum in the same day create conflicting demands on labor time? As noted earlier, within the limits imposed by physical conditions, good harvest in the mechanized rainfed areas presupposes timely and effective weeding. Timely weeding and thinning starts 2-3 weeks after sowing. If the whole holding or both crops are sown in the same day, the demand for weeding labor occurs at the same time for the whole holding and both crops.

The households without sufficient family labor or financial resources are faced with a labor shortage. Those who grow food and cash crops and without financial resources are put in an awkward position. Weeding sesame first, to the neglect of sorghum, affects the yield of the subsistence crop, while weeding the subsistence crop to the neglect of the cash crop (sesame) leads to a loss of cash income. The conflict does not only arise with regard to two or more crops sown on the same day. It may well arise even in the case of one crop. The tractor hire services are managed centrally and in order to meet the cultivation need of all, the farmers whose plots are located within the *meshrua* are cultivated in most cases within one day.

The farm household cannot make its own adjustments to overcome competing peak labor requirements during the peak period. It cannot, for instance, spread the date of sowing by ploughing parts of its holding during different weeks.

Off-farm activities also compete for labor time. Some of these activities, except those which require continuous labor input throughout all the seasons, are designed so that they do not compete for labor time. However, some activities, such as attendance of shops, cafés and regular employment cannot by their very nature be postponed. Socializing and gossiping in the market cafés is also time-consuming. Due to the hot weather and humidity, most of the refugees from the nearby farms meet at the cafés during the hot hours and often sit for several hours.

Social and cultural activities such as wedding ceremonies and the building and repairing of huts are always undertaken during the slack season and do not interfere with farm labor, although one social factor which does interfere with farm labor is attendance at funerals and mournings. These are time-consuming because all the adults are socially obliged to take part in funerals and mournings.

School attendance also competes for labor time. A considerable number of the refugee children are attending school between October and May. This can be seen from Table 6.14, whereby about 24% of the households each have one child attending school, about 31% have between 2 and 3 and about 6% have between 4 and 6.

TABLE 6.14. Percentage Distribution of the Sample Households by the Number of Children Attending School 1981-82.

No. of children per family	Umsaqata	Umbrush	Dehema	Adingrar	Aburakham	Wad Awad	Total
1	21.7	31.1	19.1	28.0	27.1	12.5	23.0
2	20.0	20.0	29.8	20.0	15.2	25.0	21.2
3	16.7	6.7	10.6	8.0	3.4	12.5	9.5
4	5.0	–	6.4	–	3.4	–	2.7
5	–	–	–	–	1.7	3.1	0.7
6	3.3	–	4.5	2.0	1.7	9.4	3.1
7	–	–	–	–	–	–	–
None	33.3	42.2	29.8	42.0	47.4	37.5	38.9
Total	100.0	100.0	100.2	100.0	99.9	100.0	100.0

When the academic institutions are not in session, students take part in farm labor. However, in the long run, education tends to create repugnance to manual work and even hostility to country life among the former students. According to the village elders, school-leavers contribute least to agricultural work and this was noticeable during our survey.

For those households whose farms are located far from the villages, a considerable part of the working day is spent travelling to and from the farm. The six villages in the Qala en Nahal refugee settlements were created to reduce the distance of the holdings from the villages, but there are still some households which spend much of the working day travelling. (See Table 6.15)

Table 6.15 shows that some holdings are located far from the villages. If we assume that the average length of the working day at peak periods is between 9-10 hours and that an average person within the nutritional and weather conditions in the area can walk about 4 km per hour, those farmers whose holdings are located about 5 km away spend about 25% of the working day walking to and from the farm. The productivity of labor may also be reduced after the farmer had trudged through difficult and muddy paths to reach his farm. This may also discourage or prevent some of the vulnerable groups from taking part in farm labor.

LABOR STRATEGIES

Since most of the refugee households, as we saw earlier, operate in a context of labor and capital/money shortage, the appropriateness of their strategy in allocating their own and their familys' stock of labor not only between leisure and work but between the different economic activities is crucial in determining the households' access to subsistence and other income.

How do the households allocate their stock of labor among the different economic activities? It is important to note here that since the households have differential access to productive resources—land, labor and capital—their labor strategy is also variable.

Here we argue that after the subsistence needs are met, the households allocate their surplus stock of labor to those activities where the perceived returns are highest. However, in evaluating the returns, the households often take into account the kind of risks and uncertainties involved in each possible alternative activity. The risks and uncertainties involved in the possible alternative activities seem to have a greater deterring effect on the households with an unstable 'subsistence fund' than on the relatively well-to-do households whose subsistence security is not within the 'subsistence margin' but above it. Thus production among the poor households is limited to the generation of subsistence food and to the procurement of a minimum cash income (obtained either from the proceeds of crops or from other activities) for the purchase of commodities which they do not themselves produce and for the discharge of their social obligations associated with birth, marriage, death, etc.

TABLE 6.15. Percentage Distribution of the Sample Households by Farm Distance.

Distance Km	Umsaqata	Umbrush	Dehema	Adingrar	Aburakham	Wad Awad	Total
Less than 1	4.5	12.5	30.3	7.5	12.2	15.6	13.0
1-2	20.4	37.5	33.3	15.0	20.4	34.4	25.6
2-5	40.9	28.1	30.3	57.5	51.0	43.7	43.0
5-8	27.3	18.1	6.1	12.5	14.3	6.2	14.8
Over 8	6.8	3.1	–	7.5	2.0	–	3.5
Total	99.9	99.8	100.0	100.0	99.9	99.9	99.9

However, the aim of production among the well-to-do households includes the achievement of higher returns at the cost of higher risk and uncertainty which households without a sufficient resource base can rarely afford to undertake. Unlike the poor households, the economic position and social status of the well-to-do households allows broader scope of maneuver and, owing to their savings from previous harvests, a one season's crop failure does not threaten their subsistence security. They are also considered creditworthy by virtue of their social status and can easily secure a loan to tide over a crisis.

The poor households live from hand to mouth and their overriding concern seems to be risk aversion rather than return maximization. Without going into detailed theoretical discussion, we shall try to demonstrate this empirically.

In the refugee land settlements of Qala en Nahal, a relatively very high value cash crop (sesame) and a very low value staple crop (sorghum) are grown. Calculations of costs and returns made at the 1982/83 prices of the two crops in the area show that a household that grows sesame at the cost of sorghum would earn about £S.35 more per feddan than a household that grows sorghum. The average yield of sorghum per feddan between 1954-55 and 1981-82 in the area was 340 kg, while the average yield of sesame per feddan between 1968-69 and 1981-82 was 140 kg. The estimated labor required per feddan on sesame and sorghum are 30.5 and 27 man/days, respectively, which means that sesame requires 3.5 man/days more per feddan than sorghum. However, the low labor input required by sorghum does not compensate for the higher producer price commanded by sesame. If we assume a yield of 340 kg of sorghum per feddan, the return at £S.18 per 100 kg is £S.61.2, while if we assume 140 kg of sesame per feddan, the return at £S.75 per 100 kg is £S.105. The average wage per man/day in the 1982-83 season was £S.2.50. The household that grows sesame can hire the 3.5 extra man/days required at £S.2.5 per man/day and still its return per feddan would be £S.35 more than the household that grows sorghum at the neglect of sesame. This difference of return is considerable for those who have 10 or more feddan holdings.

Those households which are primarily concerned with the maximization of return would grow sesame to the neglect of the low value food crop—sorghum—while those households which are mainly concerned with their subsistence security would tend to produce sorghum without being induced by the high producer price of sesame. If they grow sesame at all, they will not do it at the cost of sorghum but to supplement their subsistence need.

This pattern of behavior is unmistakably discernible from Table 6.16. Out of the 28 land-possessing very poor households, only about 29% grew sesame. Among the 38 poor households with holdings, about 63% grew sesame while among the 54 medium and 30 high-income households about 80 and 97%, respectively, grew sesame. Out of the very poor, poor, medium and rich households 71%, 37%, 20%, and 3%, respectively, grew only sorghum at the neglect of the high value crop—sesame. However, except for one household among the middle and four among the rich households, all of those who grew sesame also grew sorghum.

TABLE 6.16. Percentage Distribution of the Land-Possessing Households that Grew Sesame by Income Group.

Income Group	Umsaqata	Umbrush	Dehema	Adingrar	Total
Very poor	14.3	22.2	14.3	80.0	28.6
Poor	33.3	57.1	83.3	70.0	63.3
Middle	78.6	75.0	70.0	88.9	79.6
Rich	100.00	100.0	100.0	83.3	96.7

To some extent this may reflect the fact that the social division of labor is not very developed in the sense that almost all the households with land try to fend for their own subsistence requirement. Both the poor and the rich households are aware of the fact that it is more profitable to grow sesame and to buy sorghum for food, but still they are not willing to neglect sorghum. This is mainly because the refugees, having gone through gruesome experiences, seem to mistrust outsiders, including the market forces that operate independently of them. To fail to grow sorghum is to depend on the undeveloped and unreliable rural market, which all of the refugees, including the rich, wish to avoid at any cost. By producing their own food the households control the material basis of their maintenance and reproduction of labor. According to them, it is only after they have secured their subsistence, that they can think of higher returns, but *never* at the cost of subsistence.

Thus the main difference between the rich and poor households' production decision is that of an ability rather than an attitude. The poor households' resource base is so limited that it does not allow planning beyond the realization of subsistence income. It is important to note, however, that the poor households do not accept their present situation, but rather struggle to change it. We asked the households why they do not produce only sesame and buy sorghum from sesame proceeds. All of them, including the rich households, argued that under the present uncertain market conditions there would be nothing more irrational than to hand over one's basis of survival to a third party which one cannot easily control. Some of the households also argued that 'what if all other farmers in the region decide to grow only sesame? Are we then going to feed our children on paper money? According to them a cash crop brings only money, whereas a food crop maintains and reproduces life.

Under the existing relatively underdeveloped market conditions and shortage of transport facilities, especially during the rainy season, it is rational to produce one's own subsistence needs and then allocate the surplus labor or other resources to activities where the returns are highest. However, for the majority of the very poor and poor households, there seems to be no surplus of labor or resource which exceeds the input necessary to meet the households' subsistence needs.

As we saw before the households' strategy for allocating their labor resources can be summarized in the following. Some of the households work on non-farm activities and hire farm labor. Some of the households work on the family farm only to meet their subsistence needs, while there are some households that work on the family farm in order to secure their subsistence needs and to promote profits. There are also households that simultaneously allocate their stock of labor among alternative activities so as to spread risk. A considerable proportion of the households combine one or more of these strategies.

RESPONDING TO PRICES

In order to further illustrate whether or not the production decision of the refugee farmers is determined by the principle of subsistence security or whether it is affected by changing producer prices, we forwarded hypothetical questions to the respondents. They were asked how they would react to a number of hypothetical changes in the prices they received for the two major crops they grow in the settlement of Qala en Nahal. Alternative I assumes a 40% increase in the producer price of sesame, while the price of the food crop—sorghum—is held constant. Alternative II assumes an increase in the producer price of sorghum by 40% while no change occurs in the price of sesame. Alternative III assumes both the prices of sorghum and sesame increase simultaneously and it is further assumed that the terms of trade between the two crops are kept unchanged. Since the values of the two crops are not comparable, a 40% rise in the price of sorghum as assumed in hypothesis II can never induce those households who are sensitive to prices to produce sorghum at the cost of sesame. The same is true for hypothesis III.

The most important is the reaction of the households to hypothesis I. The distribution of the land-holding households according to their response to hypothesis I by income group is given in Table 6.17. The results show the same pattern of behavior as in Table 6.16. Out of the total very poor, poor, middle and rich households, 4%, 21%, 23%, and 61%, respectively, would increase sesame production at the expense of sorghum while about 89% of the very poor, 58% of the poor, 56% of the middle-income and 29% of the rich households reported that their production pattern would remain unchanged from that of the previous year, irrespective of the drastic increase in the price of sesame. The results show that the rich households are more responsive to changed producer price while the very poor and the poor households seem to be primarily preoccupied with their subsistence security—the production of sorghum.

The price of sesame rose drastically between 1980-81 and 1981-82, and we asked the land-holding households if they were aware of the price changes. Their replies showed that they were aware of them. We asked them later how

TABLE 6.17. Hypothetical Response to Producer Price Change by Income Group (Per cent).

Hypothesis I	Response	Umsaqata	Umbrush	Dehema	Adingrar	Total
Poorest						
	Sesame ↑ Sorghum ↓	–	–	–	20.0	4.0
	Sesame ↑ Sorghum ↑	14.0	–	14.0	–	7.0
	Sesame → Sorghum →	86.0	100.0	86.0	80.0	89.0
Poor						
	Sesame ↑ Sorghum ↓	22.0	–	25.0	30.0	21.0
	Sesame ↑ Sorghum ↑	33.0	29.0	17.0	10.0	21.0
	Sesame → Sorghum →	44.0	71.0	58.0	60.0	58.0
Middle						
	Sesame ↑ Sorghum ↓	47.0	8.0	20.0	13.0	23.0
	Sesame ↑ Sorghum ↑	20.0	33.0	–	25.0	21.0
	Sesame → Sorghum →	33.0	58.0	80.0	63.0	56.0
Rich						
	Sesame ↑ Sorghum ↓	66.0	40.0	80.0	50.0	61.0
	Sesame ↑ Sorghum ↑	–	20.0	–	33.0	9.0
	Sesame → Sorghum →	33.0	40.0	20.0	16.0	29.0

Source: Questionnaire Survey (n. very poor = 28, poor = 38, middle = 54, rich = 30).
Legend:
Sesame ↑ Sorghum ↓ = will work harder on sesame at the cost of the food crop—sorghum.
Sesame ↑ Sorghum ↑ = will work harder on both crops.
Sesame → Sorghum → = will work as before (no change).

they reacted to the substantial increase of sesame producer price when they sowed their crops in the 1982-83 season. The results are given in Table 6.18.

The results are very interesting because there is a clear relationship between their reaction to the hypothetical price changes and to the real change in sesame producer price. The same pattern of production behavior is revealed here as in Table 6.17, whereby the majority of rich households increased sesame production at the cost of sorghum while almost all of the very poor households, the overwhelming majority of the poor households and a clear majority of the middle-income households continued producing as in the previous year without being induced by the price changes. Among the rich households only very few failed to respond to the higher producer price.

These facts clearly show that the production decision of the very poor, poor and the majority of the middle-income groups is largely determined by the principle of subsistence security. They are security maximizers rather than return maximizers. However, it is crucial to emphasize that this is imposed on them by the objective conditions, i.e., by the shortage of a sufficient resource base. The fact that even the rich farmers do not totally ignore sorghum production suggests that it is only after meeting their subsistence needs that they try to maximize return at the costs of higher risks and uncertainty.

RESPONDING TO THE MARKET

For the subsistence farmers cash crops are not just a means of raising their real income but are also a means of earning money which can be used to buy goods and services that cannot be produced within the subsistence sector. These include clothes, kerosene, sugar, tea, coffee, salt and other food stuffs, and tools such as hoes, sickles, knives, axes, and utensils. Another factor which draws the refugee farmers into the market is lack of availability of institutionalized credit facilities. In order to pay their debt, many of the households are forced to sell their crops or pay in kind to the debtors. However, sale of crops is not the only way that money can be acquired; sale of labor, livestock and livestock products and trade can be equally important sources of money.

To assess the level of penetration of market relations, we used two criteria. The first is the proportion of land under cash crop and the second is the marketed proportion of total output. The limitation of the first criterion is that even when no cash crop is produced, some of the farmers can still sell part of their food crop to buy commodities, to make good their debts or to pay an obligation to the government or to the community. This is overcome by including the proportion of total output of sorghum marketed.

The subsistence nature of the very poor households is unmistakable; about 71% of the land-possessing households produced only sorghum. Among the poor, about 37% produced only sorghum, while among the middle and high-income groups about 20 and 3%, respectively, grew only sorghum. This

TABLE 6.18. Percentage Distribution of the Respondents by Responses Reported to Have Been Made as a Result of Increased Sesame Producer Price from 1981-82 to 1982-83.

		Umsaqata	Umbrush	Dehema	Adingrar	Total
Poorest						
	Sesame ↑ Sorghum ↓	–	–	–	–	–
	Sesame ↑ Sorghum ↑	14.0	–	–	–	4.0
	Sesame → Sorghum →	86.0	100.0	100.0	100.0	96.0
Poor						
	Sesame ↑ Sorghum ↓	11.0	–	–	20.0	8.0
	Sesame ↑ Sorghum ↑	22.0	–	25.0	–	13.0
	Sesame → Sorghum →	67.0	100.0	75.0	80.0	79.0
Middle						
	Sesame ↑ Sorghum ↓	20.0	33.0	–	6.0	15.0
	Sesame ↑ Sorghum ↑	47.0	–	10.0	31.0	25.0
	Sesame → Sorghum →	33.0	67.0	90.0	63.0	60.0
Rich						
	Sesame ↑ Sorghum ↓	67.0	40.0	80.0	50.0	61.0
	Sesame ↑ Sorghum ↑	7.0	20.0	–	33.0	13.0
	Sesame → Sorghum →	27.0	40.0	20.0	17.0	26.0

TABLE 6.19. Market Orientation of the Land Possessing Sample Households in the Four Villages of Qala en Nahal by Proportion of Land under Cash Crop—Sesame (per cent).

	Very Poor	Poor	Middle	Rich
100%	–	–	1.8	13.3
75%	–	–	–	20.0
50%	17.8	13.1	42.6	50.0
25%	10.7	36.8	35.2	13.3
<25%	–	13.1	–	–
None	71.4	36.8	20.4	3.3
Total	99.9	99.8	100.0	99.9

clearly shows that the higher income groups are more market-oriented than the lower income groups. Out of the middle and high income groups about 2 and 13%, respectively, produced only sesame at the cost of sorghum. These are households that had enough food savings from the previous seasons. Out of the rich households, about 20% also had 75% of their holdings under sesame. Since labor is a scarce factor, the households with substantial income from non-farm activities can increase the yield of sorghum per unit of land by applying the optimum labor input required; thus to produce their self-consumption requirements, they do not need to have large areas under food crop.

TABLE 6.20. Percentage Distribution of the Sample Households by Proportion of Sesame Harvest Sold by Income Group in the Four Villages of Qala en Nahal.

Proportion Sold	Very Poor	Poor	Middle	Rich
100%	100.0	66.7	74.4	75.9
75%	–	8.3	20.9	3.4
50%	–	25.0	4.6	3.4
25%	–	–	–	3.4
<25%	–	–	–	–
None	–	–	–	13.8
Total	100.0	100.0	99.9	99.9

Table 6.20 shows the proportion of marketed sesame by income group. Sesame is mainly produced for the market but a few of the rich households have their own camel oil press and process the crop at the settlements and sell sesame oil. The by-product, sesame cake, is used for animal feed.

Some households also pay processing charges to the camel oil press owners to extract oil from their sesame produce for their own consumption. Table 6.20 shows that the overwhelming majority of the households produce sesame for sale. However, except the very poor households, some of the other households reported having processed some of their produce. Among the rich, about 14% did not sell their sesame crop but processed it instead to sell oil at a higher price. Most of these are shopkeepers and *asara* (camel oil press) owners.

TABLE 6.21. Percentage Distribution of the Sample Households by Proportion of the Sorghum Harvest Sold by Income Group in the Six Villages.

Proportion Sold	Very Poor	Poor	Middle	Rich
None	71.4	68.4	67.9	50.0
25%	10.7	2.6	3.8	19.2
50%	17.8	26.3	20.7	26.9
75%	–	2.6	7.5	3.8
100%	–	–	–	–
Total	99.9	99.9	99.9	99.9

Table 6.21 shows that sorghum is primarily produced for self-consumption among the very poor, poor and medium-income groups, while about 50% of the rich households that had grown sorghum reported having marketed between 25% and 75% of their total sorghum produced. Among the very poor, poor and medium-income groups about 28%, 31%, and 32%, respectively, sold between 25 and 75% of their sorghum. It must be noted that among the medium and high-income groups, a subsistence crop is sold if the output is above the households' self-consumption requirements, while among the poor and very poor households, a subsistence crop can be sold even when the output is far below the households' annual subsistence need. Our findings show that the refugee farmers are not purely subsistence producers but are also commodity producers.

There are four possibilities for marketing agricultural produce in the settlements. The refugee farmers can sell their crops to refugee traders within the settlements, to outside traders who visit the settlements occasionally by truck, to traders in Gedaref town, or in the Friday market of Bazura which is about 35 km southeast of Umsaqata.

In 1981-82 about 52% sold their crops in the settlements, while about 46% reported selling their crops in Gedaref town. Only about 2% sold their crops in the neighboring villages. The latter are all from Aburakham and Wad Awad.

The market orientation of the refugee farmers is not only limited to the sale or purchase of agricultural produce, the growing numbers of shops, camel oil presses, restaurants, tea shops, bakeries, vegetable shops, butchers and laundries are but some of the living examples of the level of development of the market forces that are operative in the settlements.

The settlement of Qala en Nahal and the other two settlements of Aburakham and Wad Awad are connected to Gedaref through untarmacked road which becomes almost unusable during the rainy season. During the dry season, the journey between Gedaref and Umsaqata, the settlement headquarters, takes about 2½ hours. During the rainy season, the same trip can take up to 3—5 days. There is a daily bus service between the villages and Gedaref during the dry season. During our survey, which coincided with the harvesting season, there were lorries that came to and left the scheme at irregular intervals.

CHAPTER 7

Mechanization and Self-Reliance in the Settlements

The primary objective of the rural refugee land settlements is to achieve refugee self-reliance. The achievement of self-reliance in food production and in other requirements is mainly a function of the refugee households' resource base. As was noted in the previous chapters, within the limits imposed by physical conditions, growth in agricultural output in the refugee land settlements can mainly be explained in terms of inputs of land, labor and capital. The requirement of capital in African traditional agriculture is insignificant because neither mechanical nor draught power is used. Thus the two prime inputs are land and labor. However, in the rural refugee land settlements in Eastern Sudan, tractor power is used for cultivation and thus capital has become an important input.

Under the present system, all the capital and operating costs such as the purchase and replacement of tractors, spare parts, fuel, oil, lubricants, and other associated infrastructural costs are met by the UNHCR and other donor agencies. However, since neither the UNHCR nor the other donor agencies can be expected to inject large amounts of capital into the schemes indefinitely, the long-term economic viabilty of the rural land settlements depends on their ability to generate from their own resources sufficient capital and foreign exchange to enable them to replace old tractors, to purchase implements, spare parts, fuel, oil and lubricants, to pay wages, etc. Unless the settlements can generate the necessary capital, it is inconceivable that they would ever achieve self-reliance without imposing a financial burden on the donor agencies as well as on the GOS.

It will be the aim of this chapter to discuss the underlying policy reasons that led to partial mechanization, to describe how the system has operated over the period it has been in existence, to discuss the financial, technical, and management implication of small farm mechanization on refugee self-reliance, and to attempt to discuss possible alternative cultivation methods which are low cost, simple and compatible with the technical know-how and the sociocultural and financial conditions of the beneficiary communities.

In this chapter mechanization implies the substitution of mechanical power (tractor) for human or animal power. Since the six refugee rural land settlements in Qala en Nahal are the oldest among the refugee land settlements in the eastern region of the Sudan, our analysis will be based on Qala in Nahal. However, our findings will throw some light on the basic factors and problems confronting not only the particular settlements covered by the survey but also the other schemes in the region which are implemented along similar lines. A study of the impact of mechanization on small-scale farms in a community with a diverse socioeconomic and cultural background varying from pastoralism and agropastoralism to sedentarized farming can shed light on some of the crucial issues involved in African rural development.

THE BACKGROUND TO MECHANIZATION

Development in the Gedaref region began during World War II, when there was shortage of grain supply in the world and in the surrounding regions. (Agabawi: 1968, 75; O'Brien: 1983, 10) In 1944 the colonial government introduced the first tractors to produce sorghum in the rainfed areas. Initially, the government intended to avoid dependence on wage labor by mechanizing all operations. However, it was later found that it was not easy to mechanize post-sowing operations. Therefore, the latter had to be carried out manually, and a tenancy system was introduced in 1947-48 whereby the management cleared and plowed the land and the post-sowing operations were carried out by the tenants who in return received 50% of the produce.

In 1956 the Government abandoned sharecropping in favor of allotments to private tractor owners who received cultivable land in 1,000 feddan units. Since the mid-1940s, production in the area was carried out by the use of tractors and seeder boxes mounted on wide-level disc harrows (WLDH). The existing sorghum and sesame varieties have precluded mechanization of post-sowing operations, especially harvesting.

All the rural refugee land settlements in the eastern region are located in the Gedaref area, and agricultural production in the settlements is based on a partially mechanized system. However, since cultivation is mechanized, the mechanized operation represents only one part of the production operation.

Why is cultivation mechanized in the refugee rural land settlements? The transfer of the refugees from the transit camps near Kassala town to Qala en Nahal was not preceded by a feasibility study and the reason for resorting to the use of tractors to the neglect of other sources is nowhere spelled out. Under normal circumstances, agricultural development projects like Qala en Nahal require a detailed feasibility study of the site involving aerial survey, test of soil fertility, climatic conditions, availability of water, compatibility of the proposed activity with the technological, sociocultural and economic conditions of the beneficiaries and so on. A scientific plan is then drawn up on the basis of the information received and the recommendations of such studies.

The large refugee influxes that occurred in the end of the 1960s and early 1970s required urgent relocations of the refugees from the border areas and a detailed project feasibility study was not possible. Thus, at least initially, the decision to mechanize cultivation in the rural refugee settlements seems to have originated from a tentative measure adopted under an extreme situation: thousands of families needed to be settled; trained draught animals and ox-ploughs did not readily exist; and the settlers were very unfamiliar with the physical condition of the area. Mechanizaion represented an immediate and expedient solution. Since the UNHCR was to meet the capital and operating (including management) costs, the long-term financial, technical, and management problems that might ensue after the withdrawal of the UNHCR were not seriously considered in light of urgency of the situation.

The second reason that may explain the introduction of mechanical power (tractors) into the rural refugee land settlements is indicated by the following statement. The Draft Implementation Regulation to the Asylum Act states that

> The Minister shall allocate agricultural land within the settlement area for individual refugees during their stay in the country and *according to the Government's investment system.*
> (Draft Implementation Regulation to the Asylum Act, 1974) (Emphasis added.)

Even though this statement was made in 1974, about four years after the establishment of the settlement, it seems that it is the same policy that has led to the introduction of partial farm mechanization. The refugee rural land settlements are located within the rainfed central clay plain of Kassala Province where approximately 90% of the land is cultivated by utilizing 80 h.p. tractors and 4.55 cm WLDH. The Government's investment system in the area, as we saw earlier, has since the 1940s been based on partial mechanization. Hence, the GOS considered it natural and consistent with local practice to base agricultural production in the refugee land settlements on partial mechanization. However, one crucial factor which was overlooked by the decision-makers was the question of *the size of the holdings.* In the central clay plain, land is distributed to individual tractor owners in at least 1,000 feddan units, and to cooperatives and registered companies in 5,000 or more feddan units. (Agabawi: op.cit., 77) Large holdings are more suitable to the effective use of tractors than small holdings. The refugees' holdings, as we saw before, vary from one to over 10 feddans. The large tractors have no doubt proved appropriate in the large farm units in the Gedaref area, but it is possible that the use of the same machine can be entirely inapproapriate or ineffective in small scale agriculture.

The Cultivation System

The mechanization scheme was implemented by the GOS and the establishment costs were borne by the UNHCR. In order to meet the need for cultivation, a fleet of 21 tractors (9 Byelerus and 12 Massey Ferguson) with 20 WLDHs were placed at the service of the 6 villages in Qala en Nahal to be managed by a settlement manager appointed by the Office of the Commissioner for Refugees (COR). (Hunting: 1976, 17) Both the GOS and the UNHCR felt the necessity to create an institutional and organizational structure through which the large and modern farm technology was expected to fit into the farming condition of the small farmers. It was decided to create a centeralized tractor hire service (THS) from which the refugee farmers would receive free cultivation during the first two seasons; later a charge would be levied to recover part of the cultivation costs. It was also planned that the refugee farmers would gradually meet the running costs of the tractors and also generate surplus to meet the capital costs of tractor replacement and consequently relieve the GOS and the international donor organizations from the financial and management burden.

The tractors were based in the village of Umsaqata and distributed to the other five villages during the cultivation seasons. Until 1980 each village was assigned three tractors. The three tractors allocated to each village were assigned by lot to three different *meshrua*. Before 1974 it was the *sheikhs* (clan heads) who allocated the tractors within the *meshrua*. However, in 1974 a new institution—the *Legina*—was established and the latter played a key role in the allocation of the tractors within the village. The involvement of the *sheikhs* and later the *Legina* in the allocation and fee collection of the THS was an attempt on the part of the management to utilize the communities' traditional structures.

The cultivation system operated in the following way. Owing to the land soil condition of the clay plain, the farmers would wait for the first rains so that the hard soil could soften, allowing effective cultivation. Despite the very small and fragmented holdings, each household's holding is cultivated as a separate entity.

TRACTORS COME TO QALA EN NAHAL

The first cultivation began in 1970 but no record of the total area cultivated in that season was available from the scheme administration records. The total acreage cultivated by the tractors in the period 1971-1982 is given in Table 7.1.

As can be seen from Table 7.1, in the three villages of Umsaqata, Salmin, and Umbrush a total area of 13,353 feddans was cultivated in 1971. In the following year a total of 28,723 feddans was cultivated, an increase of about 115%. One reason for the drastic increase was that the three villages Adingrar, Umzurzur and Dehema, which were established between 1971-72, had begun to cultivate land. However, even the cultivated area in the villages of Salmin, Umbrush, and Umsaqata had increased by 90, 82 and 54%, respectively, from that of the previous year.

The total area cultivated by the tractor hire service was further increased by about 37% in 1973. This indicates that many of the families that were uncertain about the economic benefits and social security that could spring from farming now saw concretely the foundations of a stable society being laid by the good yields achieved by those who cleared and cultivated in 1972. This stimulated many families to follow suit. The yields for the 1972 season were, according to an estimate made by a UNHCR deputy representative for the Sudan who visited the Qala en Nahal in January 1972, 'between five and six sacks of sorghum and three sacks of sesame per feddan'. (The Water-Road: 1972,10) In their pre-investment study, Hunting *et al.* in 1976 also stated that sorghum and sesame yields in the period 1971 and 1973 were 6–8 and 2.5–3 sacks, respectively.

Since the Hunting report is based on official records of yields, it is necessary to treat such information with caution.

However, it must be noted that the high yields obtained in the period 1971-73 are also confirmed by the settlers themselves, who speak of bumper crops that year, but quote yields between 3-4.5 sacks of sorghum and about 2 sacks of sesame per feddan. According to the settlers this was made possible by virgin land, by an efficient manager and by new tractors. The period 1970-73 was characterized by adequate supply of foreign exchange for capital investments, for the purchase of spare parts, fuel, oil, lubricants, wages for mechanics and tractor operators and by efficient management. Hunting *et al.* also note that 'During the establishment period (1971-73) vigorous management and adequate finance ensured that the planned production targets were met'.

After the good harvest of 1972 the UNHCR deputy representative in the Sudan felt that the refugees should pay for the use of tractors during the coming season. The idea of levying tractor charges was bitterly opposed by the refugees. They thought that the UNHCR had the duty to provide them with such a service free of any charge not only because they were refugees but also because they were in their opinion unable to pay such charges. There was no doubt that many of the households were not in a position to pay, but even the relatively better-off households joined hands with the poor to protest against such charges.

The Handover and its Aftermath

After the good harvest of 1972, Qala en Nahal was presented as a success story and the UNHCR felt that the question of handing over the settlement to its implementing partner, the GOS, was on the agenda. In February 1972, the High Commissioner for Refugees visited Qala en Nahal; a brochure prepared by the UNHCR in August 1972 stated that the High Commissioner

TABLE 7.1. Total Cultivated Area by Tractors in the Six Refugee Villages of Qala en Nahal 1971-82 (Feddans).

Season/ village	Salmin	Umbrush	Adingrar	Dehema	Zurzur	Umsaqata	Total
1971	5,957	2,926	–	–	–	5,370	13,353
1972	9,630	5,315	1,680	1,800	2,100	8,268	28,723
1973	10,875	5,890	3,420	6,655	3,553	8,997	39,390
1974	2,225	4,110	1,545	1,795	4,310	2,510	16,495
1975	2,800	995	955	800	350	835	6,735
1976	1,500	1,000	1,000	500	1,000	2,000	7,000
1977	2,275	2,020	1,790	1,080	3,550	5,610	16,325
1978	6,501	3,654	2,272	1,918	3,125	3,588	21,058
1979	5,550	3,440	1,355	2,125	2,955	3,787	19,212
1980	–	–	–	–	–	–	13,900
1981	6,682.5	8,035.0	5,832.5	7,515.0	7,305.0	9,695.0	45,065.0
1982	7,967.5	6,122.5	5,115.0	5,690.0	5,980.0	8,150.0	45,572.5

> was able to see both from the air by helicopter and on the ground the vast scope of the project and the very tangible progress that was being made towards its completion. His visit took place in an atmosphere of optimism that the efforts to pioneer a viable settlement in an apparently inhospitable region, geographically and climatically speaking, *were to be crowned with success and an end to UNHCR's material involvement was in sight. As he often said about the role of his office, the High Commissioner could look forward to working himself out-of-job.* (Emphasis added.)
>
> (Water-Road: op.cit., 11)

This statement clearly indicated that, according to the judgement of the UNHCR, the refugees had attained a level of subsistence comparable to that of neighboring nationals and there was no need for the UNHCR's material involvement in the project any longer. However, the same bulletin also noted that when the High Commissioner arrived at the settlement, the elders from the six villages gathered to welcome him but also to forward their complaints about the problem of water supply, about the untimely withdrawal of World Food Program rations, about problems of land allocation and to discuss the need for better school accommodation. The complaints of the elders indicated that according to their judgement not only was the condition unripe for withdrawal of international assistance, but they thought that what was given to them was insufficient and they demanded increased aid. However, the village elders' complaints notwithstanding, the UNHCR proceeded with its plans to hand over the settlement to the GOS. Direct responsibility of the settlement was handed over to the GOS in 1973. The latter in return handed over the administration of the settlement to the People's Local Government in Qala in Nahal town about 40 km from the Qala en Nahal refugee villages.

When the decision to hand over responsibility to the GOS was taken

> . . . there had been no final evaluation of the viability of the settlement or of recurrent costs, nor any written hand-over agreement formally delineating the role and responsibility and financial commitment of both parties.
>
> (Beyer: 1976)

According to the traditional mandate of the UN Office of the High Commissioner, the aim of international assistance for organized rural refugee settlements is to enable the refugees to attain a subsistence level comparable to that of neighboring nationals through projects which are initially financed by the UNHCR.

As can be seen from Table 7.1 and Figure 7.1, following the hand over of the settlement to the Local People's Government in 1973, there was a drastic decline of the total area cultivated by the tractors in the following season and

Figure 7.1 Total cultivated land Index 1971-1982.

an attempt was made by the management to recover some of the cultivation costs by levying a charge of £S.2 per 10 feddan holding or 20 piasters per feddan. The charges were collected in advance of actual cultivation. After the UNHCR's financial pull-out, the conditions of the tractors and the farm machinery deteriorated so much that the total area cultivated declined drastically from 39,390 feddans in 1973 to 16,495 feddans in 1974. The sorry state of the farm machinery is reported by several consultants who visited the settlement between 1974 and 1980. (See Tuttas: 1976; Beyer: 1976; Hunting: 1976; Euro Action Accord: 1980) Tuttas, a UNHCR consultant, visited the settlement in April, 1976 and stated,

> We visited the tractor station in Umsaqata and found it in a deplorable state. The workshop was void of any equipment; it was a hut, insufficient of size, too small to do any work. . . . Outside we saw 30 tractors, none of them in a working condition, all in different stages of decay. There were 13 Byelerus, 17 Massey Ferguson 165. There were also 17 disc planters, all in the same sorry state as the tractors.
>
> (Tuttas: 1976, 9)

Hunting, the UNHCR consultant, who visited the settlement in April 1976, also described the state of the farm machinery as hopeless and stated that

... all the Byelerus tractors were out of order and only one of the other 12 tractors, all Massey Ferguson, was in full running order'.

As can be seen from Table 7.1 and Figure 7.1, there was a slight increase in the total area cultivated in 1977; this was as a result of UNHCR's and COR's intervention in overhauling the Massey Fergusons. However, the deterioration of the farm machinery began again in 1979 and continued through 1980. The sporadic outside financial intervention was not sufficient to rectify the defects that existed in the system.

In May 1980, the tractor fleet was inspected by a Sudanese agricultural engineer who reported that out of the 12 Massey Ferguson 185 and 165 tractors, all the latter and five of the former required replacing. In October 1980, EA-A sent a machinery specialist to inspect the condition of the tractors and stated that of the tractor fleet

> Only one 185 has a battery and working hydraulics. Of the remaining tractors, none have batteries or hydraulics.... The unusual and characteristic defects were that the draught control quadrants were fractured and useless on nearly all the tractors.
>
> (EA-A: 1980, 4)

He further noted that many of the defects were due to lack of spare parts but much of the sorry state of the equipment was also attributable to poor organization and lax supervision in the workshop.

The inefficiency of the THS following the withdrawal of the UNHCR can be observed from Table 7.2. 'Crop Observation Transepts' made by the EA-A consultant in October 1980 showed that of the total area observed about 47% was uncultivated due to lack of tractor service, 7% was ineffectively cultivated and another 7% was cultivated by alternative methods which included *seluka* (plough stick), ox plough and private tractor. The report also noted that 'the alternative cultivations... all had a high yield potential because the crops were established in June'. (EA-A: 1980, 3)

TABLE 7.2 Results of 'Crop Observation Transepts' 1980 (Areas in Feddans).

Settlement name	Total	Uncultivated	Ineffective Ploughing	Alternative Cultivation
Umbrush	320	190	15	42
Zurzur	360	90	20	11
Adingrar	490	228	52	42
Salmin	260	110	30	16
Dehema	335	170	15	20
Umsaqata	139	110	0	9

The effect of the deterioration of the tractors on farm income was very serious. As noted by Hunting,

> ... with failure of the 1975-76 cropping programme, income from sorghum and sesame production was nil for many of the refugees.
>
> (Hunting: op.cit., 16)

As can be seen from Table 7.1 and Figure 7.1, the total area cultivated by the THS in 1981 increased from 9,450 feddans in 1980 to 45,065 feddans, an increase representing about 377%. This drastic change was mainly possible by EA-A's active financial and management intervention in the mechanized refugee farming system in Qala en Nahal after 1980.

Small Holdings but Large Tractors

In order to allow maximum field efficiency and to reduce costs per unit of output, the introduction of farm mechanization must be preceded by an appropriate organization of the farm so that the tractor would fit into the farm set-up (Anker: 1955, 239). In the refugee rural land settlements each farmer's holding, irrespective of size, is cultivated and planted separately and this has led to high tractor operation costs.

> ... because of the constant need to carry out a large number of 450 degree turns thereby wasting time and recultivating land which has already been covered.
>
> (Agrisystems: 1981)

Agrisystems in their consultancy work for the UNHCR in 1981 suggested that by changing the 205m × 205m square *hawasha* into a 100m × 420m rectangle, one could reduce the number of turns by almost 50%. This reorganization of the farm cannot be carried out as long as the present shape of the *hawasha* is maintained and as long as each farmer's land is cultivated separately.

If adequate planning had been exercised at the period of the scheme's inception, it would have been very easy to divide the individual allocations into rectangles. Such a reform will now not only cost money but it will be opposed by many of the land-possessing households, which is probably why the administration of the scheme has not tried to implement it.

The cultivation of each farmer's holding as a separate entity has inflated operation costs. For example, if 10 farmers each with 10 feddans of cultivable land could pool their *hawasha* together for the purpose of cultivation instead of cultivating their *hawasha* separately, the operating costs could be reduced by 23% and field efficiency could be increased by about 23%. The operating costs could further be reduced if more farmers would pool their holdings together. A report on a Technical Appraisal Mission in December 1980, for example, concluded that

> It should be emphasized that the efficiency of larger tractors can only be achieved on larger land areas of a minimum of 300 feddans.
>
> (UNHCR and COR: 1980, 12)

To understand the refugee farmers' attitude towards pooling their holdings together for the purpose of cultivation, we asked them whether they would be for or against such a temporary reorganization; their replies are given in Table 7.3. The results show that the majority of the farmers in the four villages of Qala en Nahal are against it, while in the relatively new settlements of Aburakham and Wad Awad a considerable proportion of the sample households are for it. The traditional structural organization of small farm production has evolved over a long time under the influence of social, political, economic and technical conditions, thus farm size cannot easily be manipulated without political, social and economic effects.

PROBLEMS IN QALA EN NAHAL

The deterioration of the tractors and of the agricultural machinery led to the failure of the THS and consequently to the near collapse of the Qala en Nahal rural refugee settlement in the period following the withdrawal of UNHCR's material involvement and before Euro Action Acord's financial and management intervention. Given the resource base, this is a reflection of the incompatibility of the use of tractors with the organization of the small farm and the technological, economic and sociocultural conditions of the refugee communities. It is also a reflection of the false dichotomy between refugee aid and development which has hitherto been the guiding principle of international assistance to refugees.

Problems arose with tractors for four reasons: the small size of holdings; the refugees' low level of education and technical know-how; the low farm incomes and consequently the inability of the settlements to generate capital and foreign exchange which would allow it to meet the capital and recurrent costs; and the way in which refugee aid was not linked to the development need of the refugee-affected area. From an analysis of these four aspects, we hope to examine the implication of the introduction of tractors, which are prodigal consumers of scarce foreign exchange and maintenance and operation of which require special technical skill, for the long-term viability of the settlements.

To allow maximum field efficiency so as to reduce costs per unit of output and to increase total output, the introduction of farm mechanization must be preceded by an appropriate organization of the farm so that the tractor would fit into the farm set-up. In the refugee rural land settlements each farmer's holding, irrespective of size, is cultivated and planted separately and this has led to high tractor operation costs.

TABLE 7.3. Percentage Distribution of the Sample Households according to their Attitude to Pooling their Holdings together for the Purpose of Cultivation.

Village	Willing	Unwilling	Total
Umsaqata	25.0	75.0	100.0
Umbrush	18.2	81.8	100.0
Dehema	14.7	85.3	100.0
Adingrar	5.0	95.0	100.0
Aburakham	31.0	69.0	100.0
Wad Awad	50.0	50.0	100.0

As long as the tractor service remains heavily subsidized, the disadvantage of cultivating the small plots separately will be somewhat hidden. Tractor hire charges are £S.1.5 per feddan irrespective of the size of the holding. The problem will arise when outside finance is discontinued and farmers will be expected to pay the full cost of cultivation and haulage.

The operating costs and the inefficiency of the tractors on the 10 feddan holdings is further exacerbated by fragmentation of holdings. As can be seen from Table 7.4, out of the total farm units cultivated by the THS in 1981, only 41% were of 10 feddan units; 10, 32 and 16% were of 7.5, 5 and 2.5 feddan units, respectively, while about 1.2% were of 20 feddan units. The corresponding figures for 1982 are 38, 11, 30 and 22%, respectively, excluding the Sudanese land outside the scheme. The consequence of this fragmentation of holdings on the tractor-operating costs and on tractor field efficiency is enormous.

Technical Problems

The introduction of mechanical power (tractors) to pastoral and agropastoral communities without first creating the necessary know-how among the beneficiaries is tantamount to introducing an activity which cannot be sustained without outside intervention. The use of mechanical power, not only in agriculture but generally, was quite unknown to the refugees in Qala en Nahal and no efforts were made to provide them with the vocational training to enable them to assimilate the innovation. Instead of creating opportunities for the refugees to learn how to operate and maintain the tractor fleet, the service was *given* to them, i.e., all the operators and mechanics were from outside the settler community. The decision to use tractor power was also made from the outside.

As Schumacher once pointed out,

> If aid is given to introduce certain new economic activities, these will be beneficial and viable only if they can be sustained by the already existing

TABLE 7.4. Farm Units Cultivated by the THS, Total Net and Gross Cultivated Area 1981 and 1982.

Village	20 fd units (8.4 ha)	10 fd units (4.2 ha)	7.5 fd units (3.15 ha)	5 fd units (2.1 ha)	2.5 fd units 1.05 ha)	Net cult. area (fd)	Recult. area (fd)	Gross area cult. (fd)
1981								
Salmin	–	386	96	224	131	6,027.5	327.5	6,682.5
Umsaqata	–	538	110	294	186	8,140.0	777.5	9,695.0
Umbrush	34	284	68	231	140	5,535.0	1,250.0	8,035.0
Adingrar	–	153	69	353	122	4,117.5	857.5	5,832.5
Dehema	22	371	38	290	104	6,145.0	685.0	7,515.0
Zurzur	4	273	102	158	98	5,200.0	1,052.0	7,305.0
Total	60	2,005	483	1,550	781	35,165.0	4,950.0	45,065.0
1982								
Salmin	–	470	95	231	205	7,080.0	887.5	7,967.5
Umsaqata	–	445	97	267	169	6,935.0	1,215.0	8,150.0
Umbrush	–	239	93	251	174	4,777.5	1,345.0	6,122.5
Adingrar	–	148	97	264	199	4,025.0	1,090.0	5,115.0
Deheme	–	174	89	224	210	4,052.5	1,637.5	5,690.0
Zurzur	–	270	105	195	152	4,842.5	1,137.5	5,980.0
7th unit 'A'	–	256	24	182	67	3,817.5	722.5	4,540.0
7th unit 'B'	–	121	13	68	42	1,755.0	252.5	2,007.5
Total	–	2,123	613	1,682	1,218	37,285.0	8,287.5	45,572.5

Source:
1981 EA-A Report on Tractor Cultivation Program File No. Sud. 14/7 October, 1981, Khartoum.
1982 EA-A Progress Report on EA-A Involvement in Qala en Nahal Refugee Settlement, 1982-1983 Cultivation Season, May, 1983.

> educational level of fairly broad groups of people and will be truly valuable if they promote and spread advances in education, organization and discipline. There can be a process of stretching—never a process of jumping. If new economic activities are introduced which depend on special education, special organization, and special discipline, such as are in no way inherent in the recipient society, the activity will not promote healthy development but will be more likely to hinder it. It will remain a foreign body that cannot be integrated. . .
>
> (Schumacher: 1974, 157-8)

Not only was the existing educational level of the settlers unable to sustain mechanization, but worse still, no attempt was made to generate such an educational level that gradually could have created the conditions to integrate the innovation. Hence, it is not surprising that the mechanization scheme failed.

The introduction of tractors was not preceded by a skills survey among the settlers to identify if there were mechanics and operators among them.

TABLE 7.5. Percentage Distribution of the Respondents, by Method of Cultivation in Eritrea.

Type/village	Umsaqata	Umbrush	Dehema	Adingrar	All villages
Animal power	94.0	93.0	100.0	100.0	97.0
Plough stick	–	–	–	–	–
Hoe	–	3.4	–	–	0.8
Own tractor	2.7	3.4	–	–	1.5
Hired tractor	2.7	–	–	–	0.8
Total	99.4	99.8	100.0	100.0	100.1

Out of the total sample households, about 35% reported that they had never used any form of power—neither tractors nor animal power—for cultivation in Eritrea. This indicates the considerable proportion of the settlers who came from pastoral communities. Out of the 65% of the total sample who had practiced farming in Eritrea, about 97% had used animal power to cultivate their land. The use of tractors was almost totally unknown except to about 2% of the refugees who practiced farming in Eritrea; these are only 1.5% of the total sample households. This clearly indicates that when the decision was taken to mechanize cultivation in the refugee land settlements, no consideration was given to the background and cultural practice of the settler community.

One of the major causes of the deterioration of the THS were the very frequent breakdowns due to poor maintenance, mainly caused by lack of qualified mechanics and operators. The Government wage rate, about £S.85 a month for mechanics, was too low to attract any skilled person, given the harsh weather conditions in the area. Before EA-A's taking over of the THS in 1981, all the workshop staff members were Sudanese, who were very poorly compensated for their labor and who, whenever better employment opportunities appeared, tended to leave the settlement.

When EA-A took over the THS in Qala en Nahal, it tried to utilize whatever skills existed among the settlers and, whenever this was not possible, refugees from outside the settlement were recruited. Despite the low wage rate, EA-A could easily recruit highly qualified workshop personnel. Apart from the workshop manager, who was an expatriate, the rest of the workshop staff members were Eritrean refugees from different parts of the Sudan. According to the workshop manager, most of the workshop staff are 'model workers' who perform their duties with great care and enthusiasm. The machinery expert who visited the workshop in Qala en Nahal before the EA-A takeover stated that

> Many simple things which could be done with present resources have not been done to safeguard the laid-off machinery. Tractor tyres have been left in the reversed condition, injectors left disconnected and unprotected.
> (Accord Program for the Management of the Mechanized Refugee . . . 1980, 5)

Even though it is very difficult to state with certainty whether or not a member of a community whose ultimate survival depends on the efficient management and maintenance of the agricultural machinery would behave in such a reckless manner, the evidence suggests that refugee mechanics and operators would have been more concerned about the machinery for the simple reason that they identify their communal interest with the well-being of the farm machinery. This can be demonstrated by the following EA-A statement:

> The Government rate of £S.85 a month was hopelessly inadequate compared to commercial rates. Undoubtedly mechanics have worked on this project at rates of pay below what they could have earned elsewhere in order to help their fellow refugees.
> (EA-A Progress Report: 1981, 10)

It is difficult to expect the same kind of altruism from a person employed for no other reason but to earn money. In order to meet the cultivation need of the settlers, certain tractor operators continue working 'until 3:00 a.m. without pay because they are working for their own people'. (Agrisystems: 1981, 41)

TABLE 7.6. Umsaqata Workshop Staff 1981 and 1982.

Type	1981 Number	1981 Nationality	1982 Number	1982 Nationality
Workshop manager	1	British	1	British
Grade 'A' mechanics	3	Eritrean	3	Eritrean
Grade 'B' mechanics	3	Eritrean	3	Eritrean
Grade 'C' mechanics	4	Eritrean	2	Eritrean
Welders	2	Eritrean	2	Eritrean
Electricians				
Mechanic assistants	1	Eritrean	2	Eritrean
Type repairman	1	Eritrean	1	Eritrean
Assistant welder	1	Eritrean		
Apprentices	3	Eritrean	6	Eritrean
Total	19		19	

In order to secure the continuity of the THS, EA-A has recruited apprentices from the settlers. There were six apprentices in the workshop in 1982. An 'in-service' training was also introduced in 1982 to upgrade the technical skill of the workshop staff. EA-A has no doubt provided the necessary logistics service and an efficient organizational framework and thus has managed to overcome one of the important constraints in the THS at least for the present. Whether the problem is solved forever or will reappear following EA-A's withdrawal from the project is a question which we shall raise later.

Financial Problems

The financial costs involved in the mechanization of farm operations are costs incurred in acquiring a machine, in depreciation, in repair and maintenance, in fuel, oil, lubricants and shelter and in labor. The total operation costs of the THS in the 1982-83 season were in the range of £S278,693. (See Table 7.7)

After the hand over of the settlement to the GOS, the need for spare parts, fuel and machinery replacement required foreign exchange which was often in short supply in the Sudan. The Sudan is classified by the United Nations as one of the least developed countries in the world and is faced with critical problems of stagnant rate of growth, foreign trade deficit, growing external debt and debt service payments and rising inflation. The country is heavily dependent on imported manufactured goods and is faced with a shortage of foreign exchange to service loans. The running costs of the THS in relation to the resources of the People's Local Government and in relation to the financial capacity of the beneficiaries are very high. Thus it was not difficult to foresee that the THS would deteriorate for lack of resources following the phasing out of international assistance.

TABLE 7.7. Total Operation Costs and Costs of Different Items as Percentage of Total Cost per Annum (£S.) of the THS.

Item	Cultivation Total Cost	%	Haulage Total Cost	%
Depreciation	85,306.56	36.1	13,667.50	32.2
Workshops	28,842.42	12.2	4,930.80	11.6
Spare parts	52,182.90	22.1	8,959.58	26.1
Fuel/lubricants	34,425.00	14.6	11,760.42	27.7
Transport	7,882.98	3.3	–	–
Insurance	3,644.46	1.5	746.48	1.8
Labor	23,970.00	10.2	2,380.00	5.6
Total	236,248.32	100.0	42,444.78	100.0

The drastic decline of, for instance, cotton production—a major foreign exchange earner in the irrigated schemes—is mainly caused by financial problems and particularly by lack of foreign exchange which was needed for machinery replacement and for meeting the operating costs. According to the 1982 World Bank Report,

> Existing infrastructure and plant equipment were operated without adequate provision for replacement or spare parts for maintenance and operation. Eventually, the resource base was depleted. Canals became silted or otherwise impaired, communication and transport facilities ran down and the availability of operational farm machinery was significantly reduced. In the ensuing years (1978/79) through 1980/81) irrigated cotton yields and output collapsed.
>
> (Document of the World Bank: 1982, 65)

A country which is faced with such financial and foreign exchange constraints cannot be expected to spend the scarcely available foreign exchange in the THS in the refugee land settlements. Since foreign exchange earnings depend on cotton exports, it is very clear that both the GOS and its people would benefit more if the foreign exchange were used to overcome the capital constraint faced by the irrigated schemes than when it is used to finance the THS. Thus, it is not an exaggeration to state that the THS that was created by generous investments contained the seeds of its own destruction from the outset.

In taking over the settlement, the GOS was

> committed inevitably to large recurrent operating expenses for which funds did not exist and which could not be covered by charges for water

and use of tractors, which had been strongly resisted by the refugees themselves.

(Beyer: 1976)

Hunting *et al.* also note that since 1974 one of the major causes of failure of the THS was inadequate budgeting which had led to

. . . a rapid deterioration in the tractor services provided and a consequent inability to meet the minimum cultivation requirements of the settlement.

(Hunting: op.cit., 12)

From 1974 onwards, an attempt was made to recover a small part of the operational cost by levying tractor hire charges on those households which were considered to be in a position to bear the burden. (See Table 7.8)

TABLE 7.8. Tractor Hire Charges per Hawashas (10 Feddan Plot) 1971-1982.

Year	Charge in £S. per Hawash
1971	Free of charge
1972	Free of charge
1973	Free of charge
1974	2
1975	5
1976	5
1977	8
1978	8
1979	10
1980	10
1981	10
1982	15

Source: Scheme Administration, Collector's Account No. 36. 1974-1982, Umsaqata.

However, the amount collected from the tractor hire service charges when related to the total operating costs represents an insignificant part of the total cost. (See Tables 7.7 and 7.9)

The tractor operating cost per feddan in the 1982-83 season was, for example, £S.5.4, while the tractor hire charge was only £S.1.5 per feddan. The latter amounted only to 28% of the total operating cost per feddan.

The financial constraint of the THS was overcome by EA-A's intervention in 1981. In 1981 and 1982 EA-A's expenditure on capital and recurrent costs was

TABLE 7.9. Revenue from the THS 1979-82.

Year	Revenue (£S.)
1979	7,582.18
1980	7,594.25
1981	18,090.00
1982	38,000.00
Total	71,266.43

Source: Collector's Account No. 36, 1979-1982. Administration Records, Umsaqata.

in the range of US$2,692,300. As noted earlier, because the Sudan, like many other Third World countries, is faced with serious economic problems and with acute shortage of foreign exchange, it would have been inconceivable for it to refurbish the THS at such huge costs.

DEVELOPMENT WITHOUT BENEFICIARY'S PARTICIPATION?

> Development does not start with goods; it starts with people and their education, organization and discipline. Without these three all resources remain latent, untapped potential.
>
> (E.A. Schumacher: op.cit.)

> Refugees themselves have been ignored throughout the decision making process in the three phases of relief, rehabilitation, and development.
>
> (Karadawi: 1981)

The refugee land settlement at Qala en Nahal is a typical case study whereby a genuine attempt was made to stimulate the beneficiaries to unleash their potential productive power by supplying them with considerable material goods, but without ever attempting to integrate them into the process of decision making. The refugees were instead relegated to the background and only received what was being given to them without being able to understand how the services operated or where the assistance came from. Many took it for granted that the supply of international assistance would continue until the problem in Eritrea was solved politically. This was because the refugees were excluded from taking part in planning and because the objectives of the settlements were not sufficiently explained to them before their transfer. According to the well-meaning perception of the decisionmakers and donors, supply of sufficient agricultural inputs and other services was believed to enable the refugees to become self-reliant, but this did not occur because, among other things, in Freire's formulation the locus of decisions was kept 'outside the society undergoing change'. (Freire: 1979)

This may explain why the refugees resisted bitterly the levying of water-rate and tractor-hire charges. In March-April 1974, a UNHCR Branch Office Mission visited the settlement and the refugees forwarded their complaints to the mission about water fees and tractor hire charges. The mission noted that,

> Refugees are under the impression that UNHCR was there to finance them forever. A group of 400 refugees in Zurzur village had refused to participate to date in cultivation and had maintained that the refugees according to the 'International Laws of the Red Cross' were not supposed to work, and the UNHCR had the duty to support them. These and others also complained about the stoppage of WFP food since July, 1973, and demand resumption, despite the fact that the settlement, handicapped refugees apart, was self-sufficient in this regard.
>
> (Report on Mission to Qala en Nahal and Gedaref . . . 1974)

Such a dependent mentality was mainly a result of the way in which aid was delivered and of the lack of participation, rather than the lack of ability to pay the nominal fees. If the refugees had taken part in planning, implementation and management, they would have very easily understood the situation since neither the GOS nor the donor agencies were there to meet the running costs of the settlement indefinitely. Thus the question of refusal would have never arisen. This would have also enabled the refugees to resist against the introduction of economic activities which in their opinion were incompatible with their low level of education and technical know-how, and their sociocultural and economic conditions. Participation at the initial stage would have also enabled them to negotiate for an adaptation of farm technology which is low cost, simple to operate, can be produced from local materials and which is rooted in their sociocultural background. The exclusion of the refugees from decisionmaking seems to have generated a desire among them to be excluded from responsibility to meet the running costs of activities which were introduced without their participation.

The question of motivation is very significant with regard to refugees because, as shown in Chapter 2, the refugees are victims of violence and often their dignity and self-respect have been affected. Hence, settlement must enable them to regain their self-respect and dignity. This cannot be achieved only by the supply of material goods but by also integrating the refugees into the structures of decision making. As Baker lucidly notes,

> . . . people are not pawns to needs and drives . . . Needs and drives are part of motivation, but individuals in balancing needs, drives, interests, and aspirations make choices for themselves, they are actors in the development process.
>
> (Baker: 1983, 219)

It does not seem to us that this was ever realized by the settlement planners, by those who financed it and by those who managed it. Securing the refugees' participation in management and other decisions has two advantages. First, it helps the refugee to regain his dignity, and second, it enables him to become his own motivating force in creating an economically and socially viable community.

> Development brings freedom, provided it is development of people. But people cannot be developed; they can only develop themselves. For while it is possible for an outsider to build a man's house; an outsider cannot give pride and self-confidence in himself as a human being. Those things a man has to create himself by his own actions. He develops himself by what he does; he develops himself by making his own decisions; by increasing his understanding of what he is doing; and why; by increasing his own knowledge and ability; and by his own full participation as an equal in the life of the community he lives in.
>
> (Nyerere quoted in Baker: ibid.)

Qala en Nahal is, as noted earlier, a case study of non-participation, in which an attempt to develop the settlers from without failed to achieve long-term satisfactory results. It is also vivid evidence that the African refugee problem requires an imaginative new approach which must give the refugees the opportunities to develop themselves. This, of course, presupposes that the new structures and economic activities introduced by the provision of aid are not only intelligible to the beneficiaries but are also directly linked to their local institutional and cultural milieu. This does not in any way belittle the importance of material assistance. The provision of international aid is, indeed, a prerequisite for the development of refugees, but our contention is that if aid imposes structures or activities which cannot be sustained without external assistance, this will in the long run create dependence and discourage participation rather than promote development. Hunting for instance, notes that,

> . . . relations between the scheme management and the refugees have not been good. This is partly because there is too little involvement on the part of the settlers in the day-to-day running of the settlements . . . Too much, therefore, depends on the efficiency of the mangement organization and too little responsibility rests with the refugees themselves.
>
> (Hunting *et al.*: op.cit., 16)

This, according to the same report 'has encouraged the development of a refugee mentality and a willingness to rely too much on the efforts of others'.

A harmonious relationship between management and the refugees is also necessary for a smooth performance of the THS and other settlement activities. Following the phasing out of UNHCR's assistance, the settlement was left without any manager

> . . . despite the COR's recommendation that local government should pay a full-time project manager, no such was appointed and the settlement had been handed to local district-level officials who neglected it.
>
> (Beyer: 1976)

When a new manager was appointed later, the relation between refugees and his office became so tense that there was no possibility for any cooperation.

> . . . with a change of manager and hand-over of responsibility to the Ministry of People's Local Government, production fell off rapidly, due to lack of finance to purchase adequate spares and fuel, and to some extent, poor management.
>
> (Hunting: op.cit., 17)

THE FAILURE TO LINK REFUGEE AND DEVELOPMENT AID

According to Osman *et al.*, the GOS had hoped that,

> Qala en Nahal would act as an important generator of local zonal development. . . But the gap in organizational boundaries of refugee aid organizations and development oriented organizations in addition to the economic incapability of the host government led to the virtual collapse of the settlement when UNHCR decided to phase out its assistance in 1973.
>
> (Osman *et al.*: op.cit., 12-13)

According to the traditional mandate of the UNHCR, provision of assistance to refugees beyond the subsistence level lay outside the realm of its jurisdiction. There was also fear that assisting the refugees beyond the standard of living commensurate in the area would arouse jealousy among the local population and might in extreme situations lead to an open conflict. Provision of assistance to both the local population and the refugees in order to raise their quality of life and provision of assistance to host governments with the aim of offsetting the burden imposed on their infrastructural services also lay outside the traditional mandate of the HCR.

According to the division of powers that existed among the refugee-assisting and development agencies, there was a dichotomy between refugee aid and development assistance. In as much as the poor local population lay outside the concern of the traditional mandate of UNHCR, the refugees also lay outside the concern of the organizations that provided development assistance. It took time for the international community to realize that refugee aid and development assistance are two sides of the same coin, and refugee-related projects should from the outset be development-oriented and should fit into the overall development planning of the host governments so that not only the refugees but the local population can benefit from such projects. This approach is advantageous not only to the refugees but also the countries of asylum and to the countries and agencies which provide refugee aid and development assistance.

Qala en Nahal is a good example of the inadequacy of the traditional approach of setting up spacially segregated refugee settlements which are prejudicial to the refugees' possibility to integrate themselves into the development process of the host country. According to the traditional response '. . . Assistance is not always provided to develop beyond the level of subsistence'. (UN General Assembly, A/Conf. 125/1, 31 January, 1984, 4)

As we noted earlier, UNHCR programs ceased when the need for development set in, whereas, if humanitarian aid were development oriented from the outset, the organizational boundaries of refugee assisting and development agencies would have not been erected. Qala en Nahal is a classic example which shows that self-reliance and economic and social integration of the refugees into the development process of the host country cannot be achieved without abandoning the traditional approaches and without viewing the problem of refugees in the context of the over-all development need of the country of asylum and without long-term commitment of the international community. The experience of Qala en Nahal also shows that the road to economic and social integration of refugees is indeed a long and ardous one.

If the host country is provided with reasonably sufficient assistance and assuming it has a policy which is favorable to the refugees' social and economic integration, it will be able to integrate its response to a new refugee influx within the affected region's development process. Such an approach may also enable the host government

> . . . to avoid the temptation of setting up camps or settlements artificially separated from host communities, which foster among the refugees a state of dependency on outside assistance and which may eventually stifle the initiative of whole communities, thereby lessening their ability to help themselves.
>
> (ICVA Statement at ICARA II: 1984, 2)

As noted by Osman *et al.* '. . . Qala en Nahal was an artificial settlement in which refugees were put in a segregated project'. (Osman *et al.*: op.cit., 12)

The new approach can also reduce the perpetual financial and management burden imposed on the organizations and governments that provide refugee aid by integrating the refugee problem into the host country's development process which may from the outset enable the refugees to become productive members of the host community. The GOS and the international organizations have spent scarce resources in Qala en Nahal; the refugees are neither fully integrated into the region's development process, nor are they closer to self-reliance. The settlement still and will depend for a long time to come on outside assistance. This was exacerbated by the introduction of partial mechanization when the ability of the refugees to produce surplus and the GOS's ability to meet the recurrent and capital costs were extremely limited.

The major causes of the deterioration of the THS in the period preceding EA-A's intervention can generally be said to be associated with: the small size of the holdings, and technical, financial and management problems which are in turn linked to the false dichotomy between refugee aid and development.

CAN MECHANIZATION BE JUSTIFIED?

The factors that justify farm mechanization are mainly increased production resulting from: increased acreage, better seedbed preparation, improved timeliness of planting and saving of labor time. Do these factors also justify the use of tractors in the rural refugee land settlements in the eastern region of the Sudan?

In economies where there is land abundance and labor scarcity, capital is used to substitute the scarce factor, labor. As a result, larger areas are brought under cultivation which means an increase in total production even when there is no increase in yield. As we saw in Chapter 5, the refugee rural land settlements are characterized by acute shortage of cultivable land, and mechanization of cultivation cannot for the majority of the households lead to increased acreage. However, a qualification is in order here. If the alternative were manual cultivation, mechanization would definitely lead to increased acreage for those who hold over 5 feddans.

One man can only manually cultivate, maintain and harvest an area of 2-3 feddans in the area. The average male family labor unit in the settlements is 1.5 and an average household cannot cultivate more than 4.5 feddans manually. However, given the size of the holdings in the settlement, the use of tractors as opposed to animal power cannot lead to increased area under cultivation. The work output of oxen per day in the Clay Plain is estimated at about one feddan. Thus, a pair of oxen can meet the cultivation need of several households per season, and the use of tractors in the refugee settlements cannot be justified on this ground.

It is often believed that when mechanization is substituted for other forms of power, it can lead to better returns due to improved quality of seedbed preparation. (See Gemil and Eicher: 1973, 20; Anker: 1955, 240; Mcfarquhar and Hall: 1970, 26) The soils in the Central Clay Plain, as we saw earlier, are self-cracking and hard and dry, and tractor power might facilitate better seedbed preparation. However, the evidence suggests that the use of 75 h.p. tractors and the WLDH with seeder attachment 'results in uneven, shallow seedbed of poor tilth causing poor and uneven germination and shallow root growth'. (Document of the World Bank: 1978, 7) A report prepared for the UNHCR by Agrisystems also states that

> The continuous use of the WLDH at the same cultivation depth is considered by some authorities to lead to a breakdown of soil structure and the formation of a plough pan which restricts water and root penetration. (Agrisystems: 1981, 12)

Crop return comparisons from animal traction and tractor mechanization from experiments carried out on heavy and light soils in the Nuba mountains also show that the net returns per feddan were considerably higher with animal traction than with tractors. (See Table 7.11) Spooner, also using information from oxen cultivators in Qala en Nahal, states that

> Oxen ploughing gave good soil penetration up to 15 cm compared to the 5 cm generally experienced with the tractors.
> (Spooner: 1981, 131)

The third justification of farm mechanization is improved timeliness of planting. In the Central Clay Plain of the Sudan, due to rainfall distribution and soil conditions, the cultivation season is very short. According to the Sudanese and refugee farmers, sowing of sorghum begins during the second week of June assuming there are early rains, while sesame is planted between June 15 and July 15. Agrisystems also estimates the cultivation period as extending between June 15 and August 20. (Agrisystems: 1981, 39) These estimates assume early rains, which is not often the case. In 1981, for instance, cultivation began on June 28 while in 1982, cultivation did not begin before July 15. This shows that the planting period can be shortened drastically by late rains. In such a situation, production can be considerably increased by improving timeliness of planting. Is this happening in the refugee land settlements? Although the THS no doubt enables some farmers to plant their seeds in proper time, many cannot have their plots ploughed at the optimum time. As can be seen from Table 7.10, in the 1981 season, cultivation began on June 28 and continued for 14 weeks until October 4. This occurred despite 10 hour shifts and maximum field efficiency. Those farmers who received early and late cultivations complained of untimely cultivation, and these were a considerable proportion of the total households who hired tractors. The farmers who by chance receive timely cultivation may, no doubt, increase their agricultural production but unless each farmer or a small group of farmers own tractors together and this is very unrealistic, the majority of the farmers'

TABLE 7.10. Area Cultivated per Week, 1981

Week No.	Average working days/week	Net area cultiva. (fedd.)	Accu.%	Recult. area (fedd.)	Accu.%	Total area cult. (Fd)	(Accu.*)	Nos. of* farmers	Area cult./ working day (fd)	No. of farmers day worked
1	6.75	6,105.0	17.4	—	—	6,105.0	13.6	697	904	103
2	5.83	6,247.5	35.2	—	—	6,247.5	27.5	919	1,072	158
3	3.58	4,082.5	46.8	—	—	4,082.5	36.6	553	1,140	154
4	4.92	5,092.5	61.3	—	—	5,092.5	47.9	773	1,035	157
5	3.75	3,697.5	78.8	—	—	3,697.5	56.1	474	986	126
6	4.58	3,582.5	82.0	40	0.8	3,662.5	64.2	562	800	123
7	4.08	2,512.5	89.2	375	8.4	3,262.5	71.4	457	800	112
8	2.50	850.0	91.6	420	16.9	1,690.0	75.2	237	676	95
9	4.25	507.5	93.0	1,130	39.7	2,767.5	81.3	330	651	78
10	1.67	210.0	93.6	240	44.6	690.0	82.8	92	413	28
11	2.75	510.0	95.1	385	52.4	1,280.0	85.6	130	465	32
12	4.67	442.5	96.4	790	68.4	2,022.5	90.1	240	433	43
13	4.58	620.0	98.1	1,085	90.3	2,790.0	96.3	295	609	64
14	2.33	705.0	100.0	485	100.0	1,675.0	100.0	171	719	49
Total	56.24	35,165.0		4,950		45,065.0		5,930	625	105

* Read this instead as 'Nos of farm units.' Despite the fact that refugee farmers are legally prohibited from possessing more land than was originally allocated to them, there are many cultivating more plots than their original allocation. The refugee farmers demanding tractor hire service pay their fees to the administration and the list is submitted by the latter to the EA-A which cultivates the land without checking who the actual owner is. In order to avoid being detected the farmers who cultivate more than one plot pay the fees in the name of the original owner who had left the settlement long ago or in any other name. The administration is interested in the fact that those who pay the charges receive cultivation and EA-A's main concern is to effectively and efficiently provide service to those who have demanded such service by making good the tractor charges in advance. The fees are collected by the administration and not by EA-A. According to the EA-A report given in the table above 5,930 farmers received tractor service in the 1981 season. Although this figure includes the number of farmers whose farms were recultivated due to failure of seed germination, the figure is still misleading because according to the 1981 EA-A survey there were only 18,050 people in Qala en Nahal. If we divide this by the average household size excluding the dependents 18,050 = 3,610 families. If we include the no. of dependents, the figure is 18,050 = 3,167 families. Out of this, again according to its own finding, 17% were landless, i.e. 614 families. That means there were only 2,996 which had land. But as indicated in the table, altogether 5,930 families benefitted from the tractor service while the actual number of refugees who had land in the same season were only 2,996. It is possible that the increase can be firstly, due to the number of the refugees whose farms received second cultivation because of failure of germination and secondly, due to the number of Sudanese farmers who had land within the scheme which was indiscriminately cultivated together with that of the refugees. Despite this it is more correct to give the number of farm units that were cultivated by tractors rather than to give the number of farmers. In the presence of secret land transfers and transactions no one can ever be sure about who reaps of the fruits of tractor cultivation.

holdings are liable to be cultivated either before or after the optimal dates of planting. This problem is inherent in any centrally-managed THS.

The other justification of farm mechanization is saving on labor time. Does mechanization of cultivation enable the refugee farmers to overcome labor bottlenecks or does it lead to labor displacements? In discussing the impact of mechanization of farm labor requirement, it is necessary to distinguish between partial and full mechanization of farm operations. (The question of whether mechanization is employment creating or employment destroying is a controversial question in African agricultural development. For contrasting points of view on the impact of farm mechanization on employment, see Belshaw: 1969; Clayton: 1972; and Mcfarquhar & Hall: 1970.

Partial farm mechanization in the refugee land settlements has not led to displacement of agricultural labor. In fact, it has led to larger areas being weeded and harvested. However, since cultivation takes place at a time when agricultural labor is laid off, there is a certain degree of labor displacement occurring during the first three weeks after planting. Under an efficient management this takes about 10-14 weeks depending upon various natural and technical conditions; however, those farmers whose plots receive late cultivation often work for wages in the farms that were planted earlier. Weeding starts 2-3 weeks after planting, and if we can speak of agricultural labor displacement, this occurs only during the first 2-3 weeks after planting. However, on balance partial mechanization in the rural refugee land settlement has not led to saving of labor time, but instead to increased seasonal labor demand for weeding and harvesting. This is partly due to the fact that mechanization has enabled some of the rich households to extend the area under cultivation and partly due to the rigidity of the THS. Planting cannot be spread so as to overcome peak labor requirement because the decision of the day of planting is not in the hands of the refugee farmers. Since the whole holding is planted together on one day, the peak labor requirement occurs simultaneously throughout the plot, and many households are therefore forced to employ wage labor to overcome peak labor requirements.

Another justification for mechanization is that it creates employment for some members of the community as administrators, operators, mechanics and supervisors. In February 1982, there were 79 EA-A employees in Qala en Nahal in activities directly related to mechanization. Beside the 19 workshop staff there were one agricultural advisor, one assistant administrator, one cashier, one storekeeper, four permanent drivers, two landrover drivers, seven site foremen, one assistant site foreman, one builder, 31 guards, eight checkers, and four maids. However, although all of these are refugees from Eritrea, only a few apart from the guards and the drivers are from the settler communities themselves.

Mechanization also offers training opportunities to some members of the community in question who after acquiring the necessary skills can seek employment either within their own communities or elsewhere. The THS in

Qala en Nahal is training some apprentices but, as we shall discuss later, the question of retaining the skilled laborers within the scheme is a crucial issue which requires greater attention.

Even though there may be some advantage stemming from the introduction of partial farm mechanization in the rural refugee land settlement, none of these advantages can justify the use of tractors to the neglect of other sources of power in light of the small size of the holdings, the very low farm incomes, the lack of capital, and the very low level of education and technical know-how among the refugee farmers.

MECHANIZATION CREATES DEPENDENCE

History teaches but it is men who must draw lessons from it lest they be caught unawares and repeat the same mistakes as in the past. The performance of the THS shows the state of dependence created by mechanization.

The structure created by the decision to mechanize cultivation has unequivocally demonstrated its inability to generate the necessary conditions for its sustenance and reproduction. In other words, it is a structure devoid of self-propelling inner dynamics which easily falls apart whenever outside aid is withdrawn from it. Its situation is comparable to that of a patient who breathes with the help of a respirator and ceases to breathe whenever the respiratory aid is withdrawn. The THS operates well whenever foreign aid is pumped into it and almost collapses whenever outside aid is terminated. As Schumacher lucidly pointed out,

> From an economic point of view, the central concept of wisdom is permanence. Nothing makes economic sense unless continuance for a long time can be projected without running into absurdities.
>
> (Schumacher: op.cit.)

If adequate scientific planning had been exercised, it would not have been difficult to foresee that the program would lead to a blind alley. But it seems to us that long-term financial, technical and management issues were completely disregarded.

This section argues that the problems that led to the deterioration of the THS following the phasing out of international assistance in the past will recur following the withdrawal of EA-A unless an alternative is found to tractors.

The continuity of the THS is first determined by the settlement's ability in the long run to generate sufficient surplus to obtain the capital and foreign exchange needed for tractor replacement, for the purchase of spare parts, fuel, oil, lubricants, wages, etc. At present, the overwhelming majority of the households are not producing any surplus. In 1982, as can be seen from Chapter 8, only 26% of the total sample earned over the viability floor, while about 74% of the sample earned below the minimum income necessary to meet their annual consumption need. The generation of surplus in itself may not sometimes be enough because there may be a shortage of fuel in the country which can nullify a whole season's production. That was why EA-A had to import fuel in 1982 directly from one of the oil-producing countries in the Middle East. In extreme situations the country can limit or even stop import of tractors in order to save foreign exchange.

Given the high rate of inflation in the Sudan, the recurrent costs are likely to increase drastically in the future. In 1980, the operating cost of a 60 h.p tractor and 3.7 WLDH was about £S.2.50 per feddan, while in 1982, the cultivation cost with the same machinery increased to £S.5.4 per feddan. In 1984, the operating cost per feddan has risen to £S.6. (Wallace: 1985, 4)

The Sudan has serious economic problems and a lack of the foreign exchange needed for machinery replacement and for meeting the operating costs. Thus it is both unfair and impossible to expect the Sudan to meet the costs of tractor mechanization in the refugee rural settlements following the phasing out of international assistance.

At present the full cost of the THS is borne by EA-A. The revenue collected from the refugee farmers for tractor hire service is not used to meet part of the recurrent cost nor is the charge placed in special funds to meet the future need of the THS. Although the revenue collected at the subsidized rate of tractor hiring is insignificant compared to the recurrent cost, it would have probably been wise to place it in a special fund which could be used after EA-A's withdrawal.

The total annual cost of operating the tractors is in the range of £S.278,693.10. To cover this, it would be necessary to levy tractor charges of £S.5.4 per feddan for cultivation and £S.0.70 per sack of haulage. For most of the refugee farmers, this would represent an unbearable burden—and it is likely that the poor families would be forced to resort to alternative forms of traditional cultivation. The tractor service will then be only available to those who can afford to pay. The cultivation season, as we saw in Chapter 6, coincides with the hungry season when many families have already exhausted their stock of food. Such prohibitively high tractor charges would lead to indebtedness and further accelerate the already existing social and economic differentiation in the communities.

The present tractor charges, although comparatively low, still represent a great burden to the poor families because the charges are often paid by borrowing from the merchants or rich refugee farmers at 100-150% interest.

Under the present cultural practices and given the limited land resource, it is hard to envisage a situation in which all the refugee farmers presently using the tractors would ever generate sufficient surplus income to meet the full tractor operating costs. The THS will require outside financial support for the foreseeable future.

The second critical factor that determines the continuity of the THS is the technical knowledge in the refugee communities about the tractors and the other machines. That the settlers lack the special technical know-how is in clear. However, what is debatable is whether an innovation should be only introduced in communities where there already exists sufficient knowledge to sustain it? Cannot the required knowledge be acquired in the process of utilizing the innovation? If the beneficiary community has access to training facilities and participates in all forms of decisionmaking, there may be a possibility in the long run to generate the skill and discipline necessary to sustain the innovation. The THS is centrally managed however, and does not often provide a possibility for the majority to acquire the necessary educational level to sustain the innovation.

The EA-A has temporarily solved the problem by employing refugees with the necessary skill from outside the settler community and by recruiting a few children from the latter as apprentices. Will this create the necessary skill and discipline to keep the THS in its present or improved condition? It is difficult to be certain, but still it is possible to make some 'educated guesses'. Our discussion with the skilled refugees in the settlements revealed that the majority hopes to get better employment opportunities outside the settlements or to go abroad for further studies. Although EA-A was, during our survey, the agency least affected by the refugee resettlement program to the US and Canada, there is no guarantee whatsoever that the workshop staff will remain in the settlement following EA-A's withdrawal. Hence, it is very likely that the same problems will recur if EA-A decides to withdraw its management and financial input. To retain the present skilled manpower, the THS has to be able to pay the workshop staff at the commercial rate in the area. Unless there is financial support from outside, this does not seem possible in the near future. As we saw earlier, due to the overfragmented nature of the holdings, the tractor operation costs are far higher in the settlements than they are in the 1,500 feddan commercial farm units in the area. The demand for skilled labor in the oil-rich Middle East countries leads thousands of Sudanese to emigrate every year, creating a shortage of skilled labor which in turn leads to increased wages for skilled labor. The question is, can the settlements, in spite of higher production costs and far less income obtained from the overfragmented holdings, compete with the rich commercial farmers to retain the skilled manpower?

Assuming EA-A hands over the THS to the People's Local Government, the latter will not only be faced with financial problems but also a policy problem with regard to the level of wages to be paid to the workshop and other staff members. At present, in order to retain the skilled labor, EA-A is paying the workshop staff more than is stipulated on government scale; what will happen following the handover? Can the People's Local Government be expected to maintain a dual system whereby the refugee mechanics are paid more than the Sudanese mechanics working for the local government? This is unrealistic.

What is most likely to happen is that the new management will be forced to reduce the wages of the workshop staff to the level of the government scale. The result will be that most of the skilled refugees will seek employment outside the settlement. At present, as the THS is implemented by a voluntary agency, the wages paid to the staff of the THS are not dependent on agricultural production. The employees are guaranteed that their wages will be paid irrespective of the size of the crop. If the operation costs following the handover are to be met by the refugee farmers, the wages of the workshop staff will necessarily depend on the seasonal performance of the scheme, which undoubtedly will vary from season to season. Frequent poor harvests clearly indicate that not only will the refugee farmer be unable to pay the wages to the workshop and other staff, but the latter will be very reluctant to stay in the face of such uncertainties.

In the short run, some of the workshop staff may not, due to political commitment and patriotism, respond to the demand for their skill, but since most of them are establishing their own families, the economic pressure may in the future force them to abandon their altruism and work wherever there is higher wage.

The third critical factor for the viability of the THS is management input. One of the major causes of decline of the THS was lack of effective management which failed to exercise control over the flow of resources, maintenance of the machinery and allocation of the service. Good quality management is a prerequisite for the viability of the THS as proper usage of spare parts and fuel is essential. Furthermore, there must be supervision of operation so as to secure a maximum plowing rate. Under the present management system, the working age of a tractor is estimated at seven years but this is directly dependent on the quality of management. Bad management can considerably shorten the working life of a tractor. Lack of control over the flow of resources such as spare parts and fuel can also lead to increased costs which may finally threaten the very existence of the THS. There is no doubt that EA-A has at least temporarily solved the problem of management, but the question is—what will happen following its withdrawal?

Prior to EA-A's involvement in the THS in Qala en Nahal, it was mainly the *Legina* and the clan *sheikhs*, with the blessing of the scheme management, who had an upper hand in the allocation of the tractor service. One of the major achievements of the EA-A is the breaking of the *sheikh*-structure in regard to the distribution of tractors. Under the present EA-A management of the THS, the refugees are allowed to participate in some activities, but the major financial and technical management decisions are taken by the expatriates. The area in which refugees participate are first the distribution of tractors among the villages and within the villages among the *meshruas*. Second, the drivers, their assistants and guards of the village unit shops are all recruited from the village itself. Third, disputes arising in regard to tractors are settled by the village elders in collaboration with the EA-A staff members. Although these measures have totally ironed out all forms of unfair and unjust practices, the problem of the future still remains unresolved. Who will manage the THS after EA-A's withdrawal? The refugees themselves? The People's Local Government?

As noted earlier, although the beneficiaries' participation in development decisionmaking is considered to be a precondition of successful implementation of any agricultural innovation, there is no evidence that the refugee farmers with their present financial position, educational level and management skill, would be able to sustain the THS on their own.

Farm mechanization requires special management skills and due to the brain-drain from the Sudan, it is unrealistic to expect the Sudan to divert its highly trained personnel from other forms of assignment to the refugee settlements. Owing to the harsh climatic conditions and the low wage rates paid by the local government, it will be very difficult to recruit qualified Sudanese to work in the settlement. (The emigration of Sudanese to the oil-producing Arab Middle East countries has increased drastically since the mid-1970s. The estimation varies from source to source. For instance, Birks and Sinclair estimated the number of emigrants in 1975 to be between 26,000 and 46,000. While for 1977-78 el Din estimates the number at 231,000 and el Goul's estimation for the same year is within the range of 500,000. (Quoted in the Document of the World Bank: 1982, 117-118) Between 1976-77 and 1977-78 about 8,000 public employees left the country without notice and as a result lost their jobs.)

What may happen following the withdrawal of EA-A's financial and management inputs is that the standard of management may decline, leading to increased costs or decreased revenues, which may threaten the viability of the THS and, consequently the need for outside assistance may recur. Apart from contradicting the fundamental objective of self-reliance, this was not what the international organizations and host government intended to achieve.

THE POOR FARMERS ARE MARGINALIZED

The THS and its efficient management mainly benefits the rich refugees with large cultivable areas. Not only do the landless derive no direct benefit from the THS, but the provision of improved THS has led to the marginalization of the poor farmers and to the eviction of the former sharecroppers. Before EA-A's takeover, a considerable number of the landless farmers were cultivating land belonging to farmers who had large tracts of cultivable land which, due to lack of means of cultivation, they could not themselves utilize. Following the improvement of the THS there was no need for them to keep the sharecroppers. In fact, an opposite trend has emerged whereby the rich farmers are cultivating, on the basis of sharecropping, land belonging to the poor farmers who due to lack of labor or food during the hungry season cannot weed their own farms. This shows that mechanization has created wealth on the one hand and marginalization on the other. The marginalized farmers have turned into a cheap labor pool, enabling the rich to achieve higher agricultural income partly due to low wages and partly due to an increased demand for food. The resulting higher prices enable the rich farmer to accumulate capital. This capital is often lent to the middle and low-income farmers at exorbitant interest rates.

The marginal and landless farmers do not directly benefit from the efficient running of the THS in Qala en Nahal. However, due to the rich farmers' increased acreage resulting from the proper management of the THS, there is now a greater demand for seasonal agricultural labor than before. The marginal and the landless refugees sell their labor power to the rich farmers within the settlement and in the surrounding Sudanese villages, i.e., unlike the refugees in the other land settlements in Eastern Sudan, the former do not need to travel to the rainfed agricultural areas in search of employment. This has economic and social advantages. Economically the marginal farmer, after having worked for wages during the day time, can work on his small plot in the late afternoon. Socially he can live with his own family and can enjoy the available social services in the settlement, especially health services which are not easily available outside of the settlement. As was discussed in Chapter 6, most of the refugees in Qala en Nahal, unlike the refugees from the other settlements, work in the settlements and in the surrounding villages. The extension of the tractor service by the EA-A to the surrounding Sudanese villages in Qala en Nahal has also led to increased demand for labor in weeding and harvesting. Nevertheless, owing to the highly seasonal nature of agricultural production in the area, the demand for labor comes to an end with the peak season. Due to lack of non-farm income-generating activities during the off-season, the situation of the marginal and poor farmers cannot be improved unless there is a special project designed to help them become self-reliant or unless the land bank is raised so that they would be allocated cultivable land and derive direct benefit from the THS.

ALTERNATIVE METHODS OF CULTIVATION

Field efficiency could be increased and operation costs could be decreased if the shape of the *hawasha* (holdings) could be changed or if the small holders could pool their holdings together either on a cooperative basis or just for the purpose of cultivation. Changing the *hawasha* into a rectangular shape would involve serious organizational problems and may also lead to conflict among the holders because the quality of the holdings now varies after so many years of cultivation. Those who have worked their holdings in the previous seasons properly may not want to exchange them for weed infested plots. Pooling of the small plots together for the purpose of cultivation and then restoring the boundaries would also create boundary conflicts and not be acceptable to the refugee farmers.

Theoretically, formation of cooperatives at a village level and cultivation of the fragmented holdings as a single large unit, whereby the cooperative would possess tractors, implements and other necessary equipment and facilities, would seem to represent a viable alternative. To run the program efficently, it would be necessary to employ a manager and other technical staff from outside the settler community. However, eventually it may be possible to replace the manager and the technical staff with trained people from the cooperative members. This kind of cooperative system has various advantages but at the same time poses substantial organizational problems. The author discussed this question with the village elders in the six sample villages and in all the villages the clear majority argued that the differences of resources—labor, land, and capital (seeds, hand tools, livestock, money to hire laborers, etc.)—that exist among the refugee farmers would make it difficult to achieve harmonious working and effective relationships among the cooperative members. There is also nothing which indicates that the financial, technical and management problems that are faced under the present system would not recur. The refugee farmers have no experience in cooperative movement. They are used to individual holdings in Eritrea. However, it is important to emphasize that if low cost agricultural implements which are produced locally and which are compatible with the refugees' present abilities are *not* introduced, then the future of the settlements lies in the formation of cooperatives. However, since attitudes and cultural practices are difficult to change, our discussion below assumes that the organization of the refugee farmers into large cooperatives, even though highly desirable, is not possible in the near future. (This does not imply that the task of organizing the small farmers into cooperatives is impossible, however, for such a movement to succeed it has to come from the refugees' own initiative and must not be imposed from above.)

The aim of scientific investigation is to describe a certain reality (object of the study), to explain why that particular reality is the way it is and, based on these descriptions and explanations, to discover some general patterns, so that the researcher and others using the same or similar method will be able to predict with a certain degree of certainty the trends of development in the future. The future, within the existing limitations, being to a great extent a result of human action or omission, a study in development is incomplete if it does not go beyond explanatory and descriptive levels and offer an alternative viewpoint which may be a guide to human action so as to influence the outcome in the future.

The primary objective of the refugee rural land settlements is that they should achieve self-reliance and not be a long-term burden on the host government or/and the international donor agencies. How does the use of tractors for cultivation relate to the achievement of self-reliance? An agricultural production which depends on mechanization is by definition incompatible with self-reliant agriculture. If agricultural production is based on the use of mechanical power (tractors), and since the production of tractors occurs outside agriculture (in industry), the former becomes dependent on industry and must produce surplus to buy the required agricultural machinery, fuel, lubricants and to hire skilled labor to operate and maintain machinery. If agriculture cannot produce this surplus, the resources have to come from outside the agricultural sector, and this often leads to dependence. In the early stage of capitalist development in Europe, industry and agriculture were to a great extent mutually dependent. However, in the majority of African countries, mechanized agriculture depends on foreign industry and imported fuel which means dependence on an acutely scarce resource, foreign exchange.

In case of the refugee land settlements, mechanization is incompatible with the objective of creating self-perpetuating structures which can function independently of outside intervention. What is the alternative? Our findings show that the long-term economic viability of the refugee land settlements requires an alternative system of cultivation which must be within the reach of the means of refugee households. Since disregard of existing customs and practices can often lead to serious problems, the alternative method must develop within the existing local milieu. Such an alternative, in our opinion, must be based on the integration of livestock and crop production. It is important to point out here that our discussion of the alternative cultivation systems is not based on a comparison of profitability between tractors and animal power but rather on acceptability to the farmers and suitability of tractors to the holdings as well as on income level, technological, organizational and sociocultural considerations of the small farmers. The advantage of such a technical integration is that the production of livestock and crops will depend on each other, and this will consequently create the necessary conditions for the achievement of self-reliant agriculture. The livestock will feed on crop residues and hay. Organic manure will be used to improve soil fertility, for soil depletion is one of the major problems facing the refugee land settlements. Animal products such as milk, cream, butter, and meat will be used to improve the refugees' nutritional status. This will in return lead to improved production of crops resulting from improved productivity of labor. The majority of the settlers are former semi-nomads, and traditionally milk was an important component of their food. Hides and skin are also used for different purposes in the settler community. Livestock will also produce draught animals for traction and tilling. If the land is extended, production of fodder crops can also be included in the rotation. Since about 97% of the farm households who practiced farming in their country of origin had animals for draught power, there will be no serious problem in introducing such an activity into the settlement. This will not only benefit the refugees but even the local Sudanese farmers who may eventually learn to use animals for draught power to improve their agricultural production. Lack of 'appropriate technology' is one of the constraints that has limited agricultural production in the traditional sector in the region because the area that can be cultivated by hand tillage in the hard clay soils is very limited. Draught power would enable the Sudanese traditional farmers to increase the area under cultivation. In this way, the refugees and the local population would learn new methods and skills from each other; the refugees would not be considered as a liability by the locals but as transferers of new technology.

The advantages of oxenization over tractorization are among other things that the acquisition prices of oxen and ox plough are cheaper than tractors. The need for foreign exchange is either very little or none. The plough used by the Eritrean peasants is mainly made of wood. According to a report prepared by an agricultural expert for SCC/ESRP,

> The plough he (the Eritrean peasant) uses, the yoke, the beam and handle are made of wood; the main plough which actually does the ploughing, i.e., the mouldboard plough, is made up of a metal piece. The farming utensil is light and it suits the capacity of the draught animals. The plough corresponds to the technical level of the farmer. Being robust, it withstands the acid and stress caused by the ground, the man or the animal. And it also corresponds to the limited means of the user because he has to buy only the metal piece—as for the rest he can prepare it all by himself.
>
> (SCC/ESRP, Agricultural Development Program: 1979-80)

The management and technical skill required for oxenization are within the reach of the settler community. The ox-drawn plough is more suited to small holdings and experiences suggest that the use of oxen for land preparation is cheaper than using tractors and, consequently, that the net crop returns are higher. (See Tables 7.11 and 7.12) The majority of the settlers are former pastoralists and agropastoralists and have the skill and knowledge required to tend livestock; and a considerable proportion of the sample households are already keeping livestock in Qala en Nahal. (See Table 8.6 in Chapter 8)

It is believed that the hard clay-soil in the rainfed central plain in the Gedaref region is difficult to till with draught animals. However, tests carried out in the Nuba maintains on heavy cracking clays similar to those at Qala en Nahal show that it is feasible to use animal traction. The size of the farm units on which the research trials were conducted varied from 11 to 22 feddans. The results show the total cost incurred in tractor mechanization per feddan was about 169% more than what was incurred using animal traction. (See Table 7.11) However, since the results in Table 7.11 do not explicitly show all the details, it is necessary to treat the data with caution, but still this suggests that there is a strong argument for the introduction of animal traction in the refugee land settlements, especially in Qala en Nahal.

Oxenization can also enable the farmer to overcome labor peak requirements by spreading the date of planting; this can consequently enable him to spread risk. Oxenization can also increase the confidence of the farmer because he can himself decide when to plant. Oxen can be owned individually as opposed to tractors.

The majority of the settlers have experience in oxenization, and they claim that they can make ox ploughs with local materials. Unfortunately, the heavily subsidized THS and the dependent mentality generated by the way in which assistance is delivered seems to have somehow incapacitated the settlers from taking initiatives to develop and utilize their traditional methods of farming. They have instead become too dependent on a method which is very unreliable.

According to the Report of the Agricultural Expert submitted to the SCC/ESRP

> The Eritrean national peasant from his early stage of adolescence begins to be trained by his father how to tend livestock, how to prepare farming utensils and finally how to plough by draught animal. This means no individual of crop producing origin is unable to plough by draught animal. Animal traction remains as an alien power for only a small minority, the Beni Amer. . .
>
> (SCC/ESRP Agricultural Development. . . : op.cit., 2)

In Eritrea the ability to make a plough, to farm one's own plot and to tend livestock hold a very central position in the social and economic well-being of the peasant or pastoralist. An individual without these skills is considered to be a person with a social handicap who cannot meet the basic subsistence needs of his family—if indeed he can ever have a family. The use of tractors in the rural refugee settlements has, therefore, instead of enabling the farmers to preserve, improve and transmit their skills to their children, has led to de-skillization. The preservation and improvement of the refugees' farming experience and skill is as important as the attainment of economic self-reliance. When the refugees return to Eritrea, they will depend on animal traction rather than on tractors. Many of the refugees, especially the second generation, have by then lost their knowledge of plough making, practical farming and livestock tending. This may block or slow their reintegration into their previous communities. Thus, the use of oxen would enable the refugees to preserve and improve their knowledge of farming and livestock tending which may in turn consequently facilitate their economic and social reintegration after their eventual return. Without these skills, after their voluntary repatriation, the refugees will represent an enormous burden on their former society and the international community.

TABLE 7.11. Cost Comparisons between Animal Tractor Mechanization from the Nuba Mountain Trials 1979 (£S. per feddan)

Item of Cost	Animal Traction Heavy Soils Crop pattern I	Crop pattern II
Equipment Depreciation		
Land Preparation	1.87	1.87
Sowing	0.92	0.95
Two Weedings	0.71	0.71
Animal Husbandry	1.28	1.28
Management	0.76	0.76
Total Cost	5.50	5.60
	Tractor Mechanization (land preparation only)	
Land Preparation (2 discings)		
Equipment Depreciation	3.00	3.00
Running Cost	3.60	3.60
Sowing	completed by family labor not costed	
Weeding (Twice)	6.90	11.70
Management	1.26	1.26
Total Cost	14.80	19.50

Source:
Nuba Mountains Animal Draught Programme, 1979 Research Report.
Comparison of crop returns also shows that gross returns are exactly the same while net returns per feddan are higher in the area cultivated by animal traction than in the area cultivated by tractors. (See Table 7.11).

Our findings also show that of the sample households about 48% in Umsaqata, 51% in Umbrush, 13% in Dehema and 8% in Adingrar have cattle in the Sudan. This can facilitate the introduction of animal traction.

How do the refugee farmers feel about tractor mechanization? The attitude of the refugee farmers tends to change depending on the condition of the tractors. The majority are positive about the tractors as long as they are in running condition and as long as the operating and capital costs are borne by others. During our survey the performance of the THS was at its apex and the condition of the tractors was also perfect. The service they received was subsidized up to 72% and the farmers were very positive to tractor mechanization. (See Table 7.13) However, when the THS was on the verge of collapse in 1979, the *sheikhs* and other village elders in their meeting with the

TABLE 7.12. Crop Return Comparisons from Animal Traction and Tractor Mechanization from the Nuba Mountains (£S. per feddan)

	Sorghum		Sesame	
	Animal	Tractor	Animal	Tractor
Gross Revenue	39.00	39.00	29.80	29.80
Input Costs:				
Operations	5.50	14.80	5.50	14.80
Seeds	0.25	0.25	0.40	0.40
Dressing	—	—	—	—
Spraying	—	—	—	—
Total Costs	5.75	15.05	5.90	15.20
Net Returns	33.25	23.95	23.90	14.60

Source:
Nuba Mountains Animal Draught Programme, 1979 Research Report. Quoted in Spooner: 1981.

SCC/ESRP agricultural expert (who was in Qala en Nahal 'to make studies relating to agricultural problems which the refugees were facing and thereby suggesting solutions') unanimously identified late sowing caused by late arrival of tractors as the major problem. The agriculturalist requested the village elders to suggest a solution, and all of them suggested that the solution lay in oxenization.

The Agriculturalist stated that,

> The village elders' and *sheikhs'* suggestion as to the method of solving this problem was quite interesting. They forwarded as a suggestion that draught animal traction was applicable to the soil and if a pair of bullocks could be credited or donated for a family or two, it can sufficiently plough two to three *hawashas* of land . . .
>
> (SCC/ESRP Agr. Dev. Prog. 1979-80. 2)

TABLE 7.13 The Sample Households' Attitude towards Tractor Mechanization of Cultivation (per cent)

	Positive	Negative	Total
Umsaqata	89.9	10.2	100.0
Umbrush	91.2	8.8	100.0
Dehema	97.1	2.9	100.0
Adingrar	95.1	4.9	100.0
Aburakham	89.4	10.6	100.0
Wad Awad	89.7	10.3	100.0

It is very interesting to note that none of the elders or *sheikhs* suggested the refurbishment of the THS. The agriculturalist did not set any limit to the kind of suggestions the elders could come up with and they considered oxenization as the most appropriate technology suited to their need and means. The SCC/ESRP Report further notes that,

> It is the wish of the crop producers to plough their land by bullocks if it were not for economic problems, i.e., lack of means of holding a pair of draught animals. Consequently, it is quite obvious that if they had emigrated with their animals (save the Beni Amer from the border areas) as they repeatedly claim, all of them would have ploughed with their own bullocks and tractor ploughing could have been restricted to the vulnerable groups.
>
> (SCC/ESRP: op.cit., 3)

Before the initiative taken by SCC/ESRP, there were a few families which were using draught traction in the refugee land settlements—two families in Zurzur, two in Umbrush, one in Wad Hileu and some in Umrakuba.

After thorough discussions with the village elders, SCC/ESRP decided to give interest-free long-term loans for a few people out of the many people who had asked. The SCC/ESRP Report further states that 'the program did not merely stand on the elders' or *sheikhs* suggestion but it also rested on scientific grounds'. It was noted that all its findings suggested that application of draught traction to the soil texture around Umsaqata area was possible.

Tractor mechanization has, no doubt, resulted in the reduction of drudgery and consequently in increased leisure at least at the time of cultivation and this seems to be the main reason why the clear majority is positive about it. However, since neither the UNHCR nor the other voluntary agencies can be expected to meet the recurrent and costs of new investments indefinitely, the social benefits enjoyed by the refugee farmers alone cannot justify tractor mechanization. Some may argue that since the majority are for tractor mechanization why not respect their desire? The problem is not as simple as that. Can a poor household head who lives within the 'subsistence margin' be expected to respect his wife's desire to buy a diamond? Besides, as noted earlier, the attitude of the refugees fluctuates depending on the performance of the THS

Problems with Oxenization

It is wrong to believe that all problems will come to an end with the substitution of oxen for tractors. The acquisition price of a pair of oxen requires a considerable capital outlay which is beyond the reach of many households. However, if the international donor agencies are willing to meet the costs of tractors which are much higher, it should be possible to raise funds for the purchase of oxen. However, it must be noted that most aid is tied and since it is not possible to tie oxen programs to the industries of the developed countries, it may be difficult to secure capital for this purpose. A credit scheme could also be set up to enable the poor households to purchase oxen. "A typical settlement of 5,000 feddans growing sorghum and sesame" would need "180 trained oxen . . . to cultivate all the land in the settlement". (The Use of Animal Power Cultivation in Refugee Farms on the Central Clay Plain of the Sudan: without date, 3) As noted earlier, some households are keeping cattle in the settlements and these households may not need capital outlay to buy oxen.

One of the primary constraints on livestock production in the area is the shortage of water in the dry season. However, this problem can easily be overcome by moving the livestock to the Rahad river area and by constructing small natural *hafirs* (dams). Another problem encountered by livestock owners in the area is that of biting flies between July and September. At present, the owners move the non-milking cattle to less affected areas temporarily. According to the refugees, this can be overcome by the provision of proper shelter.

At present there is no sufficient veterinary service and diseases like 'anthrax, rinderpest, foot and mouth disease, bovine pleuropneumia' are prevalent in the settlement. (See Fre: 1984) Thus the provision of an effective veterinary service is a precondition for the successful technical integration of livestock and crop production. Another problem encountered by livestock owners in the area is shortage of forage during the dry season. This can have negative effects on draught animals because if they are not properly fed their capacity to draw the plough will be limited. This can be overcome partly by including fodder in the rotation of crops and partly by collecting crop residues such as stalks of sorghum, sesame cake and foliage from plants. Grass can also be cut and collected at the right time before its nutritive value is lost and can be saved for the cultivation season. Such a practice is very common in highland Eritrea. For the majority of the livestock owners, transhumance will still remain necessary until the GOS decides to extend the land bank available in the scheme so that growing of fodder and hay reserves (*Hizaiti* in Tigrinya) will be possible. According to SCC/ESRP's Agricultural Expert's Report,

> Forage in this area is plenty and sufficient amounts of sorghum stem could be collected in the homestead for the hottest and driest months of March, April, and May. In the summertime there is vast grazing land and the bullocks could be tended there.
>
> (SCC/ESRP's Report: op.cit., 3)

Another argument against oxenization is lack of trained animals in the area. This argument is not tenable because no animal is born trained. In Eritrea, especially in the highlands, oxen training does not really require any special skill. There are many refugees among the settlers who can train oxen and who can teach others to do the same.

Therefore, as we argued above, under the present forms of farm organization, financial resources, technical skill and management capacity of the refugees and the host government, oxenization based upon technical integration of livestock and crop production could provide an alternative to the existing system of production.

However, it is important to note that we are not by any means underestimating the relentless efforts exerted by the GOS, the UNHCR, EA-A and other agencies in helping the refugees to achieve self-reliance. The Eritrean refugees in Qala en Nahal have a diverse socioeconomic background. They included pastoralists, agropastoralists, sedentary farmers, landlords, urban dwellers, the skilled, the unskilled, etc. One of the major achievements resulting from mechanization is the fact that the settlers' (past socioeconomic background notwithstanding) understanding of the value of the land they are cultivating has increased drastically. It is difficult to establish whether this could have been achieved in the absence of mechanization. Even though we do not deem it fruitful to engage ourselves in contrafactual conditional arguments, it can still be solidly argued that an alternative method of cultivation which takes cognizance of the beneficiaries' technical, management and financial means would have been easier to operate as well as to sustain after few seasons following the provision of such facilities. Our point of departure has been that the refugee farmers' participation in achieving their own self-reliance is fundamental and that the introduction of farm technology whose sustenance and operation depends on outside assistance is by itself an obstacle to meaningful participation.

CHAPTER 8

Income in the Settlements

The aim of this chapter is to discuss the major sources and distribution of income among the sample households. This will enable us to assess the ability of the different income groups to produce enough to meet their basic needs. Measuring total income in rural areas is very complex, because it is often difficult to estimate and convert the diverse components into monetary values based on market prices. These components may, for example, include vegetables grown in the household's compound, and livestock products such as milk, butter and meat which are consumed by the household itself. When asked to state their annual income, the sample households invariably excluded these. This made it necessary to concentrate on the major sources of the household's income.

The major sources of income in the refugee rural settlements come from farm and non-farm income-generating activities. Non-farm income is here defined to include all income obtained from any kind of income-generating activity other than crop production. In the refugee land settlements these include income obtained from livestock, their products and from other livestock-related activities such as fetching water, firewood, thatching grass, building material and animal feed for sale, all kinds of trade (such as shopkeeping, money lending, café and restaurant operating, camel oil-press ownership, handicraft, local beer (*siwa*) brewing, charcoal burning and wage labor. We have included income from livestock and livestock-related activities in non-farm income because only a few households earned income from livestock and livestock products, while many households earned money by using donkeys and to some extent camels for transport. It would have been more proper to include the latter in income from trade. However, for simplicity, we have designated this income as income related to livestock as only households with donkeys and camels can engage in fetching water, firewood, building materials and thatch grass for sale.

INCOME FROM CROP PRODUCTION

In the high rainfall area of Qala en Nahal, both sesame and sorghum are grown. In the low rainfall areas of Aburakham and Wad Awad, only the staple crop, sorghum, is grown. The distribution of crop returns of the sample households in the 1981-82 agricultural season is given in Tables 8.1 and 8.2. Since crop prices fluctuate drastically from season to season depending on supply and demand, it is best to use returns in quantity rather than monetary values. (In 1981-82 the price of one sack of sorghum (90-100 kg) was £S.16 while in 1985 the price has gone up to £S.130. However, this abnormal drastic price increase is due to shortage of grain caused by drought. Otherwise the sorghum price in the eastern region was for many years extremely low compared to the neighboring countries.)

A considerable proportion of the sample households, i.e., about 25% had zero return from sorghum in the 1981-82 agricultural season. Beside the landless households which we saw in Chapter 5, there are few households who, due to crop failure, did not obtain a return from sorghum. If we exclude Wad Awad, the number of households without any return from sorghum is about 27%. The level of crop return as can be seen from Table 8.1 is higher in the villages of Qala en Nahal than in the settlements of Aburakham and Wad Awad. In the latter settlements none of the sample households reported having received over 30 sacks of sorghum in the said season, while in Qala en Nahal some households obtained up to 60 sacks. Crop return among the sample households varied from 0 to 60 sacks. Sorghum is a low value crop. In the same year, the average price of sorghum was about £S.16 per sack. (This price refers to the market price received by the farmers when they sell their crop to merchants.)

As can be seen from Table 8.2, in the high rainfall area of Qala en Nahal, sesame represents an important source of income; about 52% of the total sample households earned an income from sesame, varying from one sack to 12 sacks. Sesame is a high value crop. One sack of sesame (100 kg) was worth about £S.50 in 1981-82. The price increased drastically in the following year, up to £S.75.

About 48% of the sample households had no income from sesame. These are landless refugees, refugees whose land holdings are not big enough to allow diversification and marginal farmers whose production decisions, as we saw in Chapter 6, are governed by the 'subsistence ethic', i.e., refugees who give priority to food crop production and farmers whose plots did not receive timely cultivation.

Table 8.3 gives the total crop return of the sample households in monetary value based on the market prices that prevailed in the 1981-82 agricultural year.

The significance of sesame production is very clear from the income level of the villages as none of the households in Aburakham and Wad Awad earned more than £S.500 from crop production.

TABLE 8.1 Percentage Distribution of Sorghum Return among the Sample Households in 1981–82

Quantity in sacks	Umsaqata	Umbrush	Dehema	Adingrar	Aburakham	Wad Awad	Total
0	30.0	31.1	29.8	22.0	25.4	3.1	24.6
1– 5	1.7	2.2	4.5	8.0	6.8	3.1	4.4
6–10	11.7	8.9	10.6	12.0	22.0	31.2	15.3
11–15	11.7	6.7	21.3	12.0	22.0	15.6	15.3
16–20	8.3	17.8	6.3	12.0	16.9	28.1	14.0
21–25	10.0	13.3	10.6	10.0	3.4	12.5	9.5
26–30	8.3	6.7	8.5	8.0	3.4	6.2	7.2
31–35	3.3	6.7	4.3	4.0	—	—	3.1
36–40	5.0	2.2	2.1	6.0	—	—	2.7
41–45	3.3	2.2	2.1	6.0	—	—	2.3
46–50	3.3	2.2	—	—	—	—	1.0
51–55	1.7	—	—	—	—	—	0.3
56–60	1.7	—	—	—	—	—	0.3
Total	100.0	100.0	100.1	100.0	99.9	99.8	100.0

TABLE 8.2. Percentage Distribution of Sesame Returns among the Sample Households by Village

Quantity in sacks	Umsaqata	Umbrush	Dehema	Adingrar	Aburakham*	Wad Awad*	Total
0	50.0	52.3	48.9	38.0			47.8
1	1.7	2.3	4.3	6.0			3.5
2	3.3	9.1	17.0	12.0			9.9
3	1.7	4.5	10.6	16.0			8.0
4	15.0	6.8	4.3	12.0			9.9
5	8.3	15.9	6.4	6.0			9.0
6	8.3	4.5	6.4	4.0			6.0
7	3.3	4.5	—	4.0			3.0
8	5.0	—	2.1	2.0			2.0
9	—	—	—	—			—
10	1.7	—	—	—			0.5
11	—	—	—	—			—
12	1.7	—	—	—			0.5
Total	100.0	99.9	100.0	100.0			100.1

* Due to climatic conditions, no sesame is grown in these settlements.

TABLE 8.3 Percentage Distribution of the Sample Households by Returns Obtained from Crop Production—Sorghum and Sesame (£S.)

Crop Income in £S.	Umsaqata	Umbrush	Dehema	Adingrar	Aburakham	Wad Award	Total
0	28.3	28.9	29.8	22.0	25.4	3.1	23.5
1– 100	1.7	2.2	4.3	4.0	8.5	12.5	5.1
101– 200	8.3	6.7	8.5	10.0	25.4	28.1	14.0
201– 300	8.3	13.3	6.4	10.0	30.5	25.0	16.0
301– 400	8.3	11.1	25.5	8.0	6.8	25.0	13.0
401– 500	15.0	8.9	4.2	12.0	3.4	6.2	8.5
501– 600	5.0	11.1	6.4	14.0	—	—	6.1
601– 700	3.3	2.2	4.3	4.0	—	—	2.4
701– 800	1.7	4.4	4.3	—	—	—	1.7
801– 900	6.7	6.7	4.3	8.0	—	—	4.4
901–1000	1.7	—	—	6.0	—	—	1.7
1001–1100	5.0	2.2	—	2.0	—	—	1.4
1101–1200	5.0	2.2	2.1	—	—	—	1.7
over 1200	1.7	—	—	—	—	—	0.3
Total	100.0	99.9	100.1	100.0	100.0	99.9	99.8

If we divide the sample households into different socioeconomic categories, we see that the very poor and the poor households do not derive any considerable return from cash crop production while the medium and the high-income households derive a substantial proportion of their crop return from cash crops. Among the very poor and poor households about 86 and 78% of their crop return was obtained from sorghum, respectively, while only 14 and 22%, respectively, was derived from cash crop production.

INCOME FROM OTHER SOURCES

These are, as noted earlier, incomes from all kinds of non-farm income-generating activities.

Household Income from Wage Labor

For the landless households, except in Aburakham, income earned from wage labor represents a major source of material livelihood. According to the survey, about 75% of the total income of the landless households came from wage labor. Aburakham has a different characteristic in that only about 38% of the landless households' annual income came from wage labor and about 62% of their annual income originated from other non-farm income-generating activities, mainly trade. This shows that most of the landless households in Aburakham are from the vulnerable groups who, due to lack of able-bodied family members, cannot cultivate land and consequently cannot even work for wages.

About 45% of the sample households did not work for wages in 1981-82. These are mainly households whose income from their own production and/or other income-generating activities was enough to meet their consumption needs. They also include families which lack sufficient family labor to allow them to diversify their economic activities. In these are also included vulnerable families with physically handicapped and aged members and families that are female-headed without able-bodied household members. As we saw in Chapter 7, working for wages for those who possess land is often detrimental to the family's crop production if it is undertaken to the neglect of the family's own farm. However, there are also some skilled household heads who have regular employment and depend on hired farm labor.

Household Income from Trade

The refugee households are engaged in a broad variety of non-farm income-generating activities in order to secure their material existence. Some of these non-farm activities include shopkeeping, running restaurants and cafés, bakeries. For example, in 1983 there were 32 camel oil presses, 36 restaurants, 63 shops, 15 bakeries, 21 butcher shops, and 34 vegetable stalls in the 6 villages of Qala en Nahal owned by refugees.

As can be seen from Table 8.5, about 18% of the sample households were

TABLE 8.4. Percentage Distribution of the Sample Households by Income Obtained from Wage Labor

Wage Labor Income £S.	Umsaqata	Umbrush	Dehema	Adingrar	Aburakham	Wac Awad	All Sample
0	40.0	48.9	48.9	38.0	47.5	53.1	45.4
1–50	16.7	11.1	—	6.0	—	—	6.1
51–100	11.7	15.5	8.5	24.0	1.7	12.5	11.9
101–150	8.3	8.9	23.4	10.0	8.5	12.5	11.6
151–200	3.3	2.2	6.4	6.0	23.7	9.4	8.9
201–250	1.7	4.4	4.3	—	3.4	—	2.4
251–300	6.7	—	2.1	6.0	6.8	3.1	4.4
301–350	5.0	6.7	4.3	2.0	1.7	—	3.4
351–400	3.3	2.2	—	4.0	1.7	—	2.0
401–450	—	—	2.1	2.0	—	—	0.7
451–500	1.7	—	—	—	1.7	—	0.7
501–550	—	—	—	—	—	3.1	0.3
551–600	—	—	—	—	—	3.1	0.3
over 600	1.7	—	—	2.0	3.4	3.1	1.7
Total	100.1	99.9	100.0	100.0	100.1	99.9	99.8

engaged in trade and had earned a considerable proportion of their income from it. If we were to include the income from the sale of water, firewood, thatch grass and building materials in this category, the number of households engaged in trade would be much higher. Our findings also show that those households with substantial non-farm sources of income often obtain higher crop returns. This is mainly because they use their capital or money accumulated in non-farm enterprises for agriculture. They can, for instance, hire labor for weeding, harvesting and clearing. They can also rent or purchase land belonging to other poor households.

There are many shops and other non-farm economic activities in the settlements and this is important for various reasons. First, it reflects the growing social division of labor among the settlers. Most of these activities employ at least two people, which means that about 480 people work in them, some of whom also take part in farming during agricultural seasons. Second, it reflects the growth of the home market whereby, as more and more people become landless, they join the ranks of the agricultural laborers, who fully depend on purchased commodities for personal consumption. As more and more farmers become marginalized, due to change in the land holding system in the settlements, they are less and less able to produce their own subsistence, and their dependence on purchased commodities increases. This leads to the expansion of the home market.

Household Income from Livestock and Related Activities

A considerable proportion of the households earn income from livestock proceeds, products and from activities related to livestock. With the ever-rising demand for beef and other livestock products in the Sudan and in the Middle East, this represents a considerable source of income for a few households. Donkeys and camels are used for carrying water, firewood, thatching grass, building materials and animal feed both for sale and for the households' own use. Camels are also used for the same purpose as well as for transporting crops from the farm to the villages. During the rainy season some families sell milk in the settlements.

Although the refugees in the land settlements in Eastern Sudan are of diverse socioeconomic background, for the majority of the settlers in Qala en Nahal livestock have been the main basis of existence for many centuries. Livestock also play a key role among the settled agriculturalists and agropastoralists in Eritrea. Livestock are the major form of wealth and also have important functions which maintain social relations. In addition, livestock in Eritrea are used as a source of power in cultivation, threshing and transport. Animal dung is also used as fertilizer and for fuel, and above all animal products are used as the major if not the only source of protein. Socially, livestock are used as bridewealth, funeral sacrifice, and in feasts for births, marriages and other important occasions. Extracontractual liabilities arising from homicide are also paid in livestock form.

TABLE 8.5. Percentage Distribution of the Sample Households by Income Obtained from Trade

Income in £S.	Umsaqata	Umbrush	Dehema	Adingrar	Aburakham	Wad Awad	Total
0	86.4	80.0	91.5	90.5	74.6	62.5	82.4
1–100	—	6.7	—	4.0	3.4	—	2.7
101–200	1.7	2.2	2.1	—	5.1	6.2	2.1
201–300	1.7	—	—	—	1.7	9.4	1.7
301–400	—	2.2	—	—	3.4	6.2	1.7
401–500	—	2.2	—	—	1.7	—	1.0
501–600	1.7	2.2	—	4.0	5.1	6.2	2.4
601–700	—	—	—	—	—	3.1	1.7
701–800	5.1	2.2	2.1	—	—	—	1.0
801–900	1.7	2.2	2.1	—	—	—	0.7
901–1000	1.7	—	—	—	—	—	1.0
Over 1000	—	—	2.1	2.0	5.1	6.2	1.4
Total	100.0	99.9	99.9	100.0	100.1	99.8	99.8

When the refugees fled Eritrea some of them took their livestock with them, others abandoned them and there were others who claimed that their livestock were killed in the war. There were also a few households who reported that the Ethiopian army confiscated their livestock. Several factors determined whether the refugee households took their livestock to the Sudan. These are first, geographical proximity to the border areas, second, the nature of the incident that gave rise to flight, and third, mere chance. Those refugees whose places of origin were far from the border reported that taking their livestock would have exposed them. Hence they were forced to abandon them when they fled. Those who fled from just across the border did not have the same problem. If the military attacks were sudden and intense, the refugees fled for their lives. But those refugees who fled before the attack had time to take their livestock with them. For example, about 54% of the sample households in Umsaqata that had livestock in Eritrea reported taking them to the Sudan. Some of the households' livestock were not present when the incidents that caused flight occurred, and the shepherds later came to the Sudan with their livestock to join their relatives. Out of the 47% that reported having abandoned their livestock when they fled, a considerable proportion reported that their livestock was brought to them later in the Sudan.

We have compared the households' ownership of livestock in Eritrea and in the Sudan, and the results are given in Table 8.6. Fewer refugee households own cattle and camels in the Sudan than in Eritrea. The results in Table 8.6 show that livestock still play an important economic and social role in the settlements. However, it is important to note that data on livestock, and consequently income from livestock, are often underestimated by the refugees for two reasons. First, they want to avoid the tax payment which is levied per head. The settlement headquarters and the various *sheikhs* try to assess the number of livestock every three years by going as far as Semsem and Rahad, while the owners often try to avoid having their livestock counted. Second, counting of livestock is traditionally thought to bring bad fortune.

In order to estimate the number of livestock owned by the refugees, we examined the tax records in the administration headquarters and we found that the figures were gross underestimations. We doubted the accuracy of the figures because we saw many more goats in the villages and donkeys at the water points than the number indicated in the records. According to the tax records there were only 332 goats and 302 donkeys. We therefore decided to disregard the information in the official records and instead to ask the sample households whether they owned livestock. We cannot be sure that the households told the truth, but the uncertainty is more with regard to numbers than ownership. Furthermore, we made it clear that the information was being gathered purely for academic purposes and would not be used for taxation purposes. Therefore we feel sure that our information is more reliable than that given to government officials whose major concern in livestock counting is tax assessment. The amount of tax paid by livestock owners is very

TABLE 8.6. Percentage Distribution of the Sample Refugees by Livestock Ownership in Eritrea and the Sudan

Village	Cattle		Camels		Goats		Sheep		Donkeys	
	Eritrea	Sudan	Eritrea	Sudan	Eritrea	Sudan	Eritrea	Sudan	Eritrea	Sudan
Umsaqata	82.0	48.3	42.6	25.0	63.9	65.0	11.5	36.1	49.2	59.0
Umbrush	86.7	51.1	28.9	8.9	48.9	53.3	11.1	24.4	51.0	53.3
Dehema	57.4	12.8	12.8	2.1	59.6	57.4	8.5	40.4	40.4	46.8
Adingrar	76.0	8.0	26.0	2.0	52.0	64.0	12.0	26.0	50.0	52.0
Aburakham	39.9	—	3.4	—	30.5	32.0	11.9	18.6	33.9	25.4
Wad Awad	65.0	—	6.2	—	40.6	37.5	15.6	15.6	50.0	34.3

considerable, and the households have every reason not to reveal the real information about their livestock. (See Table 8.7)

TABLE 8.7. Livestock Annual Tax/Head in the Settlement (Qala en Nahal)

Year	Cattle	Camels	Donkeys	Sheep	Goats
1976	0.45	0.60	0.12	0.15	0.10
1977	0.45	0.60	0.12	0.15	0.10
1978	0.45	0.60	0.12	0.15	0.10
1979	0.60	1.20	0.25	0.18	0.13
1980	0.60	1.20	0.25	0.18	0.13
1981	0.60	1.20	0.25	0.18	0.13
1982	0.60	1.20	0.25	0.18	0.13
1983	2.00	3.00	0.50	0.25	0.18

Source: Administration Tax Records, Umsaqata, 1976–1983.

The data in Table 8.6 show that while the proportion of the households owning cattle and camel in the settlements has declined drastically when compared with the pre-flight period, the proportion of households owning goats, sheep and donkeys in the settlement has increased considerably. Our findings also show that the number of livestock owned per household is much less in the settlement than in the pre-flight period.

Despite the fact that livestock was the basis of existence especially for the refugees in the Qala en Nahal settlement, planning did not take this into account. In Qala en Nahal, where there is a shortage of water, the refugees are not allowed to keep their cattle within the scheme between October and June. In the other settlements, the refugees face serious problems due to lack of fodder, and as can be seen from Table 8.6 none of the households in Aburakham and Wad Awad keeps cattle. The limited land does not allow cultivation of fodder nor sufficient grazing within the scheme. It is not clear why animal husbandry is disregarded in the planning, but it is probably due to the relatively low profitability of livestock as compared to alternative land use in Kassala Province.

Many of the households have made their own adjustments with regard to livestock ownership, and a considerable proportion are deriving returns from livestock and other livestock-related economic activities. (See Table 8.8)

Among the sample households, about 33% reported earning incomes from livestock ownership varying from £S.1 to over £S.500. Our findings show that donkeys play a central role in providing a basis of material existence for the poor households, especially during the dry season when other employment opportunities are none or very few.

TABLE 8.8. Percentage Distribution of the Sample Households by Income Obtained from Livestock-related Economic Activities

Income in £S.	Umsaqata	Umbrush	Dehema	Adingrar	Aburakham	Wad Awad	Total
0	53.3	60.0	59.6	72.0	81.2	81.2	67.2
1–50	3.3	4.4	2.1	8.0	1.7	—	3.4
51–100	16.7	11.1	19.1	6.0	—	3.1	9.5
101–150	3.3	4.4	8.5	12.0	6.8	6.2	6.8
151–200	6.7	8.9	4.3	2.0	6.8	9.4	6.1
201–250	—	6.7	4.3	—	—	—	1.7
251–300	3.3	4.4	—	—	3.4	—	2.0
351–350	6.7	—	2.1	—	—	—	1.4
351–400	—	—	—	—	—	—	1.4
over 400	6.7	—	—	—	—	—	
Total	100.0	99.9	100.0	100.0	99.9	99.9	99.5

Household Income from Remittance

This includes all income obtained from relatives and friends living outside the refugee land settlement both within the Sudan and abroad. To our surprise, unlike urban refugees who live to a great extent on remittances from the Middle East, Europe and America, only a very small proportion of the sample households reported receiving remittance during the study period. (See Table 8.9) Only a few families received income from this source because the settlers are primarily former semi-pastoralists, and their children lack the necessary skill and education to enable them to gain employment in Sudanese towns or abroad. The proportion of the households that reported receiving remittance is higher in the villages of Wad Awad and Umbrush; this is because a number of these families have some children and relatives in the Middle East. But, generally remittance does not represent a considerable source of income. About 90% of the sample households did not receive income from this source during the period under study.

Total Household Income

It is difficult to estimate total household income but for our purpose it is defined to include crop returns (sorghum and sesame), income from livestock and other livestock-related activities, charcoal production, wage labor, trade, handicraft and from all other income-generating activities. (In Aburakham there were a few female-headed households that earned some income from the sale of alcohol and home brewed beer. However, this activity is strictly prohibited after the introduction of *sharia* law in 1983. If alternative income-generating activities are not introduced, these households will suffer seriously.)

Table 8.10 shows that 3.4% of the sample households had no source of income except the free rations they received from the World Food Program (WFP) and the social aid from SCC/ESRP. Out of the total sample, about 56% have a total annual income of up to £S.500, 27% have between £S.501-1,000 and 2% have over £S.2,000. Among the last, 67% are from the settlement of Umsaqata. In all the sample villages, about 23% of the sample households earned an annual income of over £S.700, whereas in the four villages of Qala en Nahal about 25% of the sample have earned over £S.700 in the 1981-82 agricultural season.

The level of total household annual income in the rural refugee land settlements is very low when compared with the average rural household income in Kassala Province and in the rainfed Gedaref area. In 1981-82 agricultural year, the average household annual income in the rural refugee land settlements was in the range of £S.558 (See Table 8.12). The corresponding average household's annual income in the rural areas in Kassala Province was £S.1295. A recent ILO-UNHCR study of *Labor Markets in the Sudan* also shows that the annual household income in the three survey villages in the rainfed areas in the Gedaref region was comparatively very high. Among the 296 sample households only about 9% had below £S.500, while 38% had

TABLE 8.9. Percentage Distribution of the Sample Households by Income Obtained from Remittance in £S. per Annum (per cent)

Income in £S.	Umsaqata	Umbrush	Dehema	Adingrar	Aburakham	Wad Awad	All sample
0	96.7	75.0	95.7	92.0	94.9	75.0	89.7
1–100	—	8.9	—	2.0	1.7	—	2.0
101–200	—	8.9	—	2.0	1.7	9.4	3.1
201–300	—	2.2	—	2.0	—	9.4	1.7
301–400	3.3	2.2	2.1	—	1.7	—	1.7
401–500	—	2.2	2.1	2.0	—	6.2	1.7
Total	100.0	99.9	99.9	100.0	100.0	100.0	99.9

TABLE 8.10. Percentage Distribution of the Sample Households by Total Income (£S.)

Income in £S.	Umsaqata	Umbrush	Dehema	Adingrar	Aburakham	Wad Awad	Total
0	3.3	2.2	4.3	2.0	6.8	—	3.4
1–100	3.3	4.4	2.1	4.0	3.4	3.1	3.4
101–200	—	2.2	6.4	6.0	8.5	3.1	4.4
201–300	10.0	11.1	19.1	8.0	11.9	9.4	11.6
301–400	26.7	20.0	17.0	16.0	25.4	28.1	22.2
401–500	8.3	20.0	19.1	14.0	13.5	12.5	14.3
501–600	5.0	8.9	10.6	16.0	11.9	9.4	10.2
601–700	8.3	8.9	4.3	12.0	3.4	9.4	7.5
701–800	6.7	4.4	4.3	4.0	6.8	3.1	5.1
801–900	5.0	6.7	6.4	6.0	—	9.4	5.1
901–1000	8.3	2.2	—	6.0	—	3.1	3.4
1001–1100	—	4.4	—	—	1.7	3.1	1.4
1101–1200	3.3	—	—	—	1.7	—	1.0
1201–1300	1.7	—	—	—	—	3.1	0.7
1301–1400	1.7	—	—	2.0	—	—	0.7
1401–1500	—	—	—	—	1.7	—	0.3
over 1500	8.3	4.4	6.4	4.0	3.4	3.1	5.1
Total	99.9	99.8	100.0	100.0	100.1	99.9	99.8

between £S.500-1,499, and about 53% of the sample had between £S.1,500 and over £S.20,000 in the 1981-82 agricultural year. (See ILO-UNHCR: 1984, 32.) However, it is wrong to compare the income of the refugee households with that of the ILO-UNHCR survey because the latter was not only based on small farmers but also included commercial farmers who possessed up to over 500 feddans of cultivable land. Furthermore, the villages included in the survey were not typical rural villages because

> since the surveys were carried out in the rainy season when access to villages off asphalt roads is very difficult—villages near the Khartoum-Port Sudan road were selected.
>
> (ILO-UNHCR: 1984, 22)

This is very significant because many such villages operate cafés and restaurants on the Khartoum-Port Sudan roadside which generate substantial non-farm income. Households away from the asphalt roads do not have such an opportunity and, if such villages were included in the survey, the results would have been considerably different.

Socioeconomic Differentiation

As noted earlier, the level of annual household income in the rural refugee land settlements is relatively very low. However, despite this, the distribution of income among the households as given in Table 8.10 is relatively differentiated. The total income of the sample households varied from £S.0 to £S.2,270 per annum. This large difference indicates that, despite the generally low level of income, some households are relatively better off than others. To show the level of differentiation among the sample households, we have grouped them into four income groups. Classification of small farmers into four income groups is unusual in the literature of peasant studies. However, since there is a substantial difference in the income level between the very poor and the poor households, lumping the two groups together would mask the differences between them.

The classification of the households into four income groups is done partly by taking the minimum annual income necessary for a household of average size to meet its basic needs and partly by taking into account the differences of income among the households. The latter is important because there is no generally valid criterion by which to classify rural households into various income groups. The income level of all the households can be very low compared to the level of income in a certain province, but if we take the income level of the households independently, it can be differentiated, and this differentiation of income is, as we pointed out earlier, a result of differential access to the resource base. The ILO-UNHCR Survey, in classifying the surveyed households into three income groups considers that less than £S.1,500 is poor, £S.1,500-9,999 is medium-income and more than £S.10,000 is rich, but these households are not operating within the same resource constraints as the refugees and it is wrong to use the same criteria for the classification of the refugee households. In limiting the size of the holding allocated to the refugee families to 10 feddans, the GOS was not trying to create refugee commercial farmers. Since the ILO-UNHCR Survey included both commercial and small farmers, the level of income is naturally higher than among the small refugee farmers. Thus the classification of the refugees households into rich, medium, poor and very poor is mainly done for analytical purposes and to show the differential access of the different income groups to resources within the given physical limitations and resource constraints in the settlements.

For our purposes the very poor households are those whose total income per year is between £S.0 and £S.350; the poor households are those whose annual income varied from £S.351 to £S.500; the medium income group are those households whose annual total income is between £S.501-900; while the rich households' annual total income is between £S.901-2,270. The distribution of the sample households according to income groups and by village is given in Table 8.11.

Our findings show that the very poor households are the landless unskilled laborers, the female-headed households without able-bodied teenage male children and marginal farmers who either, due to lack of sufficient cultivable land or family labor or lack of food during the hungry season, cannot produce enough to meet their annual need for consumption. These households constitute about 36% of the total sample. In Qala en Nahal, about 58% of the very poor households are landless, and about 64% of those with original land allocations have lost part of their holdings, their present holdings being smaller than what was originally allocated to them. Some of them have rented out, sharecropped, mortgaged or abandoned parts of their holdings. Some of them also share their holdings with their married sons. Shifts in land possession do not yet exist in the relatively new settlements of Aburakham and Wad Awad. However, in the former about 25% of the poorest households are landless. The average annual income of the poorest households is £S.232. However, this conceals the poverty that has gripped some of the households. Some households earn nothing or very little. For instance, in 1981-82 there were 10 households with no income at all who depended completely on food aid.

The poor households constitute about 23% of the total sample. Their annual income varied from £S.352-500, with an average of £S.415. In Qala en Nahal about 19% of them are landless, and among those with allotments, 39% now have less land than was originally allocated to them. Much of their land has been alienated in the same ways as noted above.

The farmers in the middle-income group constitue about 27% of the total sample, and their income varies from £S.501-900 with an annual average of £S.657. Only 5% of this category in Qala en Nahal and 15% in Aburakham are

TABLE 8.11. Average Income and Percentage Distribution of the Sample Households by Income Level (Average Income in Sudanes £s)

	Umsaqata		Umbrush		Dehema		Adingrar		Aburakham		Wad Awad		Total	
	Av. inc.	%	Av. inc.	%	Av. inc.	%	Av. inc.	%	Av. inc.	%	Av. inc.	%	Av. inc.	%
Very poor	245	32.0	247	38.0	228	40.0	209	24.0	217	47.0	268	31.0	232	36
Poor	402	18.0	444	22.0	405	28.0	416	26.0	408	22.0	424	25.0	415	23
Middle	667	25.0	699	29.0	629	21.0	648	38.0	617	22.0	681	31.0	657	27
Rich	1479	25.0	1395	11.0	1315	11.0	1381	12.0	1477	8.0	1285	13.0	1414	14
Total		100.0		100.0		100.0		100.0		99.9		100.0		100

landless. In Qala en Nahal about 65% of them have between 8 and 10 feddans of land, but about 41% now have less land than was initially allocated to them; 20% have more land while 39% have the same amount of land as their original allocation.

The rich households have economic activities which are relatively highly diversified. These include farming on quite a large scale, processing agricultural products (flour milling and oil pressing), money and commodity lending, and various other commercial activities. These households constitute about 14% of the total sample, but their annual income makes up 35% of the sample households' total annual income. Their annual income was between £S.901 and £S.2,270 with an annual average of £S.1,414. About 61% of them have more than 10 feddans of cultivable land. Only one household is landless but it has substantial income from non-farm activities. A few of the heads of the rich households are skilled laborers who employ daily laborers with the income obtained from wage labor. Since most of the heads of rich households are engaged in non-farm activities, they are the major employers of daily agricultural laborers.

Our study of income distribution among the four income groups shows that the annual incomes of the households vary considerably. The poorest section constitutes 36% of the total sample, but its annual income is only 15% of the total income. The poor households constitute about 23% of the total sample and their annual income represents only about 17% of the total. The middle-income group represents about 27% of the sample and its annual income constitutes about 32% of the total annual income. However, the annual income of the rich households constitutes about 35% of all the households' total income despite their making up only about 14% of the total sample households.

THE IMPORTANCE OF NON-FARM INCOME

The total annual farm and non-farm incomes by villages are given in Table 8.12. The ratio of the off-farm income to farm income varied from settlement to settlement. However, the ratio (except in the settlements of Adingrar and Umbrush) is over 40%, especially high in the settlements of Aburakham and Wad Awad. The land allocated to the households in these two villages is both small and ecologically highly marginal, and the households are forced to engage in a broad variety of non-farm income-generating activities to provide a basis of material existence. According to the agricultural officer in Aburakham, these activities are often carried out to the neglect of their own plots. Many of the households are uncertain about the viability of their small holdings and engage in wage labor and other non-farm activities to secure a minimum income. This behavior supports the view which we raised before—whenever a farm cannot guarantee a certain stable minimum income which will sustain the household and allow it to meet its social obligations, the household tends to engage in alternative activities which will guarantee it a minimum income. However, it must also be noted that if the farm can secure the household a minimum stable income which does guarantee the sustenance of the household, the head of the household tends to be reluctant to abandon his holding even in favor of more promising, but uncertain, income-generating activities. Whether a holding can generate the minimum income is determined by the household's past experience with the holding, by the climate and by the condition of the crop after sowing.

Even in the settlement of Qala en Nahal, a considerable proportion of the households' total income is generated by non-farm activities. It is interesting to note that this occurred despite 1981-82 being a relatively bumper season. The results would have been less surprising if there had been a crop failure that season, as the proportion of the farm income would have been smaller. Our findings show that the overwhelming majority of the households are engaged in a broad variety of non-farm income-generating activities: the majority to provide a basis of material existence; the rich minority to obtain a surplus which in turn is used in shopkeeping, money lending, renting of land, hiring of farm labor, etc.

Farm and non-farm activities are, however, very closely tied together in the settlements. About 45% of the total household income in money terms emanated from non-farm economic activities. Out of the total non-farm income, about 44% was from casual and regular employement within or outside the settlements. Non-farm activities include construction, tailoring, mat and basket making, weaving, embroidery, charcoal burning, fetching water, firewood, building materials, thatch grass and animal feed for sale, laundry and barbering. Firewood and water sales provide a basis of material existence for many families in all the settlements. Our results show that about 49% of the sample households do not fetch their own water but purchase from 'water sellers' who fetch it with donkeys. (The demand for water brought by the water sellers is so high that competition among customers sometimes drives prices very high.) Out of the total sample households, only about 18% did not obtain income from non-farm income-generating activities.

About 53% of the very poor households' annual income is derived from wage labor and 34% of the very poor households in Qala en Nahal derived 100% of their income solely from wage labor. The significance of wage labor, however, declines drastically among the higher income groups. Among the poor households, income from wage labor represents 26%. But among the middle and rich farmers, its share declines to about 13 and 8%, respectively. There are five skilled laborers who earn substantial amount of income among the rich households. Most of the middle farmers and all of the rich farmers employ daily laborers while they spend ,most of their time in off-farm income-generating activities.

The proportion of income from crop production, on the other hand,

TABLE 8.12. Proportion of Crop and Non-farm Income by Village (£S)

Settlement	Total Crop Value	% of Total Value	Average Household Crop Income	Total Value of Non-farm Income	% of Total Value	Average Household Non-farm Income	Total Value of Income	Average Household Total Income
Umsaqata	24,332	57.2	405	17,734	42.2	296	42,066	701
Umbrush	15,198	61.8	338	9,410	38.2	209	24,608	547
Dehema	13,904	58.3	296	9,931	41.7	211	23,835	507
Adingrar	19,024	66.9	381	9,431	33.1	189	23,455	569
Aburakham	9,216	34.2	156	17,758	65.8	301	26,974	457
Wad Awad	7,520	43.2	235	9,906	56.8	310	17,426	544
Total	89,194	54.6	304	74,170	45.4	253	163,364	558

This includes remittance and distribution of rations and social aid provided to the vulnerable groups, the former by the WFP and the latter by SCC/ESRP.

TABLE 8.13. Components of the Households Income (Per cent)

Income Group	Crop Return	Income from Wage Labor	Other Income-generating Activity	Total
Very poor	35.6	52.8	11.6	100.0
Poor	59.1	26.0	14.9	100.0
Medium	64.1	12.9	23.0	100.0
Rich	53.3	8.4	38.2	99.9

increases from the bottom upwards with slight decline among the rich. The greater proportion of the poor, middle and rich households' income is derived from crop production. Another interesting observation that we can make from Table 8.13 is that the higher the income group, the higher the income earned from non-farm income-generating activity. As can be seen, non-farm income activity apart from wage labor does not represent a substantial source of income among the very poor households. However, its share continuously increases as one goes up the ladder. This has enabled the rich farmers to rent, sharecrop and purchase land belonging to the marginal farmers. Farm and non-farm income reinforce each other to secure the dominant position of the rich households. One important aspect in the poor-rich households' relationship is the fact that the rich households, especially the shopkeepers, play a key role in sustaining the poor households during the hungry season. To live through shortage of food and other commodities, the poor households borrow from the shopkeepers. When the head of the household leaves the settlement to work in the rainfed or irrigated agricultural schemes, his family borrows from the shopkeepers until the head of the household returns and makes good what has been borrowed. This system leads to indebtedness of the very poor and poor households, but without it these families would not be able to get through the crises that occur often, not only during the hungry seasons, but also during periods of crop failure.

FOOD TO THE VULNERABLE

As can be seen from the above tables, some households have no sources of income. How do these families survive? After the 1980 Khartoum Conference, an agreement was entered between the GOS and the World Food Program (WFP). According to this agreement, the WFP agreed to

> ... supply the Government at Port Sudan with the following commodities —the total value of which inclusive cost of freight, insurance, superintention and storage is estimated at US$17,131,000.

TABLE 8.14. WFP Commitmentment to Vulnerable Groups in the Settlements, July, 1981—July, 1984

Settlement	No. of refugees classified as vulnerable old	current	Duration of assistance	Sorghum M/t	Dried skim milk	Edible fat M/t	Pulses M/t	Fish Protein
Es Suki	1,500	1,900	Three years	648,000	64,800	48,600	48,600	
Aburakham	250	320	" "	108,000	10,800	8,100	8,100	
Wad Awad	109	200	" "	47,000	4,700	3,500	3,500	
Qala en Nahal	400	—	" "	173,000	17,300	13,000	13,000	
Umsrakoba	100	300	" "	43,000	4,300	3,200	3,200	
Towawa	1,170	445	" "	505,000	50,500	38,000	38,000	
Umgulja	—	750						
Umgurgur	850	900		367,000	36,700	27,500	27,500	
Kohkora	—	324						
Km 26	290	580	" "	126,000	12,500	9,400	9,400	
Kashin el Girba	190	240	" "	82,200	8,200	6,100	6,100	
Port Sudan	1,000	1,000	" "	430,200	43,000	32,000	32,000	
Total	5,859	6,959		2,529,400	252,800	198,400	189,400	3,000

Source: Letter of Readiness concerning WFP, Project 2503 — Assistance to the Settlements of Refugees — Vulnerable Groups 23/6/81

(Plan of Operations Agreed upon between the GOS and UN/FAO Food Program Concerning Assistance to the Settlement of Refugees in the Sudan. Project No. 2503, p.5)

It was further agreed that the WFP assistance would be provided for three years from the date distribution began. Out of this food, a certain amount is allocated to the vulnerable groups in the settlements.

Table 8.14 shows the total amount of assistance to be provided to the vulnerable groups in all the settlements in Eastern Sudan over three years. The vulnerable groups are defined as members of the refugee community who, due to age, sickness, physical handicap, etc., cannot engage in income-generating activities, or who, if they do, cannot produce enough for their subsistence. Female-headed households without able-bodied adults are also counted as vulnerable.

In February 1983, there were 320 and 200 vulnerable groups who were receiving food rations from the WFP in the settlements of Aburakham and Wad Awad, respectively. Before the renewal of the list of the vulnerable groups in 1983, there were 400 persons receiving free food distribution in the six villages of Qala en Nahal. According to the WFP representative in Gedaref, the level of welfare in the Qala en Nahal was such that the community can, without any outside assistance, take care of its own vulnerable groups, and accordingly free distribution of rations was going to be stopped. There is no doubt that the aggregate level of income is higher in Qala en Nahal than in the other settlements, but as we saw earlier, despite the relatively reasonable income earned by some households, there are still others whose annual income is far below the minimum income required to sustain them.

During the period of the survey, although some voluntary agencies were aware that the vulnerable groups needed to become self-reliant, no concrete measures were taken to introduce any income-generating activities to them which were suitable to their situation.

CHAPTER 9

Viability and Self-Reliance in the Settlements

> Essentially, the concept of viability relates to a situation where the particular economic unit under discussion is capable of sustaining itself.
> (Chauhan *et al.*; 1973)

The major objective of rural refugee settlements is to provide refugee households with the means to enable them to earn a minimum viable income which meets adequately customary expenditure on consumption, farm expenses and social costs related to births, weddings, deaths, etc. Since crop failure due to lack of rain is common in the area, a viable income must also include margins that permit households to cope with crop failure and allow the purchase of some basic farm equipment.

THE VIABLE HOUSEHOLD

Household viability is the household's ability to sustain itself by generating a specific minimum income which permits it to meet its consumption requirements, its current farm expenses and its social obligations (expenditure on ceremonies and festivals including births, weddings, funerals, etc.) and to procure an additional cash income which permits it to meet its demands for goods and services produced outside the subsistence sector.

The criterion for determining viability must be defined in terms of a specific measure of household income. The refugee households in the land settlements were expected to derive their subsistence need from crop production, but a considerable part of their annual total income originates from non-farm income-generating activities. (See Chapter 8.) Therefore, we assess the economic viability of the households by using, on the one hand, crop returns and, on the other, crop returns plus income obtained from non-farm activities—total income. The proportion of the economically viable households will vary depending on the criterion used to distinguish between viable and unviable households.

Food and Other Consumption Requirements

Data on which to base an accurate family expenditure are difficult to obtain and the data here must be recognized as approximate. The only available data on rural family expenditure is the Household Sample Survey conducted in 1967-68 and published by the Department of Statistics in December 1970. These data are not useful to us because they are aggregated at the national level and because price inflation has rendered them out of date. Furthermore, the expenditure data were in terms of money spent and not quantities purchased. Thus we refer to different sources to estimate the annual average family expenditure in the refugee settlements.

Due to the diverse ethnic background of the settlers, it is difficult to speak of a typical dish in the settlement. In general, however, the households' diet consists of a breakfast of tea or milk with bread or *kitcha*. The majority's access to milk, especially during the dry season is very limited. The next meal at noon consists of *injera, kisra* or *geât* with lentil, tomato or vegetable sauce. Vegetables are only available in the rainy season, but there are households that keep dry ladyfingers (*bamiya*) for the dry season. During the harvest, the high and medium-income households eat meat. But during the dry season, when most households' stock of grain and cash runs out, meat becomes a luxury item accessible only to the well-off. The evening meal consists of the same items. There are also households that eat beans (*fool*).

How do we measure the standard food requirement of an average size farm household per year? Crop production data only make sense when compared with the quantity of food needed to feed a family and to allow it to meet customary expenditure on basic requirements such as sugar, tea, coffee, cooking oil, salt, soap, vegetables, kerosine, firewood, clothing and social obligations. A certain amount of surplus produce is also necessary for the farm household to cope with crop failure, to purchase basic farm tools such as axes, sickles, hoes and *seluka* and to cover the costs of hut construction and repair, transport, tractor hire charge, flour grinding charges, etc. In rural Africa, a considerable amount of the harvested crop is lost from lack of proper storage, and we shall assume here that 10-20% of the crop in the settlements is lost because of this. The refugees in the Qala en Nahal also pay taxes.

Sorghum Requirements

It is difficult to measure exactly the amount of sorghum required by farm household in the refugee land settlement. In our survey we asked the sample households whether they had produced sufficient sorghum to meet their sorghum need throughout the year in the 1981-82 season. About 53% reported having produced enough. In other words, in the 1981-82 season, 53% were self-reliant in sorghum. These were those farm households that had produced 13 or more sacks. Among land-possessing households, about 70% produced sufficient food crop—sorghum. It appears that 13 sacks is the minimum required for a farm household to be self-reliant in sorghum. Among the land-possessing households about 68%, 64%, 76%, 72%, 59%, and 75% in Umsaqata, Umbrush, Dehema, Adingrar, Aburakham, and Wad Awad, respectively were self-reliant in sorghum in 1981-82.

TABLE 9.1. Farm Households that Produced 13 Sacks of Sorghum or More in 1981–82 (Per cent)

Umsaqata	Umbrush	Dehema	Adingrar	Aburakham	Wad Awad	Total
55	59.1	51.1	60.0	42.4	56.2	53.4

We also asked the sample households to state the amount they spent on sorghum. (See Table 9.2.) About 58% did not buy sorghum in 1981-82. However, this does not mean that this group was self-reliant in food crops. As noted earlier, 53% were self-reliant in sorghum. The 4% out of those who said that they had not bought sorghum are those who borrowed sorghum from their neighbors, relatives and friends, promising to return the loan during the next harvesting season. As can be seen from Table 9.2, out of the total sample, 1.4% reported spending between £S.1-50, 27% £S51-100, 13% between £S.101-150, and 2.3% over £S.151. None of the farm households, including the landless who completely depended on purchased sorghum, spent more than £S.250. This indicates that the expenditure on sorghum in 1981-82 per farm household was about £S.250. This is again very useful in quantifying the annual household expenditure on sorghum. As we noted earlier, 13 sacks of sorghum was the minimum of sorghum needed to meet the annual sorghum need of a farm household and, if we include the 10-20% which is lost due to storage problems, the amount of sorghum needed by an average household is between 14.3 and 15.6 sacks. The price of sorghum at that time was £S.16 per sack and the amount of money needed to meet the farm household's annual requirement at the price that existed in 1981-82 is between £S.230 and £S.250. This is the same as the maximum amount spent on sorghum as indicated in Table 9.2. Therefore, we can safely assume that the annual average household sorghum requirement in the refugee land settlements is between 13-16 sacks or £S.200-250. (The price of sorghum fluctuates. During the survey, the price of one sack of sorghum was £S.16, while in March 1985 the price rose to £S.130. Thus it must be borne in mind that our study is referring to the period 1981-82.)

Over 50% of the total sample households or about 70% of the land-possessing households were self-reliant in sorghum in 1981-82, but this is not

TABLE 9.2. Percentage Distribution of the Sample Households by Expenditure on Food Crop Per Annum

Amount in £S.	Umsaqata	Umbrush	Dehema	Adingrar	Aburakham	Wad Awad	Total
0	53.3	52.3	57.4	58.0	52.5	84.4	57.9
1–50	1.7	2.3	—	2.0	1.7	—	1.4
51–100	25.0	22.7	31.9	22.0	35.6	9.4	26.7
101–150	11.7	20.4	10.6	18.0	8.5	6.2	12.7
151–200	8.3	2.3	—	—	—	—	2.0
201–250	—	—	—	—	1.7	—	0.3
Total	100.0	100.0	99.9	100.0	100.0	100.0	100.1

the case every year in all the settlements. 1981-82 was a bumper crop season and by no means typical with regard to crop production, especially in the settlements outside Qala en Nahal. (See Table 9.3.) The average farm household income in Qala en Nahal in 1982-83 does not differ considerably from the farm income obtained in the 1981-82 season except for the settlement of Adingrar. (See Table 8.12 in Chapter 8)

However, in the 1983-84 season, income earned from crop production in Qala en Nahal was not more than 30% of the preceding season, whereas in Aburakham and Wad Awad the average crop income per farm household in 1982-83 season was £S.14.7 and £S.5.8, respectively. In 1983-84 the total harvest was only 10% of the expected grain yield in Qala en Nahal. (Wallace, 1985, 7)

TABLE 9.3. 1982–83 Average Settlement Crop Income in £S.

	Umsa-qata	Umb-rush	Deh-ema	Adin-grar	Abura-kham	Wad Awad
Sorghum	266.46	239.03	256.13	147.97	14.07	5.77
Sesame	184.0	78.58	74.10	103.90	—	—
Total	450.46	317.61	330.87	251.87	14.07	5.77

Source: Agrisystems, Agricultural Survey of Refugee Settlements in the Eastern Sudan. Report of Mission Undertaken for UNHCR in Collaboration with the FAO. April, 1983.

Other Requirements

Farm households spend considerable amounts on commodities and services which they do not themselves produce. It is difficult, however, to estimate the monthly or annual required consumption of such commodities and, subsequently, the estimation of the outlays on such goods and services is also difficult.

During our survey we asked the sample farm households to state their annual expenditure on various items of consumption. However, since they did not keep records, it was impossible for them to say with certainty what their expenditure was. It was necessary for us to ask them their average daily or weekly expenditure and then compute from this their monthly and annual expenditure. Furthermore, the ability of households to purchase commodities and services is affected by the seasons, i.e., during the harvesting season most families eat meat and other exotic food items, while during the hungry season only the rich households can. Therefore, we could not assume that the households' expenditure was the same every month. But this variation was reduced by the fact that even those households short of cash could borrow commodities from the shops to be repaid during the harvesting season.

Therefore, the monthly expenditure of the credit-worthy farm households did not radically vary from season to season. This was confirmed by our investigation of the records of one shop in one of the settlements. Expenditures on clothing, hut construction, hut repair, transport, tractor charges, festivals and ceremonies were easier to remember than expenditures on small items of daily consumption. Thus, the data in Table 9.4 should be treated with caution.

As can be seen in Table 9.4, the sample farm households' expenditure on purchases of commodities excluding sorghum varied from zero to £S.800 per year. This clearly shows that expenditure on consumer goods is a function of the households' income. Although the proportion of the rich households' income spent on consumer goods is less than among the lower income groups, it is clear that the households with higher income had spent more on consumer goods and services than the lower income groups. Out of the total sample, 4.4% or the poorest section had zero expenditure. This is simply because they had no money with which to purchase anything. Out of the total sample, about 6% spent between £S.1-200, 55% between £S.201-400, 29% between £401-600, and about 6% between £S.601-800.

The average household expenditure on other commodities beside the food crops in 1981-82 was £S.419 in Umsaqata, £S.399 in Umbrush, £S.323 in Dehema, £S.337 in Adingrar, £S.311 in Aburakham, and £S.332 in Wad Awad. Across all the settlements the average was £S.355 per year.

As can be seen from Table 9.5, about 61% of the sample reported having spent between £S.1-500 on festivals and ceremonies. Out of the total sample, about 53% had spent between £S.51-200 and about 8% spent between £S.201-450. The outsider may be surprised to see such poor communities spending a great proportion of their income on festivals and ceremonies. However, it is important to realize that such events are socially necessary. In order to pay for them, many households fall prey to debts and deplete their scarce resources.

In 1981-82 the average expenditure on festivals and ceremonies by the farm households in Umsaqata was £S.115, in Umbrush £S.95, in Dehema £S.74, in Adingrar £S.55, in Aburakham £S.52, and £S.48 in Wad Awad. The average in all the settlements per household was £S.75. If we exclude the farm households that did not incur costs on ceremonies and festivals, the average is £S.123 per farm household in all the settlements.

In Qala en Nahal about 72% of the land-holding households reported having paid tractor hire charges in the 1981-82 season. The amount paid varied according to the size of the holding. The average for the farm households who hired tractors for cultivation and haulage was about £S.15. Tractor service is provided free of charge in the settlements of Aburakham and Wad Awad. The households in Qala en Nahal also pay taxes and duties. These include livestock tax, license duties paid by owners of shops, teashops, restaurants, camel oil presses, water carts, water bags, etc. These are paid once a year. The figures indicated in Table 9.7 include such duties.

TABLE 9.4. Percentage Distribution of the Sample Households by Annual Expenditure on Commodities excluding Sorghum

Amount in £S.	Umsaqata	Umbrush	Dehema	Adingrar	Aburakham	Wad Awad	Total
0	1.7	2.3	6.4	6.0	5.1	6.2	4.4
1–100	—	2.3	—	—	—	—	0.3
101–200	5.0	—	4.3	6.0	11.9	3.1	5.5
201–300	6.7	9.1	38.3	20.0	35.6	40.6	24.0
301–400	36.7	36.4	25.5	40.0	23.7	18.7	30.8
401–500	25.0	25.0	14.9	16.0	13.6	12.5	18.1
501–600	11.7	18.2	4.3	12.0	5.1	18.7	10.9
601–700	10.0	6.8	6.4	—	5.1	—	5.1
701–800	3.3	—	—	—	—	—	0.7
Total	100.1	100.1	100.1	100.0	100.1	99.9	99.8

TABLE 9.5. Percentage Distribution of the Household Sample by Expenditure on Festivals

Amount in £S.	Umsaqata	Umbrush	Dehema	Adingrar	Aburakham	Wad Awad	Total
0	31.7	29.5	31.9	54.0	42.4	43.7	38.7
1–50	1.7	—	—	—	—	—	0.3
51–100	23.3	20.4	51.1	26.0	49.1	43.7	35.3
101–150	13.3	20.4	10.6	10.0	3.4	12.5	11.3
151–200	8.3	25.0	—	4.0	1.7	—	6.5
201–250	8.3	4.5	—	—	1.7	—	2.7
251–300	3.3	—	2.1	6.0	1.7	—	2.4
301–350	3.3	—	—	—	—	—	0.7
351–400	1.7	—	2.1	—	—	—	0.7
401–450	5.0	—	2.1	—	—	—	1.4
Total	99.9	99.8	99.9	100.0	100.0	99.9	100.0

TABLE 9.6. Percentage Distribution of the Refugee Households by Expenditure on Tractor Hire Service

Amount in £S.	Umsaqata	Umbrush	Dehema	Adingrar	Aburakham	Wad Awad	Total
0	30.0	27.3	31.9	24.0	—	—	28.2
3.75	6.7	—	—	6.0	—	—	2.0
7.50	5.0	18.2	21.3	24.0	—	—	16.3
11.25	1.7	2.3	27.7	—	—	—	0.5
15.0	36.7	34.1	2.1	32.0	—	—	32.7
22.0	3.3	4.5	10.6	2.0	—	—	3.0
30	11.7	11.4	6.4	8.0	—	—	10.4
Over 30	5.0	2.3	—	4.0	—	—	6.9
Total	100.1	100.1	100.0	100.0			100.0

TABLE 9.7. Percentage Distribution of the Sample Households by Amount of Tax Paid

Amount in £S.	Umsaqata	Umbrush	Dehema	Adingrar	Total
0	31.7	31.8	44.7	40.0	36.8
1–5	1.7	2.3	31.9	2.0	8.9
6–10	33.3	47.7	19.1	58.0	39.3
11–15	18.3	13.6	—	—	8.4
16–20	5.0	—	—	—	1.5
21–25	1.7	2.3	—	—	1.0
26–30	3.3	—	—	—	1.0
31–35	—	2.3	2.1	—	1.0
Over 35	5.0	—	2.1	—	2.0
Total	100.0	100.0	99.9	100.0	99.9

The average tax paid by the households in Umsaqata was £S.9, in Umbrush £S.6, in Dehema £S.4, and in Adingrar £S.5. The average tax for the total sample was £S.6.

The average annual expenditure reported by the sample households in Qala en Nahal, excluding expenditure on sorghum, was £S.475 and £S.370 in Aburakham and Wad Awad. As we saw earlier, a household's expenditure on sorghum was in the range of £S.200-250 or 13-16 sacks. Therefore, if we include £S.225 to the other expenditures, the total household annual expenditure in Qala en Nahal is about £S.700 while in Aburakham and Wad Awad the average consumption expenditure per family is in the range of £S.600.

THE MINIMUM VIABLE INCOME

How do we measure the minimum viable income which allows a household to meet the customary expenditure on consumption, current farm expenses, and social obligations? In the preceding section we looked at the level of consumption expenditure per family in the 1981-82 agricultural year. Chauhan *et al.*, in their study of economic viability of small farmers in Sangli District of Maharashtra State of India, calculated annual household expenditure on essentials such as food, clothing and fuel and on ceremonies and festivals for sample families, and the average value was used as a viability floor to distinguish between the viable and non-viable households (See Chauhan *et al.*: 1973, 92). If we use the same method, our viable household can be defined as one whose total income exceeded £S.700 in the 1981-82 agricultural year. It is necessary to adjust this value for inflation.

In their study of the rural refugee agricultural settlements in eastern Sudan in 1982, Cree and Jonsson (1982, 28) estimated the minimum annual income required per average refugee household for meeting its 'annual household costs' to be 'in the range £S.50-£S.60 per month or £S.600-700 per annum'. Their estimate, although without details of how they arrived at their conclusions, correlates with our results of annual household consumption expenditure. (The author does not think that this is a coincidence. Jonsson was at that time a UNHCR assistant program officer in Gedaref with wide knowledge of refugee needs in the area. Cree had also a good knowledge of the settlements in Eastern Sudan because he had worked there on several occasions as a UNHCR consultant.)

Is it possible that the minimum viable income is the same as the annual average consumption expenditure per family in the settlement? What are the problems with taking such an approach? The first problem is that the existing level of consumption expenditure per family may not always correspond to the minimum viable income: when the supply of food and cash run out during the hungry season, many of the households which are not credit-worthy are forced to cut their consumption expenditure. In such a situation, the average consumption expenditure per household may not correspond with the minimum viable income which is objectively needed to sustain a household. However, this may be balanced by the fact that there are some rich households that consume luxury items throughout the year. Another problem is that, irrespective of the existing level of consumption expenditure, one will always find households living on less than the average family annual expenditure. However, it is not the *average* level of consumption expenditure that is interesting; in this case, it seems that the latter corresponds with the minimum income needed to sustain a household of an average size in the area.

To further explore means for estimating the minimum viable income, the author tried to compile data based on group discussions at different levels, case studies and other sources. (See Table 9.8)

Although the data in Column I are very important, they do not reflect the general pattern of consumption in a rural community. This is because first, the consumers are all male adults with a consumption rate which is likely to be higher than that of the average household. Second, some of the articles consumed, as can be seen from the same column, reflect to an extent urban rather than rural patterns of consumption. For example, commodities such as spaghetti, bread, kerosene, potatoes and tomatoes are not typical in rural communities. The large amount of kerosene consumed shows that kerosene was not only used for lighting but also for cooking, an unknown use in African rural communities. Third, the consumers in Column I have a much higher monthly income than the average farm household. Some of them were dressers (advanced and elementary) and some were teachers, and their income varied from £S.75-£S.150 a month. In higher income groups, although the proportion of the amount expended on consumption in respect to their total income is often less than in low income groups, higher income in absolute terms means more access to consumer goods. Hence, the amount

TABLE 9.8. Average Monthly Expenditure per Household

Item	I	II	III
Meat	26.00	—	1.94
Spaghetti	6.50	—	—
Tomatoes	14.30	—	1.10
Bread	17.72	—	5.50
Water	3.80	—	1.75
Cooking Oil	8.30	4.20	4.10
Salt	0.20	0.30	0.20
Kerosene	12.00	0.40	0.60
Flour grinding charges	2.75	—	1.25
Charcoal	6.25	8.00	3.00
Tea	1.80	3.50	1.25
Sugar	8.75	15.00	9.00
Vegetables	9.65	13.90	4.00
Lentils	2.40	—	2.00
Fruit	1.55	—	—
Potatoes	7.70	—	1.80
Soap	7.50	—	2.00
Coffee	—	5.50	3.50
Firewood	7.50	7.50	2.50
Matches	0.20	0.35	0.20
Clothes and Shoes	—	10.00[1]	3.00[1]
Social obligations	—	2.50[1]	2.00[1]
Self help	—	2.50[1]	1.50[1]
Building and Repairs	—	10.00[1]	4.50[1]
Transport	—	5.00[1]	3.50[1]
Utensils	—	2.00[1]	1.75[1]
Seed/5 feddans	—	—	2.00
THS/5 feddans	—	—	7.50
Sorghum	22.00	21.00	19.00
Total	167	112	90

[1]These figures are computed from annual expenditures to fit monthly expenditures.

Source: The data in Column I are based on average real consumption over a period of two months. Five male adult SCC/ESRP employees, teachers and dressers live in different huts but eat together and share the monthly consumption expenditure every month. Each item purchased is carefully recorded for the purpose of monthly accounting.

II. Average monthly expenditures for a couple together with their one or two children in the Rahad irrigated scheme in Eastern Sudan, *AID Project, Sudan, Rahad Irrigation Project,* US Aid, March, 1982, E-5.

III. Author's estimation based on group discussions, case studies and key informants. An average is calculated to arrive at the results. The different sources were checked against each other and there were no large discrepancies between the different sources.

given in Column I is likely to have been influenced by the relatively higher income earned by the consumers. Finally, the difference between the amount in Column I on the one hand, and in Columns II and III on the other, is so marked that it is unlikely to be representative of the customary consumption of rural communities. Therefore, it is not appropriate to use these data to measure the average monthly consumption expenditure required by an average refugee family.

The data in Column II are strikingly instructive for their approximation to our own estimation, but they are not exhaustive because various commodities that are consumed daily in the refugee land settlements are not in the list. The expenditure on some articles such as vegetables is also influenced by the specific situation in the Rahad scheme. Horticulture is included in the rotation of crops in the Rahad irrigated scheme, so there is a supply of vegetables throughout the year, unlike in the settlements where vegetables are only available during the rainy season. Thus these data are not exhaustive enough to be used as a standard requirement of consumption expenditure in the rural refugee land settlements.

As stated before, the data in Column III come from different sources and were later discussed with knowledgeable persons in the refugee comminities. We asked the key informants, for example, how many times one drinks coffee and the amount used each time. It was difficult for some to express the amount in kg or lbs but they could express easily in volume. We converted the volume to lbs by weighing it. We gathered that the consumption of such commodities as coffee, tea, sugar, soap, water and charcoal is higher in the dry season when agricultural labor is laid off. When people are underemployed in the settlement, they are at home more and consequently their consumption of such commodities increases. It is also in the dry seasons that social visits occur and this leads not only to increased consumption of such commodities, but also to people wearing better and cleaner clothes. In contrast the consumption of vegetables is higher in the rainy season simply because there are no vegetables in the dry season. All this indicates that consumption expenditure has a seasonal pattern, and this was taken into account when we calculated the monthly consumption requirements. The quantity of each commodity was then multiplied by the price of each item that was prevailing in the settlement during the study period.

According to the data in Column III, an average refugee household needs an annual income in the range of £S.1,080 in order to meet its basic needs. According to the key informants and the information brought forward in the group discussions in the settlements, the minimum viable income per refugee household is £S.1.080 per year, which is about 54% *more* than the real average household consumption expenditure revealed by our survey.

The EA-A survey and estimates made for three levels in 1980-81 in Qala en Nahal refugee settlements show that the recurrent family expenditures in 1980 prices were £S.696.48 (high), £S.489,48 (medium) and £S.347.16 (low).

These consumption expenditure levels are excluding what the EA-A survey calls 'luxury' items, such as meat, eggs, snuff and charcoal. If we include the luxury items, the corresponding recurrent family expenditures are £S.935, £S.570, and £S.347, respectively. The poor households do not consume so-called luxury items. If we take the medium level, the level of consumption expenditure per annum in 1981-82 excluding the 'luxury' items adjusted to 30% annual inflation rate is £S.636. If we take the high level consumption expenditure the annual recurrent family expenditure adjusted for 30% annual inflation rate is £S.905. If we include the so-called 'luxury' items, the medium level of consumption in 1981-82 is £S.743. It must be pointed out here that the EA-A survey and estimates do not include farm and social obligation expenditures.

In its Documentation for the June 20-23 Conference, Khartoum, 1980, the National Committee for Aid to Refugees estimated the annual refugee household expenditure at £S.900. (NCAR, Vol. II, 27) The inflation rate in the rural areas was 'estimated to be 60-70 per cent'. A limited field survey which we conducted in Gedaref and Qala en Nahal in 1982-83 showed that prices of essential commodities in the latter were only 10% more than in Gedaref. Thus, according to the NCAR's estimation the recurrent refugee household expenditure in 1981-82 was in the range of £S.1,170.

The average per capita annual income of the rural population in Kassala Province is £S.185. The average family size in the Province is seven persons. Thus, the annual average household income is £S,1,295.

The question now is which of these criteria is the most appropriate measurement of the minimum viable income in the refugee agricultural settlements, or again how do we define a viable household? Compared to the other estimates we saw above, the existing level of average consumption expenditure per refugee household in the rural refugee settlements is low. This may to some extent show that the existing level of consumption expenditure seems to be lower than what is objectively needed by the average household to meet its basic needs, which may mean that the very poor and poor households are cutting their consumption expenditure when their stocks of grain and cash run out during the hungry seasons. The discrepancy between the various estimations shows how difficult it is to determine exactly the viability floor. For our purpose, it is assumed that the viability floor in the rural refugee settlements in Eastern Sudan in the 1981-82 agricultural year was in the range of £L.700-£S.1,000. The existing level of average consumption expenditure per household was, as stated before, £L.700 per year. Thus we shall use this as the lowest bench mark to distinguish between the households whose annual total income is within or below the viability floor.

THE VIABLE FARM HOUSEHOLD

Due to lack of data on household income for several years, our analysis is based on one year's income. Furthermore, owing to the highly fluctuating climatic conditions in the area, household income and especially farm income vary drastically from season to season. In order to identify the households that were viable, we measure income in two different ways. The climatic conditions in the 1981-82 agricultural season were exceptionally good and production was therefore good. Thus, the income earned from the different income-generating activities that year can be a good measure of the available resources when utilized under favorable conditions.

Household Viability by Income from Crop Production

The distribution of income obtained from crop production (sorghum and sesame) in the 1981-82 agricultural season among the refugee households are given in Table 8.3. About 22% of the sample households in Umsaqata, 16% in Umbrush, 11% in Dehema, and 16% in Adingrar had earned over £S.700 from their crops. In Qala in Nahal, 16% of the total sample households were able to earn an adequate minimum income which allowed the farm households to meet the customary expenditure on consumption and to meet some of the current farm expenses. Therefore, 16% of the sample households in Qala en Nahal became viable by income obtained from crop production. None of the sample households in Aburakham and Wad Awad attained this level.

Household Viability by Total Income

Total income is defined to include all incomes from crop production, trade, wage labor, handicraft, livestock and livestock-related activities, etc. The only sources of income that are excluded are remittance and subsidy. We excluded these primarily because they are not related to income-generating activities in the settlements or outside the settlements. They are also very unreliable sources of income. The distribution of the sample households by total income is given in Table 8.10.

As we saw in Table 8.12, about 45% of the total income of the households is derived from off-farm income-generating activities. Subsequently, the number of the viable households considerably increases if we use total income to distinguish the viable households from the non-viable ones. According to the data in Table 8.10, about 35% of the sample households in Umsaqata, 22% in Umbrush, 17% in Dehema, 22% in Adingrar, 14% in Aburakham, and 25% in Wad Awad were viable. Out of the total sample, 23% were viable while, if we look at Qala en Nahal separately, 25% of the total sample had earned over the minimum viable income.

Off-farm income-generating activity is very crucial in the economic life of the settlements. This is especially true for Aburakham and Wad Awad where none of the sample households had reached the viability floor on the basis of the first criterion. This is mainly because the settlements are located in marginal areas and because the holdings are too small to generate adequate income for the farm households to become economically viable. Due to the ecological marginality of the area, the farm households can only grow sorghum while those in Qala en Nahal can grow the high value crop, sesame.

The farm households in the former settlements are also unable to keep either camels or cattle, which are good sources of income in Qala en Nahal.

The results, according to the two alternative criteria, show that at least in 1981-82 the majority of the refugee households were unable to earn the minimum viable income, be it from farm and/or non-farm income-generating activities. Even though most households were able to produce more sorghum than was necessary to meet their needs, the short fall was often in cash income to meet the costs incurred on goods and services which the households do not produce themselves. If a household lacks other sources of income, it is often forced to sell its food crop in order to buy other necessary commodities and to meet its social and kinship obligations.

THE VIABLE FARM

A viable farm is here defined as a farm which, under the prevailing constraints and opportunities operative in the region in general and in the settlements in particular, can in the long run enable the farm household to earn the viable income to sustain itself and to maintain the same standard of living commensurate in the region.

We assume here that the farm household does not engage in non-farm income-generating activities so that all income necessary for meeting its customary consumption, including expenditure on ceremonies and festivals and current farm expenses, is obtained from crop production. We have assumed earlier that the lower limit of the viable region is £S.700.

To estimate the amount of land resource necessary for each household to earn the necessary minimum income to maintain itself and to meet some of the costs of production, we need to know the average yield per feddan in the area. The average yield of sorghum per feddan in the Gedaref area where the refugee land settlements are located was 340 kg per feddan between 1954-55 and 1981-82. The average yield of sesame between 1968-69 and 1981-82 was 140 kg.

Thus, if farm households grow only sorghum, they must produce about 44 sacks or 3,937.5 kg of sorghum to reach the minimum limit of the viable region, i.e., £S.700. Since the average yield of sorghum per feddan in the past 28 years was 340 kg, each household must have 12 feddans of land under cultivation. However, the refugee land settlements have existed for many years and continuous cultivation has led to soil depletion and even erosion. In 1969 the Land Allotment Board advised that land in the region be farmed on the basis of an eight-course rotation of four years' crop followed by four years' resting. Therefore, we can assume that at least ¼ of the households' land must remain fallow every year. This will require three feddans of additional cultivable land which brings the viability floor measured in cultivable land to 15 feddans per household.

Crop failures are part of life in the semi-arid regions in Africa, and a viable farm must produce margins so farm households can cope with crop failure. The size of the margin necessary for such purposes is difficult to estimate. However, for our purpose it is assumed that this margin, if accumulated over three years, must be equivalent to the household's one year's consumption expenditure. This means that the household has to produce 15 sacks of surplus sorghum. This will require about 4 feddans of additional cultivable land. Therefore, for a household to be able to earn the viable income, it requires about 19 feddans of cultivable land. However, since the farm households in Qala en Nahal grow a high value crop (sesame), the amount of land needed by each household will be slightly smaller than 19 feddans.

It could be argued that since crop failure is common, it is not reasonable to provide the refugees with material protection against it. It is true that even the local population is faced with crop failure, but what is needed is to alleviate the plight of the local population and not to let the refugees share the poverty of the nationals. Solutions ought to be sought to the drought. Such an argument also presupposes that the amount of cultivable land available to the refugees is similar to that of the local population, which is far from being the case.

How does 19 feddans compare with the actual land possession in the refugee land settlements? As we saw in Table 5.6, only 11% of the total sample farm households reported having more than 10 feddans of cultivable land. Since none of the sample households specified the exact size of his possession, we tried to investigate the land records in the scheme administation's office in Umsaqata. According to this source, 4.4% of the total number of the households in the four villages in the Qala en Nahal settlement possessed between 20-90 feddans. (See Table 5.9)

The rest of the sample households in Qala in Nahal have 10 or less feddans of cultivable land. None of the sample households in Aburakham and Wad Awad possess over 10 feddans. (See Table 5.6.) This shows that about 95% of the sample households in Qala en Nahal and all of the households in Aburakham and Wad Awad do not have enough land for them in the long run to generate the income necessary to adequately feed themselves and to meet the customary expenditure and current farm costs.

As we saw earlier, the average size of land per family in the Sudanese villages in the surroundings of Qala en Nahal is 29.1 feddans. (Spooner: 1981, 109) In view of this, our estimate of the average size of land per family required in the refugee settlements is very conservative. One of the yardsticks used by host governments and by the international organizations to measure refugee self-reliance is the principle of local parity. However, it is difficult for the refugees to achieve the same material level as that prevailing in the surrounding region unless they have equal access to land and other resources.

Farm viability or the 'model farm' approach is interesting in that it shows the amount of land necessary for a household of an average size to earn the minimum viable income, but as a measurement of viability it is questionable.

This is because a high proportion of the households' income is earned outside crop production. Despite the fact that only 15% of the sample households in Qala en Nahal reported having over 10 feddans of cultivable land, about 25% of the sample households' total income exceeded the lowest limit of the viability floor.

THE VIABLE SETTLEMENT

Settlement viability refers to the ability of the refugee households to generate adequate income so as to be able to meet the long-term operational costs without financial contribution from the GOS, UNHCR and other voluntary organizations. However, since no community is expected to meet the full costs of all infrastructural services independent of outside support, settlement viability in this sense is difficult to achieve and the provision of infrastructural services, both physical and social, have to come either from the GOS or from international voluntary organizations. However, the refugees must pay, whenever possible, all the taxes and duties paid by the Sudanese so that the GOS will be able to meet the recurrent costs of the infrastructure.

At present, all the capital and recurrent costs on health, education, agriculture, non-agricultural self-help, aid to vulnerable groups, staff salary, administration costs, etc., are met by contributions from the GOS and UNHCR, WFP, and various other NGOs. The only exception is Qala en Nahal, where there has been an attempt to recover part of the cultivation costs by levying tractor hire charges, although these are far below the actual operational costs. Furthermore, the tractor hire charges are not used towards cultivation costs, but are directed to the People's Local Government in Kassala for other settlement expenditure.

In 1981-1982, the UNHCR's budget for operational costs in Qala en Nahal was £S.71,393 and £S.103,142, respectively. However, it must be pointed out that this does not include the costs incurred by EA-A on the tractor hire service and other related activities. The levels of funding for EA-A activities in the period 1981-84 were £S.656,241.58, £S.344,858.91, £S.734,325.82 and £S.566,228.17 respectively. (Wallace: 1985).

The Sudan Council of Churches/Eastern Sudan Relief Program (SCC/ESRP) is running one of the most comprehensive social service and community development programs in the refugee settlements. Their programs include health, education, social aid to the vulnerable groups, mother and child health including nutrition and an anti-tuberculosis campaign. SCC/ESRP's total expenditure on recurrent costs excluding capital costs in 1981 and 1982 in Qala en Nahal (Umsaqata) was £S.107,300 and £S.205,350, respectively. The corresponding expenditure in Aburakham and Wad Awad for the same period was £S.60.600 and £S.205,350, respectively. This is excluding the large expenditure on the anti-TB campaign.

The American-based International Rescue Committee (IRC) also runs an adult clinic in Aburakham and Wad Awad. However, their expenditures cannot be included here as we have no access to them.

The total expenditures on recurrent costs incurred by UNHCR, EA-A and SCC/ESRP in Qala in Nahal in 1981 and 1982 were £S.1,334,048 and £S.915,638, respectively. This is excluding the large costs incurred by SCC/ESRP on the anti-TB program. The corresponding recurrent costs incurred by UNHCR and SCC/ESRP in Aburakham and Wad Awad in the same period were £S.203,187 and £S.392,483, respectively. There is a drastic increase of expenditure between 1981 and 1982 in Aburakham and Wad Awad. The main increases are due to salary and transport increases which are caused by the rising oil price and increased salaries and numbers of personnel.

The large differences between the two years indicate that given the high inflation rate in the country, recurrent costs are likely to increase drastically in the future.

A report compiled by the Office of Refugee Affairs of the American Embassy in Khartoum, for example, found out in December 1983 that the total expenditure in Qala en Nahal for the fiscal year 1982-83 was £S.1,241,831. This suggests that owing to the large recurrent costs and the large annual increases due to inflation, the refugee households will be unable, independent of outside contributions, to meet the operational costs in the long run, not to mention capital costs. Therefore, the settlements will depend on outside assistance for both their expansion and survival. Their survival can only be guaranteed if comprehensive programs aimed at increased agricultural production and creative income-generating activities are introduced. The long-term need of the settlements also calls for a new approach which requires lower investment and recurrent costs and above all an approach which encourages local capacity building and participation at the grassroot level.

CHAPTER 10

Conclusion: Self-Reliance or Dependence?

The fundamental objective of the rural refugee land settlements in the Eastern Sudan was to enable the refugees to become self-reliant and to ease the financial and management burden imposed on the Government of the Sudan and the international organizations. This study has, therefore, attempted to assess the rural refugee land settlements' progress to date by identifying the factors and problems that have affected their performance and that may affect their future development.

Even though there have been some tentative successes, our study shows that the resource base at the settlements, the technology used for cultivation and the consequently large capital and recurrent costs, the skill required to operate and maintain it and, to some extent, the host government's settlement policies are such that they cannot promote self-sustained economic and social developments in the long run.

Even though the Sudan has Africa's most ambitious settlement programs and one of the most generous refugee policies in the world, it seems that the dramatic increase of the refugees since April 1984 has drastically reduced the ability of the country to cope with the problem.

Even though military activities and violations of fundamental human rights are the ultimate causes of the tremendous increase of asylum seekers, a study of the causes of flight suggests that it is an oversimplification to perceive refugee flight as solely a function of fear of political persecution. Instead, flight in the region is a result of a combination of actual, or perceived, fear of violence or persecution and deteriorated environmental conditions. When people are exposed to an actual or perceived threat, the question of whether they cross international borders, or whether they become displaced internally or whether they stay at their places of origin is determined by an interplay of various structural , geographic and sociocultural factors. This is to say that there are factors that reinforce or countervail the affected populations' decision to flee. These countervailing or reinforcing factors are, first, the distance of the possible country of asylum from the affected areas of origin; second, the basis of existence of the affected population and the sociocultural values emanating from it; and third, access to or lack of economic, political and social development in the area of origin as well as in the place of destination.

Our findings show first that flight is a decreasing function of geographical distance. Second, the propensity of people to respond to external pressure by resorting to flight is higher among pastoral and agropastoral peoples than among communities with a long history of being sedentary. Third, an area with relatively adequate economic, social and political opportunities is characterized by a stronger inertia which countervails mass exodus, partly by increasing their capacity to cope with man-made or natural disasters. It seems that people in the neglected areas do not feel that much is at stake when they flee. This suggests that development projects in the potential refugee-producing areas, initiated by developmental international organizations together with the populations in the affected areas, may countervail mass exodus.

The question of whether provision of relief assistance on the other side of the frontier creates a 'pull' factor is a tricky one. When the conditions in the place of origin, either due to natural disasters or political unrest, are expulsive and if relief and development assistance do not reach the victims at their places of origin and the areas of their present displacement, the population in such areas are potential refugees even when they do not know what they will find on the other side of the frontier. It is only when the situation at the places of origin is unbearable and emergency relief is provided across the border that the 'pull factor' may become operative.

The major part of this book has been concerned with an agricultural and socioeconomic study of the rural refugee land settlements in Eastern Sudan. Most of the literature dealing with rural African refugees states that they are comprised of women, children and the aged. However, our findings show that there is no remarkable difference between the demographic characteristics of the refugees and the rural population in the Sudan. Neither is the prevalence of vulnerable groups of families, except in the case of female-headed households, remarkably different among the refugees compared to that among non-displaced communities in rural Sudan.

For many of the refugees, settlement has brought a new way of life which is radically different from that of the pre-flight period. A comparison of the occupations of the heads of the sample households in the settlements with their occupations in the pre-flight period shows that a considerable degree of transformation has taken place. Settlement has led to denomadization of the refugees and a sedentary way of life has become the dominant form of existence. Not only has crop production become the basis of material existence, but for many households wage labor has become a means of livelihood. The sale and purchase of labor power and other commodities has become a widespread practice. Under normal historical circumstances the transition from nomadism to sedentariness is a long process, but in the case of refugee communities it seems that process is telescoped by social and economic uprootedness.

The fundamental objective of the rural land settlements is to achieve refugee self-reliance. Within the limits imposed by physical conditions, self-reliance in the rural refugee land settlements can be achieved mainly by means of sufficient land, labor and capital.

A study of the refugee household labor sources shows that even though a full scale commercialization of labor relations has not yet taken place, there are many households that sell their labor power or hire laborers to overcome peak labor requirements. Despite these developments, the household or the family still provides the social basis of subsistence production and organizational framework for the allocation and division of labor. Even though a few of the very poor and poor households employ wage labor to overcome peak requirements, about half of the middle-income group and over 90% of the rich households hire farm laborers. Our findings show that labor is one of the primary constraints on agricultural production. Weed control during July and August and sesame harvesting during the last weeks of October and the first weeks of November are highly labor consuming and the amount of labor required often exceeds the family's own stock.

In the refugee settlements physical labor availability is determined partly by demographic factors, and partly by the existing social norms and values which themselves regulate the participation of the different segments of the population in farm and off-farm income generating activities. Demographic characteristics are not static as there are shifts in the age structure of the households. Also shortages faced by the younger households are alleviated at the family's later stage of its cyclical development. However, values and social norms cannot be changed easily in the short-run. Despite high labor requirements at the peak periods, female participation in farm work, especially among the households whose subsistence fund is not threatened by one season's crop failure, is either non-existent or is very marginal.

The results of our study also show that there are some factors which limit the intensification or utilization of the potentially available family labor force on the households' farms during the period of peak requirement. In the land settlements, the poor households run out of subsistence funds at the same time as the availability of employment opportunities both within and outside the settlements are at their peak, the morbidity rate is at its highest and the need for labor on the family farm is greatest. These put the lowest and the low income groups under considerable stress.

A study of the refugees' labor strategy shows that after the subsistence needs are met, the households allocate the surplus stock of labor to those activities where the perceived returns are the highest. However, the resource base of the lower income groups allows little more than the attainment of subsistence needs and in essence the overriding objective of production among the poorest and the poor households is limited to the securing of subsistence food and to the procurement of minimum cash income for the purchase of necessary goods and services produced outside the subsistence sector and for the discharge of their social obligations.

However, among the well-to-do households, the aim of production includes the achievement of higher returns at the cost of higher risks and uncertainties. Thus, our empirical investigation shows that the production decision of the very poor, the poor, and the majority of the middle-income households in allocating their labor resources is to a large extent determined by the principle of subsistence security. They are, in other words, risk minimizers rather than return maximizers.

The second constraint on agricultural production is land. Our findings of land availability in the settlements and land distribution among the refugee households show that the amount of land available in the settlements, when related to the size of the population, is not adequate to enable the majority of the households to generate sufficient income in order to meet the customary expenditure on consumption and the current farm expenses as well as allowing them to practice fallowing so as to avoid soil depletion caused by continuous cultivation. Nor does the total amount of land within the existing schemes allow accommodation of future land demands arising from natural population growth. Thus, the newly established families either share the holdings of their parents or join the ranks of the landless agricultural laborers. The sharing of holdings has led to land fragmentation and some holdings are reduced below economic levels in this process.

Land transfer for the benefit of a third party is legally prohibited. However, in reality land has become a commodity which is alienable or acquirable at will. The problem of land shortage has created land-hunger which has consequently led to land-grabbing, whereby some of the economically and socially well-placed households have accummulated holdings greater than their original allocations at the cost of the disadvantaged groups. Landlessness has become a major problem especially in the old settlement of Qala en Nahal.

The third constraint on agricultural production in the rural refugee land settlements is associated with the use of tractors for cultivation. Under existing farm organization and settlements' resource endowments, the use of mechanical power (tractors) does not seem to be compatible with the fundamental objective of long-term refugee self-sufficiency. The use of large tractors and the wide level disc harrows on the small size of the holdings, which vary from one to 10 feddans, is not cost-effective. The low level of education and technical know-how of the refugees in the settlements mean that the skilled manpower required for the maintenance and operation of the tractors and other agricultural machinery has to be recruited from outside the settler communities. Due to the very low level of farm income and the ever growing capital and recurrent costs (including wages), the majority of refugee households are unable to meet these costs from their own savings. This is exacerbated by the fact that competition for mechanics and tractor operators in the large mechanized agricultural schemes in the Gedaref region is very high and this had consequently driven up wages to a level which is beyond the means of the settlement. The shortage of technical skills is mainly caused by emigration to the rich oil-producing countries in the Middle East. This makes it difficult to retain skilled laborers in the settlements. The problem of retaining skilled labor will arise, even if the settlements train their own mechanics and tractor operators. The tractor hire scheme is centrally managed and by its very nature it does not allow 'learning by doing'. Thus the skill to maintain and operate the tractors will remain in the hands of the few individuals who will sell their skilled labor wherever there are favorable employment opportunities. The rural refugee settlements, if left alone, will not in the long run be able to compete with the rich Sudanese commercial farmers in the Gedaref area. Thus, as long as tractors are used, the settlements will depend on outside assistance not only for their expansion but even for their survival. Consequently, the fundamental objective of creating self-perpetuating economic structures is very difficult to achieve.

This suggests that the long-term economic viability of the settlements requires the development of an alternative system of cultivation which must be within the reach of refugee households' financial management and technical skills. Experiments conducted in the Nuba Mountains on soil conditions similar to that of the refugee settlements show that animal traction is not only feasible but also highly cost-effective. Thus, one of the possible alternative systems of cultivation is animal traction based on the technical integration of livestock and crop production. This will not only facilitate the achievement of self-sufficiency but will also provide each farmer with the possibility to improve his farming skill and to transfer it to the younger generation; it will also facilitate the refugees' economic and social reintegration after their eventual repatriation.

The fourth major constraint on agricultural production in the area where the refugee land settlements are located is a low, unreliable and bad distribution of rainfall. In the settlements outside of Qala en Nahal, such as Aburakham and Wad Awad, there have been continuous crop failures since 1982 mainly due to lack of sufficient rainfall. The water-canal to the Rahad irrigation scheme passes between the two villages and if the GOS were willing to share its irrigation water with the refugees in the villages, the situation would be changed drastically. The question of sharing irrigation water is very sensitive because the Nile is Sudan's life artery and the GOS is reluctant to share such a valuable resource with aliens.

An assessment of the economic viability of the households shows that under the existing resource base, the overwhelming majority's annual total income is below the minimum viable income which is needed to meet the households' consumption requirements, current farm expenses and social obligations. Despite relatively major financial commitments on the part of international organizations and the generous refugee policy of the host government, poverty still remains the major problem for the majority of the households. Nevertheless, by African rural standards, striking progress has been achieved in the provision of social services, especially in the field of health. The prevalence of poverty in the settlements is not markedly different from that existing in many other rural areas in Africa, including the refugees' country of origin. However, there are significant differences between refugees and non-displaced rural communities. The latter have not suffered the trauma of flight and are living in their own country with pride and dignity. For settlements to retain refugee populations, it is necessary to provide the refugees with a meaningful basis of material existence. It is necessary not to perceive these efforts as compensation for what has been lost. The losses can only be regained when the root causes that led to the social and economic uprooting are eliminated and the refugees can voluntarily return to their country of origin where they, too, could again live as they formerly did—with pride and dignity.

Even though the factors which we saw earlier have affected the performance and the development of the rural land settlements, the program has achieved success in some areas. It has, for instance, succeeded in settling refugee communities which have widely diverse socioeconomic backgrounds. For the majority, settlement has brought a new way of life which is radically different from their previous one. Many of these communities had no experience of cultivation in the pre-flight period. Now even those families with no experience of a sedentary way of life have adjusted themselves to the new situation.

The settlement program has also enabled the communities to regain their confidence and self-respect. Cultivation of land and engagement in other income-generating activities does not only enable the refugees to secure their material existence, but it also enables them to restore their dignity and self-respect which have been shattered partly by social and economic uprooting during flight and partly by living on emergency relief handouts in the post-flight period in the country of asylum. To live on handouts without being able to take part in productive activities is physically and mentally stifling. The attainment of such objectives in a foreign environment among communities which have suffered the trauma of sudden flight and uprootedness is therefore indeed an achievement in itself. This was made possible by the combination of the host government's, the international organizations' and above all the refugees' relentless efforts and hard work.

However, as pointed out earlier, despite these achievements the rural land settlements have not yet attained self-reliance as was planned by both the GOS and the international organizations. Some of the settlements have been in existence for almost a decade and a half, and despite the host government's and the international organizations' intention to phase-out their material involvement after two to three years, most of the settlements are still dependent on outside assistance not only for their expansion but even for their survival. This is exacerbated by climatic conditions in which crop failures caused by among other things recurrent droughts have necessitated the provision of assistance. However, the need for assistance in the refugee settlements has even recurred in periods of bumper crop seasons in the region. The fact that the settlements which are located in the ecologically marginal areas such as Aburakham and Wad Awad experience recurrent crop failures caused by lack of rainfall is a cause for concern in the long run.

The infrastructures which were determined from outside of the refugee communities still require external assistance for their maintenance, operation and replacement. Under the present resource base in the settlements, for most households, there is very little or no possibility of saving the capital needed for the maintenance, operation and replacement of the infrastructures, and the machinery has to come from outside the refugee communities. Therefore, even though the fundamental objective of the agriculturally based rural refugee land settlements was to create viable economic systems and to ease the financial and management burden imposed on the GOS and the international community, none of these objectives has yet been fully achieved.

It is important, however, to understand that self-reliance is a goal which must be fostered and cannot be easily reached within a short period of time. Even though it is clear that it can only be achieved by a relatively long process of economic and social development, at this stage it is possible to give a reasonable assessment of the land settlements' performance. It is, however, necessary to look at this study as an interim report on the rural refugee land settlements' progress to date. This study has outlined the problems and factors which have impeded the achievement of self-reliance and prevented the phasing-out of international assistance and which may stand in the way of the settlements' future development. It is therefore important to note that these are causes for serious concern in the long run.

The Sudan has Africa's most ambitious settlement programs and one of the most generous refugee policies in the world, but still it seems that the government perceives the problem of refugees as a transient one. This is, no doubt, in keeping with the refugees' own perception of their presence in the Sudan. However, it cannot be denied that the policies and settlement programs that stem from such a perception are a hindrance to the refugees' possibility of improving their material and cultural life on an equal footing with the nationals.

The settlement policy of the government, for example, states that settlements should not provide refugees with more resources than are accessible to nationals in the area or that the refugees had in their country of origin. Since the quality of life of the local population is often low, it may be better to take measures to raise the material standard of the local population rather than to withdraw assistance if a higher material standard should be reached by the refugees. However, this is difficult to implement not only because of lack of sufficient assistance, but also because the populations in the non-refugee affected areas may demand the same benefits as those extended to the refugee affected areas.

The principle of not providing the refugees with more resources than they had in their country of origin probably reflects the government's perception of refugeehood. The rationale of this principle is mainly to avoid the emergence of an economic situation that would decrease the refugees' propensity to repatriate themselves after the eventual improvement of the situation that forced them to flee. This also shows that the government perceives the presence of refugees as being temporary awaiting voluntary repatriation. This kind of policy may be detrimental to the refugees' ability to integrate themselves economically and socially. As long as the refugees are in the country of asylum, it is important to eliminate all obstacles that hinder their possibility to participate in the socioeconomic life of the country on an equal footing with the local population.

If the situation that forced the refugees to flee ceases to apply, it is the prerogative of the government to return them to their country of origin: economic entrenchments notwithstanding. Art. 11(a) of the Regulation of the Asylum Act is very explicit on this question, stating that

> A refugee may be expelled . . . if the reasons which made him seek asylum have ceased to apply and it is possible to return him to his original country.

Nor is this policy favorable to the refugees' economic and cultural integration since they may lack the incentive to plan for the long term.

The second settlement policy also states that settlements must be set up in such a way that they do not 'dispossess nationals in the area from land or opportunity'. Since the GOS has accepted the responsibility to not only allow the refugees to stay within its territory but also to try to enable them to become self-supporting, the refugees will compete with the local population for scarce resources. The objective must be instead to increase the opportunities so that both the refugees and the local population will be able to improve their economic and social life. If one strictly follows this policy, one will be forced to apply the principle of spacial segregation, whereby refugee settlements, in order not to dispossess nationals from land or opportunity, will be located in distant and isolated areas. This would limit the refugees' possibility to integrate themselves and to contribute to the development of the country.

Refugee settlements located in isolated areas are faced with the following problems: the establishment costs may be high, the local population may not be able to enjoy the social services provided by the international community for the refugees, it will be difficult to bring the produce to the market, it will limit the possibilities for refugees and the local population to learn from each other, and the structures created by heavy investments cannot easily be taken over by the local population following eventual repatriation of the refugees.

Another settlement policy also states that settlements must be attractive enough to retain people who have no initial feeling of belonging there, but warns that the settlements must not attract a further influx. The last part shows that the government is worried about the fact that settlements may become 'a pull-factor' for other refugees. The problem is how a balance can be struck between, on the one hand, making the settlement attractive to the settlers and, on the other, making it unattractive to new refugees. It is understandable that the GOS fears that good economic opportunities and social amenities in the settlements may 'pull' new waves of refugees. However, the question is: can the objective of self-reliance be achieved at the same time as there is a policy that tries to keep the economic life of the settlement below a certain level for fear of 'pulling' a further influx or for fear of decreasing the refugees' propensity to repatriate?

There are also other restrictions that may be detrimental to the refugees' efforts to achieve self-reliance. For example, Art. 9 (2) of the Asylum Act limits freedom of movement of the refugees to the 'place of residence specified for' them. The African experience shows that 'the more successful settlements have allowed refugees freedom of movements'. (Chambers: 1981)

If the refugees want to work ouside the schemes, they can easily obtain a travel permit from the settlement management and can move in the rural areas freely. However, there is more control if they want to travel to the cities. The major problem that stems from such a restriction is related rather to the problem of land-shortage in view of an increasing population. The refugees are not allowed to move in search of new cultivable land outside the settlement scheme. Since the GOS, when planning the land settlements, did not take into account the future demand for land arising from natural population growth and from immigration, and since the refugees are barred from expanding beyond the designated areas, some of the old settlements like Qala en Nahal have clearly shown their inability to absorb the rising numbers.

The surplus refugee population cannot move freely into the cities because the industrial sector is itself in a state of crisis. Therefore the refugees must either work their small holdings very hard, even when the marginal productivity of their labor is miniscule, to increase output per unit of land or become migrant laborers in the irrigated or rainfed agricultural schemes. However, in view of the seasonality of agricultural production and abundance of laborers during the trough season and the low and unreliable rainfall in the area, the rising numbers cannot be absorbed in either of these alternatives without leading to a deterioration of their standard of living because of the climatic conditions and the types of crops grown in the area. The climatic conditions limit cultivation to once a year, thus 'cropping frequency' cannot be increased and the climatic conditions set a limit to the forms of exploitation of agricultural resources. The traditional way of easing population pressure and soil degradation in the area has been to bring new areas under cultivation. But the refugees are barred by law from leaving their 'place of residence', at least for the purpose of bringing new areas under cultivation. It is therefore in this respect that the problem of freedom of movement assumes important significance with regard to long-term economic viability of the settlements.

As shown above, refugee status does not also imply that one can freely enter the labor market. A refugee must acquire a work-permit from the Department of Labor before he can enter the labor market. (Art. 14 (2) of the Asylum Act) However, it is important to point out that this is mainly true for the urban labor market, as the author saw no such restriction being enforced in the rural areas in Kassala Province. The Sudan has pressing economic problems and it is justifiable to formulate its policies in such a way as not to jeopardize its own development efforts. However, the country's development is not necessarily promoted by treating the problem of refugees as an isolated phenomenon. The interests of the refugees, the local population and the government would probably be better served by linking the question of refugee self-reliance to the overall development need of the country.

To transform the refugees from a liability to an asset and to enable them to become an important factor in the process of national development, three conditions must exist simultaneously. First, the performance of the national economy must improve so that the country is able to cope with the challenge and the refugees are able to become productive members of the host community by putting into practice their creativity and industriousness. Unfortunately, the large influxes are occurring at a time when the economy of the country is on the verge of collapse and when the world economy is experiencing one of the most serious crises since the Great Depression of the 1930s. However, the international community has a responsibility to help the Sudan to cope with the challenge of development and to alleviate the plight of the refugees, for these two tasks are two sides of the same coin.

The second important factor is the policy of the government. Does government policy treat the problem of refugees as a separate and distinct question or as an integral part of the country's development problems? Even though, as pointed out earlier, the Sudan has very generous refugee policies there are many obstacles that must be removed before the refugees can compete with the local population on equal footing.

The third important factor is the role policy assigns to the refugees. No matter how skilled and industrious refugees may be, their enthusiasm and their ability to release their productive energy can be stifled by a policy that does not encourage them to become their own motivating force in the development process. There is a tendancy among all concerned with refugee matters to assume that increased assistance alone is a panacea that can ameliorate the social and economic conditions of the refugees and their hosts. Even though increased material assistance is crucial, it is not the only variable on which the alleviation of the economic and social plight of the refugees depends. The right of the refugees to participate in identification of locally felt needs, in planning, program design, implementation, administration and project evaluation must be recognized. It cannot be said that at present the refugees in the settlements are effectively participating in these and the other activities which affect their lives directly or indirectly.

APPENDIX 1

Methodology

THE STATE OF RESEARCH INTO REFUGEES

> Refugees constitute one of the greatest but least well-appreciated and least well documented tragedies of present-day Africa.
>
> W.T.S. Gould

Given its magnitude, the African refugee problem and particularly the problem of refugees in the Sudan has received scant scientific attention and much less than it deserves. Organized settlements are being attempted in a number of African countries with the most ambitious programs in Sudan. This study project represents a partial attempt to evaluate the conditions and progress of this program. The literature dealing with organized settlements in Eastern Sudan consists mainly of mission reports, feasibility studies by consultants and internal reports which are not easily accessible to outsiders. However, the accessibility of such materials varies depending on the policy of the organization, and although some of these documents have been useful sources of data in this study, they often deal with very specific questions as spelled out in the 'terms of reference' by the organizations which order them. Mission reports and consultancies are often carried out under crushing time pressure, tend to be based on observations and impressions made during short visits, and can never be a substitute for a scrupulous scientific investigation. This may not apply in each case but is generally true. (One exception is B.C. Spooner's report for EA-A in 1981.)

John R. Rogge's article 'The Quala en Nahal Refugee Resettlement Scheme' appeared in the *Sudan Notes and Records* in 1975 and, since the study was carried out not long after the establishment of the settlement, it mainly dealt with the description of the settlement process, the provision of the services and some problems of implementation.

In 1976, Hunting Technical Services Ltd. in association with Sir M.

Macdonald and Partners and Shankland Cox and Partners carried out a pre-investment study in Eastern Sudan. The main aim of the study, among other things, was to investigate the feasibility of settling refugees in Gedaref, Showak, Jebel Meharigat, Aburakham and Wad el Shaeer in the Eastern region. Their 'terms of reference' also included the investigation of the Qala en Nahal refugee settlement to determine its capacity to absorb additional refugees. This study contains some interesting data on the situation of the refugees in the Qala en Nahal settlement during the period of its decline. Euro Action-Accord (EA-A) first become involved in refugee assistance in 1976, but until 1980 its involvement was marginal. In 1980, it decided to intensify its assistance on the basis of long-term program in the refugee sector. This necessitated a closer investigation of the situation of the refugees so as to identify needs where EA-A could play a role. A consultant, B.C. Spooner, was recruited to carry out an investigation with the following specific 'terms of reference',

> —To design a system of tractor and land management in Qala en Nahal which will serve to ensure a viable and efficient tractor service giving maximum potential benefit to all refugee farmers.
> —To identify areas which will benefit from the assistance of EA-A particularly in relation to long-term self-sufficiency possibilities for the settlement.
> EA-A Project Identification Mission Board Paper and Policy Recommendation: March, 1981

The study was completed in March, 1981 and has laid the foundation for EA-A's long-term involvement. This unpublished internal document was of tremendous help in providing background materials to our research and has enabled the author to compare it with some crucial data which were obtained from official records. Even though Spooner's scrupulous work provides a wealth of information, his analysis was to some extent limited by the specific objectives set by the 'terms of reference'. However, unlike other consultancy work known to the author, Spooner's is in depth and has captured some of the most essential features of the refugees' life in the settlement without, however, subjecting his data to detailed analysis. EA-A's internal annual reports have also provided some important data on the tractor hire services and other related areas.

Cree and Johansson's unpublished paper 'Self-reliance in Agricultural Settlements in Eastern Sudan' (1982) is a general and practical attempt made to analyze self-sufficiency in the refugee settlements under the given resource bases. Although this work is interesting, the authors did not carry out an empirical study of the various settlements apart from wage-earning settlements in Es Suki.

METHODOLOGY OF THE STUDY

The aim here is to present the sources of the data, the means and the procedures used for data collection and to discuss the factors that can affect the reliability of the data collected and the measures taken to minimize the effect of the biasing factors.

CHOICE OF TYPE OF SETTLEMENT

During the time of our research there were three types of organized settlements in the eastern and central regions of the Sudan—rural land settlements, rural wage earning settlements and semi-urban settlements. Among the 23 villages, six were wage-earning settlements. (Kashmel Girba, Kilo 26, Fatah el Rahman, Awad el Sid, Kilo 7, and Umgulja) The villages of Fatah el Rahman, Awad el Sid, and Kilo 7 are located near the Suki scheme in Blue Nile province in the central region. All the wage-earning settlements except Umgulja are inhabited by Eritrean refugees. The latter is inhabited by refugees from Tigrai. Sixteen out of the 23 villages were land settlements and were all located in Kassala province. These were Umsaqata, Umbrush, Dehema, Adingrar, Salmin, and Zurzur (collectively known as Qala en Nahal), Umgurgur, Korakora, Abuda, Um Ali, Wad Awad, Aburakham, Elhawata, Mufaza, Tenedba, and Um Rakoba. (See Fig. 2.8) The last two villages were inhabited by Ethiopian refugees from Tigrai while the rest are inhabited mainly by Eritreans, apart from a few exceptional cases. During our survey, Elhawata and Mufaza were in the process of being consolidated. There was also one semi-urban settlement—Tawawa—inhabited by Ethiopian refugees. Beside these villages, there was one transit camp (Wadsherifie) which accommodated new arrivals from Eritrea. Since March, 1984, about 14 transit camps have been established where new arrivals can remain to receive emergency relief.

It was decided that the study areas must include old and new settlements as well as settlements in marginal and suitable areas. To be included, a settlement must have been in existence for at least two agricultural seasons, must consist of a minimum of 300 families, and a majority of settlers must be Eritreans. (For the settlements inhabited by Ethiopian refugees, (see Bulcha: Uppsala University, Department of Sociology forthcoming).

Accordingly, the four old villages of Qala en Nahal, namely Umsaqata, Umbrush, Dehema, and Adingrar which are located in the relatively agriculturally suitable areas and the two relatively new settlements of Aburakham and Wad Awad, situated in ecologically marginal areas, were selected systematically.

MEANS OF DATA COLLECTION

The data on which this research is based are derived from primary and secondary written records, interviews with randomly selected sample households and interviews with government, NGOs' officers and key informants. Since the author has lived among the refugees, the method of participant observation was used to supplement the other methods of data collection.

At a general level, information was collected from UNHCR's headquarters in Geneva, EA-A in London, Khartoum and Qala en Nahal, World Food Program in Khartoum and Gedaref, Sudan Council of Churches/Eastern Sudan Relief Program (SCC/ESRP) in Stockholm and Gedaref, International Rescue Committee (IRC) in Gedaref and the Office of the Commissioner for Refugees (COR) in Khartoum and Gedaref. The scheme administration records in the various settlements were also important sources for some crucial basic data. The records of the administraion of the various schemes were thoroughly examined with the aim of gathering data to highlight some of the problems and to countercheck information obtained from elsewhere. The data were supplemented by information collected from interviews with officials in the schemes and employees of the various voluntary agencies in different activities in the settlements.

Most of the available consultancy work on the refugee settlements and other related areas were also closely studied and some useful data were obtained from such reports. In order to gain a wider understanding of the problem, we have tried to collect data from all the Ministries concerned which are directly or indirectly dealing with refugees.

The second and major type of information was obtained from interviews with 294 randomly selected sample heads of households in the land settlements, whereas the third type was composed of data gathered by less formal interviews with the *Legina,* with clan *sheikhs,* and with systematically selected key informants. The latter mainly comprised merchants, students, teachers, health officers, refugees and some highly knowledgeable old men. In addition, we also tried to gain a wider and more complete understanding of the society surveyed by combining the anthropological approach of participant observation with field work. The latter helped the author to gain insights which were useful in formulating interesting questions during the informal interviews, in interpreting the data collected, and in focussing on the most important socioeconomic issues.

Sampling Framework

Most surveys in Africa are conducted on the basis of random sampling on an unknown universe (unknown population). As a result, some researchers engaged in African studies express scepticism about the validity of the use of survey research as a means of data collection. This difficulty does not apply to our investigation because the SCC/ESRP clinics at the settlements have complete records of the families in the settlements. SCC/ESRP is a voluntary agency which is responsible for mother and child health (MCH) and for the anti-TB clinics in most of the settlements in Eastern Sudan. In its attempt to eradicate tuberculosis among the refugees and the local population in the surrounding areas, its TB team has carefully counted the number of families in each village. Each village is divided into zones, and each family within each zone is assigned a particular number which is placed at each family's gate.

Since there is a continuous follow-up and since the survey was carried out at the peak season (harvesting season) when the number of emigrants was none or very little, the record was considered relatively complete. Even those who had illegally immigrated into the settlements were included in their list. For the SCC/ESRP personnel, it did not matter whether people had moved into the settlements with or without the permission of the authorities concerned. Thus, the sample households were drawn from the SCC/ESRP anti-TB-clinics.

The scheme administration also keeps records of the settlers and in some of the settlements, like in Qala en Nahal, there were sketches of the villages which could be used to locate the selected households in the sample. However, a careful examination of the records in the scheme administration's office revealed that the population records were either out of date or highly variable from year to year. This can be seen from Table 1 below, according to which the population in the six villages of Qala en Nahal was unchanged between 1970 and 1972 and between 1976 and 1977 while in fact it decreased sharply from 1972 to 1976. This indicates that on one hand, the records were not updated every year, and on the other, many families have, without the authority of the administration, entered or left the villages. This implied that the list of the sample households could not be drawn from the scheme administration records.

TABLE 1. Estimated Distribution of the Population by Village 1970-81 according to the Offical Records.

Village	1970	1972	1976	1977	1980
Salmin	4,091	4,091	3,461	3,471	4,400
Umsaqata	3,629	3,629	3,276	3,276	4,606
Dehema	1,213	1,213	1,270	1,270	3,222
Adingrar	2,513	2,513	2,089	2,089	3,446
Umbrush	2,832	2,832	1,745	1,745	3,786
Zurzur	4,000	4,000	1,438	1,438	2,696
Total	18,278	18,278	13,289	13,289	22,156

Source: Scheme Administration Records: Agricultural File M/A/L/2/A/1 Umsaqata 1970-1980.

The Procedure of Conducting the Survey

Research in the developing world is fraught with many practical complex problems. The first step was to apply for a research permit. A research permit was issued by the Office of the Commissioner for Refugees in Khartoum (COR) and by the National Research Council. The COR wrote letters to the security, to the Assistant Commissioner in Gedaref, and to the Project Manager in Showak. The Assistant Commissioner in Gedaref in return wrote letters of recommendation to the various settlement managers requesting them to collaborate with the author.

When the author arrived at the settlement, he submitted the letter of recommendation to the managers and called on their support in matters which were within their means. The author explained the purpose of the research and the means of data collecting. After their approval, the author requested them to arrange a meeting with the *Legina*. Th managers called a meeting of the *Legina* in each village and explained that the conducting of the survey was authorized by the GOS and requested them to inform all the residents to collaborate with the author and the enumerators. After this, the managers left us alone with the residents' committee for further discussions. In each village surveyed, we explained to the *Legina* in great detail the aim of the study and the procedure to be followed for collecting the necessary information,. Their questions were mainly concentrated on the surveyors' identity (for security reasons), on the living conditions of the Eritrean refugees in Europe, on the world press about theEritrean question, the kind of solidarity and support the Eritrean struggle enjoyed abroad, etc. They also asked whether they would derive any benefit from the results of the survey. Because of the fact that the author and the enumerators were all Eritreans, their identity could easily be established. In fact, the author met several old friends, classmates, and relatives among the residents and this was of great help in enlisting the collaboration of the residents and in increasing their confidence in the survey.

The question of whether the residents would derive any benefit from the results of the survey was very crucial because the answer to this question could, to a great extent, affect the reliability of the information elicited. This is more so because the refugees had lived on handouts contributed by the international community, and they had a tendency to relate any survey to the provision of material assistance.

To overcome this source of bias, we went into great detail to make them believe that the study was independent of any agency that has anything to do with the provision of assistance. We frankly told them that they would not derive any material benefit from it. We told them that our sole aim was to find out the truth about their conditions of living and simultaneously emphasized the fact that we totally lacked the means of improving their conditions of existence. However, we informed them that our findings would be published and made available to all those who would be interested. In almost all the settlements, the members of the committee said that they would have taken us for liars if we had said otherwise and decided to collaborate. All of them also expressed their joy that the surveyor was a fellow countryman. In most other surveys, Eritreans worked only as enumerators, hired by foreigners.

In order to increase their confidence in the survey, we informed the *Legina* that the respondents would remain strictly anonymous. We also explained to them in great detail that the randomly selected households as such were not interesting to us; they were only a subset of a population whose selection did not depend on their particular characteristics. In a few cases, in order to convince the committee, the sample households were selected in their presence. We also told the *Legina* to reassure the residents that their answers would remain confidential.

After their approval, the *Legina* either called a meeting of the clan heads (sheikhs) or went around to inform them to cooperate with us. In the six villages of Qala en Nahal, there were 144 of them. Each clan head in turn informed his people to cooperate with us. Before carrying out the actual survey, the questionnaire was tried out on a few refugee households. This was done to test the relevance of the questions and the appropriateness of their formulation. A few adjustments were later made, i.e., a few questions were modified or excluded and a few others were also included.

After all these technicalities, we went to the SCC/ESRP TB clinics to collect data about the universe. From the universe it remained to determine the size of the sample in each village. After having selected the first household by the use of a random table or by casting lot, every n^{th} of the households in each zone was selected for interviews. The proportion of the sample was 8% in Umsaqata, 7% in Umbrush, 9% in Dehema, 9% in Adingrar, 10% in Aburakham, and 10% in Wad Awad. Since the huts were not always in rows, their haphazard arrangement made identification of the selected sample households difficult. In some of the villages, it was necessary to hire the SCC/ESRP's home visitors as guides to identify the selected huts. Since the home visitors were the ones who carried out the family counts and numbered the huts and were the ones responsible for the delivery of medicines and follow-ups, they could easily locate the sample households.

The enumerators were instructed to interview the household heads. When the man was not present, the answers could be given by the woman. In the women-headed households, we interviewed the woman as head of households. If neither was present, we passed over to the other n^{th} and returned to them in the evening. If we failed after two visits, we took the next family. The same principle applied for refusals. There was only one refusal but he was later convinced by the clanhead to cooperate and agreed to answer our questions.

The same general procedure was smoothly followed in all the settlements except in the village of Wad Awad. In this village, some of the committee members were unwilling to allow us to carry out the survey and we subsequently decided to abandon our decision to include the village in the survey. However, after the SCC/ESRP social workers' intervention, the committee agreed to call a general meeting of all the villagers. The meeting was held without our participation and the villagers unanimously decided in favor of the survey. Those who were reluctant apologized and agreed to cooperate. However, since some were very reluctant to let us visit their huts, we reached a compromise, whereby we submitted the list of the sample households to the committee and the latter agreed to summon them for interviews a few days later. All the heads of the sample households came for an interview and the interview was carried out in the storekeeper's office.

After our arrival in Gedaref, we contacted the UNHCR's sub-office and received a list of highly qualified and trained enumerators. The author employed three of the most qualified ones who spoke English, Tigrinya and Tigre. They also understood Arabic. They were former university students who had fled from their country of origin during and after 1975. Some additional, trained enumerators were also employed in various settlements. This was very helpful because it pleased the residents, since it gave some income to a few members of their community. This also increased the residents' confidence in the survey.

Since the enumerators' understanding of the questionnaire was believed to be a prerequisite for eliciting the required information, the questionnaire was scrutinized in the presence of all the enumerators. In order to be able to assess their performance and in order to help them understand the questionnaire, they were asked to interview each other and it was only after the author was convinced that they had mastered the procedure and the technicalities that they were sent to the different zones. They were also told to follow instructions strictly when they approached the interviewees and were told to ask for permission to come into the compound and later explain the purpose of the survey. The author was always available to answer questions whenever necessary. The author accompanied some of the interviewers to assess their performance and to provide further guidance whenever needed. We went through all the answers with each enumerator every afternoon and evening.

The Interview

In survey research, the researcher must choose between interview and questionnaire methodologies. Questionnaires are usually used in industrialized societies, where almost all can read and write, but are inappropriate for African rural studies because the majority of the population are illiterate. In our investigation, personal interviews with the help of enumerators were considered appropriate. In order to minimize costs and to facilitate data collection, processing and analysis, we considered structured (closed-end) questions to be appropriate as opposed to unstructured (open-end) questions. The advantage of the structured interview according to Galtung is, among other things that '. . . it creates a common complete comparability' (Galtung: 1969). The disadvantage according to him, is'. . . that they are inflexible and do not permit freedom of response.' In order to avoid the latter disadvantage we included in the end of the majority of the questions 'others' which permitted 'freedom of response.'

Whether the questions in the interview schedule could generate the relevant data that could enable us to fulfill our stated aim was discussed at the post-graduate seminar, and the questionnaire was also administered in a pilot group. The latter helped us to exclude, include and modify a few questions.

To some refugees, the concept of random sampling was to some extent incomprehensible. For example, they could not understand why only their neighbors and not they themselves or why only they and not their neighbors were included in the sample. We explained to each family in great detail that the individual *per se* was not interesting to us; he was only interesting in as much as he was a member of the community we were studying. Only when we brought the questions of time and financial costs that would be required for total enumeration, did they understand the reason for partial enumeration. The use of casting lot is not alien to their tradition either. For instance, in the Eritrean highlands, land is distributed among the villagers by lot (see Chapter 2).

When we came to interview an individual who was among friends, the latter sometimes wished to be present when their friend was being interviewed. This may have an advantage of control in the sense that their presence would inhibit the interviewee from lying, but the disadvantage was that they may have censored themselves. It was difficult to ask the friends to leave; it was often easier to ask the interviewee to follow the interviewer to a shed. After some days, we could even ask those present to leave because we were accepted as members of the community.

In administering the questionnaire, we faced no particular problems because the scheme managers, the voluntary agencies, the village committees and the residents had extended to us their unreserved support and cooperation. Before our arrival in the settlements, and especially in Europe, many expressed their doubts that the authorities would ever allow us to carry out our survey freely without intervention. When we started our work we found out that not only was the scepticism groundless, but also that the settlement managers and the COR officials were extremely cooperative and positive. In fact, from the beginning to the end we faced no problems of intervention. Whenever we requested any support, it was given to us without any delay. In fact, the settlement managers did not hesitate to allow us to examine their files, even late after office hours. This attitude, in our opinion, was unique because in the developing world many researchers often complain of obstructive intervention by the authorities concerned.

We were also told that if we did not have female enumerators and because the man is the sole spokesman of the household, the women in the settlements would refuse not only to answer our questions but would even prevent us from entering into their premises. Wilson, for instance argues that

> in some countries, the male head is the exclusive household spokesman, and no explanation of the working of tables of random numbers will move him to abrogate that right
>
> (Wilson: 1958, 231)

Contrary to such assertions, in conducting the survey not only were the women in the settlements willing to answer our questions, but some of them were even more lucid and less ambiguous than some of the men. In fact, many of the women whom we interviewed wanted to discuss many questions outside the questionnaire. In fact, the answers provided by women, especially on crop income and consumption, seemed to be more dependable. The question of not having female enumerators would have been a serious problem if we had women-specific questions such as problems encountered during child birth, sex habits, etc.

Transport not to settlements but between the villages would have been very difficult, if the SCC/ESRP mobile teams had not transported us between the villages to be studied. The scheme administrators and the other voluntary agencies also cooperated with us in this respect.

RELIABILITY OF THE DATA

The central question which required attention is the truthfulness of the information obtained through the questionnaire survey. There are many biasing factors involved in obtaining information through interviewing.

Various foreign scholars who use survey research to collect data on African rural societies often give language as a major barrier to eliciting reliable information. (See Pausewang: 1973; Rudengren: 1981; Ijomah: 1970) Usually, when foreign scholars direct research projects the problem of language represents a major barrier. Many of the concepts employed by social scientists are usually difficult to translate into the local language literally. This barrier can relatively well be overcome if the research efforts are fully directed and implemented by people who are versed with the language and social structure of the society surveyed. Both the author and the enumerators speak the same language as the interviewees, and no problem of communication was experienced in our survey research. Therefore, it is believed that no wrong answers were received resulting from misunderstanding of the questions, be it by the enumerators or by the respondents.

The view that the rural people in the developing countries are courteous to strangers and that as a result the answers given are often deliberately designed to please the stranger is widely held among social scientists. Wuelker, for instance, notes that, 'a European will always receive rose-tinted answers to his queries for fear of offending him' (quoted in Pausewang: op.cit., 108). This is not true in every case. It is rather determined by the nature of the information sought. If one is trying to collect objective data which is not in any way related to the personal interest of the surveyor, or to his organization or his country, there is no reason why the respondent would believe that the surveyor would be pleased or disappointed by his answer. A typical example would be if the UNHCR representative went to the refugee settlements and asked the residents what they think of UNHCR.

In our case, there was not any reason to believe that courtesy had played any role in biasing the information received. Since our identity and our independence was made clear to the respondents, the latter had no reason to believe that we would be pleased or disappointed by their answers.

The respondents may, due to fear, suspicion, reluctance, vested interests, etc., give wrong information. A typical example of this is a respondent who deliberately lies, wishing to avoid income tax or hoping to qualify for food distribution. There is little one can do to remedy this source of bias except by counterchecking the truthfulness of the answers given, and this is not often possible to do, especially when data for comparison are totally lacking. In our survey research, the fact that our respondents were refugees was by itself a source of some problems. There is a tendency on the part of the refugees to believe that the international community owes them a living, and subsequently they have a tendency to underestimate their income and overestimate their misery. This does not at all mean that there are no families that live under miserable conditions, but usually even the well-off refugees complain equally. Hence, in our opinion, although all measures were taken to make the refugees believe that no material benefits would be gained from the results of the survey, probably some families have underestimated their income. Rich families may deliberately have withheld some information, not because they were afraid of income tax or because they hoped to qualify for food distribution, but for the desire to maintain a low profile. The rich refugees do not gain anything by declaring that they possessed up to 100 feddans of cultivable land when possession of more than 10 feddans is prohibited by law.

To avoid or minimize underestimation, we tried to establish some inbuilt crosschecking whereby the respondent was first asked to state his total income and then the individual components of the given total. A special problem, however, was data dealing with livestock and income obtained from livestock. They are probably deliberately underestimated by the refugees since animal tax is levied per head, and the refugees will naturally try to avoid this. Further, counting of livestock is considered as a harbinger of bad luck, and owners are very reluctant to reveal the size of their livestock heads. However, it must be noted that the unreliability is related to the number of livestock owned and not to actual ownership per se. The reason for doubting the reliability of the statistics on livestock arose from the fact that there was a large discrepancy between the number of livestock kept in the administration records and the number of goats and donkeys that we saw in the settlement. To be able to estimate the degree of error in this regard, the author returned to the villages several weeks after the completion of the survey. On this second visit, the author tried to collect data in an informal way and this time people were more open and friendly than ever. Since it was felt that the number of the donkeys reported was an underestimation of the actual figure, we selected three key informants from each block in one of the villages. We asked them to prepare a complete list of the families in every block and then asked them to state whether or not each family in every block owned one or several donkeys. A comparison with the administration records showed that there was a great discrepancy between the two. A comparison with our results (although much less) also showed a difference of about 17%. This countercheck could not be carried out in all the villages but convinced us that the number of livestock and, subsequently, the income reported to have been received from it was probably true only with a wide margin of error. Unfortunately, the same counterchecking was not possible in regard to other data, because information on crop income, for instance, is not as visible as donkey ownership.

The respondent may also give wrong information because his perception of reality is incorrect. However, this is mainly dependent on the clarity and nature of the question asked. Since our questions dealt with the conditions of existence and actual social relations in the settlements, we do not believe that the information collected was affected by the inability of the respondents to understand their situation.

Therefore, because of the precautions detailed above, it was felt that the majority of the answers were of a truthful nature. As stated earlier, some researchers engaged in rural African studies question the usefulness of survey research, however, it must be noted that their works do not offer any better alternative of data collecting. The question in our view is not whether survey research is applicable to the developing world or not. The question is rather, in the absence of reliable data and other means of data collecting, whether or not survey research can yield useful results. Our experience in the field shows that if one is well versed in the sociocultural background and in the language of the society surveyed and especially if one tries to combine the field work with critical observations so as to gain a wider understanding of the social structure in question, survey research can yield very useful data. The decisive point, in our opinion, is the nature of the questions asked and the way they are communicated to the persons from whom the information is elicited. However, it must be noted that survey research seems to be more appropriate in eliciting factual data and one should be extraordinarily careful with its use in the collection of attitudinal data.

In order to further assess the reliability of the data the author, as noted earlier, returned to the settlements and stayed in each up to one month. During this time, the author requested a few of the households if they would be willing to be reinterviewed because we said that we had lost the answers and all those who were asked volunteered. The answers received in the second round were quite similar to the ones given earlier. There were slight differences in a few answers, but the difference was not at all significant to the extent of affecting the reliability of the data. This, of course, does not prove much, since the respondents may only have repeated their earlier answers. However, since the questions were so many and detailed, the fit was astonishingly good.

Bibliography

Unpublished Primary Sources

EA-A Crop Transepts and Land Survey, 1980, Kartoum.

EA-A Sub-branch off., Umsaqata. EA-A Survey, 1981.

EA-A Sub-branch off., Umsaqata. Employment Register 1981-1983.

Interview - 294 sample households

Interview - *legina,* sheikhs and key informants in the six villages.

Interview - scheme manager at Qala en Nahal refugee settlement.

Interview - Aburakham and Wad Awad scheme manager.

Interview - *legina* and sheikhs at the Sudanese villages of Umsaqata and Dehema.

Discussions - Bashir el Ahmadi, Commissioner for Refugees, Kartoum, P. James, Director - EA-A, Khartoum, R. Yuill, Project manager -EA-A, Umsaqata, L. Johansson, UNHCR ass.prog. off., Gedaref, Ismail Ibrahim., ass.commissioner for refugees, Gedaref.

SCC/ESRP branch office, Gedaref. Agricultural Development Program 1979-1980.

SCC/ESRP branch office, Gedaref. Annual Budget for the Fiscal Year 1980.

SCC/ESRP branch office, Gedaref. Annual Budget for the Fiscal Year 1981.

SCC/ESRP branch office, Gedaref. Budget Summary for SCC/ESRP 1982.

SCC/ESRP branch office, Gedaref. Comments on the 1982 Budget for SCC/ESRP.

SCC/ESRP branch office, Gedaref. Comparison Budget with Actual Expenses of Full Year 1981.

SCC/ESRP branch office, Gedaref. Employment Register 1978-83.

SCC/ESRP branch office, Gedaref. Medical Monthly Reports for the Months of January-December, 1979.

SCC/ESRP branch office, Gedaref. Medical Monthly Reports for the Months of January-December, 1980.

SCC/ESRP branch office, Gedaref. Medical Monthly Reports for the Months of January-December, 1981.

SCC/ESRP branch office, Gedaref. Medical Monthly Reports for the Months of January-December, 1982.

Scheme Adm.Records, Umsaqata. Adingrar Agricultural Register No. 5.

Scheme Adm.Records, Umsaqata. Agricultural File M/A/L/57/A/1 1972-79.

Scheme Adm.Records, Umsaqata. Agricultural File M/A/L/2/A/1 1975-1983.

Scheme Adm.Records, Umsaqata. Dehema Agricultural Register No. 3.

Scheme Adm.Records, Umsaqata. Collector's Account No. 36. 1974-82.

Scheme Adm.Records, Umsaqata. Salmin Agricultural Register No. 2.

Scheme Adm.Records, Aburakham. Land Records 1980-83.

Scheme Adm.Records, Umsaqata. Land Records 1969-83.

Scheme Adm.Records, Umsaqata. Scheme Administration Tax Records 1976-1983.

Scheme Adm.Records, Umsaqata. Scheme Administration Records 1969-83.

Scheme Adm.Records, Umsaqata. Umbrush Agricultural Register No. 4.

Scheme Adm.Records, Umsaqata. Umsaqata Agricultural Register No. 1.

Scheme Adm.Records, Umsaqata. Zurzur Agricultural Register No. 6.

Published Primary Sources - UN and other Documents

Ministry of Agriculture, Food and Natural Resources. Mechanized Farming Corporation. *Agricultural Statistics.* Bulletin No. 2. Khartoum, November, 1979.

Ministry of Agriculture, Food and Natural Resources. *Current Agricultural Statistics* CAS 1, 3 (June, 1979).

Ministry of National Planning. *Economic Survey 1983/84*. Khartoum, 1984. (Arabic).

Ministry of Agriculture, Food and Natural Resources. Department of Agricultural Economics. *Yearbook of Agricultural Statistics 1977*. Khartoum, June 1977.

Gen.Ass.Res. 428 (V), 14 December, 1950.

United Nations General Assembly Res. 319 (IV).

United Nations *Convention relating to the Status of Refugees,* 28 July 1951.

United Nations General Assembly A/Conf./25/1, 31 January, 1984.

United Nations *Official Records of the General Ass.,* Twenty-third Session, Supp. *No. 11 (A/7211)*, 1968.

United Nations *Official Records of the General Ass., Twenty-fourth Session, Supp. No. 12 (A/7212)*, 1968.

United Nations *Official Records of the General Ass., Twenty-fifth Session, Supp.* No. 12 (A/8012), 1970.

United Nations *Official Records of the General Ass., Twenty-sixth Session, Supp. No. 12 (A/8412)*, 1971.

United Nations *Official Records of the General Ass., Twenty-seventh Session, Supp. No. 12 (A/8712)*, 1972.

United Nations *Official Records of the General Ass., Twenty-eighth Session, Supp. No. 12 (A/9012)*, 1973.

United Nations *Official Records of the General Ass., Twenty-ninth Session, Supp. No. 12 (A/9612)*, 1974.

United Nations *Official Records of the General Ass., Thirtieth Session, Supp. No. 12 (A/10012)*, 1975.
United Nations *Official Records of the General Ass., Thirty-first Session, Supp. No. 12 (A/31/12)*, 1976.
United Nations *Official Records of the General Ass., Thirty-second Session, Supp. No. 12 (A/32/12)*, 1977.
United Nations *Official Records of the General Ass., Thirty-third Session, Supp. No. 12 (A/33/12)*, 1978.
United Nations *Official Records of the General Ass., Thirty-fourth Session, Supp. No. 12 (A/34/12)*, 1979.
United Nations *Official Records of the General Ass., Thirty-fifth Session, Supp.* No. 12 (A/35/12), 1980.
United Nations *Official Records of the General Ass., Thirty-sixth Session, Supp. No. 12 (A/36/12)*, 1981.
United Nations *Official Records of the General Ass., Thirty-seventh Session, Supp. No. 12 (A/37/12)*, 1982.
United Nations. *UN 1981 Yearbook. International Trade Statistics Vol. 1.*
United Nations *Protocol relating to the Status of Refugees*, 31 January, 1967.
UNHCR. *Report on UNHCR Assistance Activities in 1982/83 and Proposed Voluntary Funds Programs and Budget for 1984*. 1 Aug., 1984.
1949 *Statute -of the Office of the UNHCR.*

Unpublished Government and other Secondary Sources

Adedeji, Adebayo, *ECA Statement to ICARA II*, Geneva, 9-11 July, 1984.
Adepoju, Aderanti, *Refugees in Africa: Problems and Prospects.* Paper presented at the Symposium 'Assistance to Refugees: Alternative Viewpoints', 27-31 March, 1984, Oxford.
Ahmad, A., 'Farm Mechanization and Agricultural Development: A Case Study of the Pakistan Punjab'. Unpublished Ph.D Dissertation. Michigan State University, 1972.
Agrisystems S.R.L *Agricultural Survey of Refugee Settlements in the Eastern Sudan.* Report on Mission Undertaken for UNHCR in Collaboration with FAO, prepared by J. Cree, April, 1983 (mimeo).
Agrisystems S.R.L *Report on Mechanized Agricultural Production on the Rural Refugee Settlement Scheme Kassala Province*. Prepared for UNHCR, Sept. 1981 (mimeo).
All Africa Conf. of Churches and WCC. *Statement for the Second International Conf. on Assistance to Refugees in Africa.* Geneva, 9-11 July, 1984.
Barnet, Tony, 'The Labour Market in the Irrigated Areas of the Sudan.' In *Draft Report of the UNHCR/ILO Project on Income-generating Activities for Refugees in Eastern and Central Sudan.* Submitted to the Khartoum Workshop, 17-20 April, 1983.
Belshaw, D.G.R., *Technological Innovation in Agriculture: The Economist's Role.* Paper read to a Conference on the East African Agricultural Economics Society on Technical Innovations in E.A. Agriculture, Nairobi, 1969.

Benedict, P. et. al., *Sudan Rahad Irrigation Project.* USAID. PN. AAJ-610. (mimeo).

Beyer, G.A., *Report on Mission to Sudan.* Sudan Desk, UNHCR Geneva, May, 1976. (typescript).

Bulcha, Kibreab, Nobel and Stohl, Refugees and Development in Africa. Notes from an on-going Research project. SIAS, Uppsala 1984 (mimeo)

Chambers, Robert, *Rural Refugees in Africa: Past Experience, Future Pointers.* Paper for the Khartoum Refugee Seminar 11-14 September, 1982.

Chambers, Robert, *Rural Refugees in Africa.* What the Eye does not see. Paper for the African Studies Ass. Symposium on Refugees 13-14 Sept., 1979. London: 28 Aug. 1979.

Cree, T. and Jonsson L., *Self-reliance in Agricultural Settlements in Eastern Sudan.* Paper presented to Khartoum Conference September 11-14, 1982.

CuEnod,J. et.al., *Assistance Review Mission to the Sudan 3-18 Nov. 1982.* Sudan Desk, UNHCR, Geneva, Jan., 1983 (mimeo).

Department of Statistics. *Household Sample Survey 1967-68.* Khartoum, 1970.

Dines, Mary, Ethiopian Repression in Eritrea in *The Eritrean Case,* Proceedings of the Permanent People's Tribunal of the International League of the Rights and Liberation of People's Session on Eritrea. Milan, Italy, May 1980.

Drake, H. Max, *Pitfalls of Survey Research in Africa.* Paper prepared for the Annual Meeting of the African Studies Association held in Boston, Oct., 1970.

El Bushra, Judy, *Report of a Survey of Educational Needs among Eritrean and Ethiopian Refugees in the Sudan.* Khartoum, 1982. (mimeo).

Fre, Zeremariam, *Qala en Nahal on the Move:* Euro-Sudano-Eritrean Approach to Agricultural Development, A Two Month Report, Aug.-Sept., 1981. (mimeo).

Fre, Zeremariam, *The Integration of Pastoralism and Semi-mechanized Farming: The Example of an Eritrean Experience in Eastern Sudan.* Agricultural Extension and Rural Development Center, University of Reading. (mimeo).

Goitom, Eyob, "Adaptation and Interpretation: The Case of the Eritrean Refugees in the Three Towns. 1974-1979." B.A. Honours Diss. Department of Geography, University of Khartoum, 1980.

Goodwillie, Susane., *Refugees in the Developing World: A Challenge to the International Community.* UNHCR, Geneva, 5 Aug. 1983. (mimeo).

Hartling, P., *Introductory Statement by the UN High Commissioner for Refugees to the Second Conference on Assistance to Refugees in Africa.* Geneva, 9 July, 1984 (typescript).

Hunting, *Refugees Resettlement Project in the East-Central Sudan. Pre-investment Study.* Report sponsored by the UNHCR. Aug. 1976 (mimeo).

IBRD/World Bank. *Sudan: Investing for Economic Stabilization and Structural Change.* Report No. 3551a-Su, Feb. 16, 1982. (mimeo).

IBRD/World Bank. *Sudan: New Halfa Irrigation Rehabilitation Project.* Report No. 2608a-Su. Northern Agricultural Division Eastern Africa Projects Development, April 25, 1980. (mimeo).

IBRD/World Bank. *World Development Report,* 1981 New York. Oxford University Press, 1981.

ICVA. *ICVA Statement for the Second International Conference on Assistance to Refugees in Africa.*

Ijomah, B.I.C., *The Problem of Quantitative Research in Africa.* Paper presented at the African Studies Association Conference, Boston, Oct. 21, 1970.

Jacobs & Paar, *An Assessment of the Economic Integration and Impact of Urban Refugees in Port Sudan,* Gedaref and Kassala. Office of Refugee Affairs. Embassy of United States, Khartoum, Aug., 1983. (typescript).

James, D.P., *The Quala en Nahal Refugee Settlement Project.* Report on Tractor Cultivation Programme. EA-A, Khartoum, 1981 (typescript).

James, D.P., *Progress Report on EA-A's Involvement in Qala en Nahal Refugee Resettlement,* 1982-83 Cultivation Season. EA-A, Khartoum, May, 1983 (typescript).

Karadawi, A. & Ibrahim, Ismail, *Refugee Settlement Programme in the Sudan: A Country Case Study.* Office of the Commission for Refugees. Khartoum, 1982. (mimeo).

Kursani, Ibrahim, *Eritrean Refugees in Kassala Province of Eastern Sudan: An Economic Assessment.* 20 August, 1984. (mimeo).

Meeting of Experts on Refugee Aid and Development. Mont PElerin, Switzerland, 29-31 Aug. 1983 (typescript).

Mertes, Alois, Federal Republic of Germany *Statement to the Second Conf. on Assistance to Refugees in Africa.* July, 1984. (typescript).

Ministry of Agriculture, Food and Natural Resources, Statistics Unit. *Area, Production and Average Yield of Main Crops in the Sudan 1977/78-1981/82.* Khartoum 1983. (typescript).

Ministry of Agriculture, Food and Natural Resources. Mechanized farming Corporation Statistics and Follow up Division 1954/55-1975/76,Khartoum.

Ministry of Finance and Economic Planning (Planning). *Rural Labour Study in Northern Sudan.* UNDP/IBRD Planning Assistance and Training Project. Khartoum, July, 1983. (mimeo).

Ministry of Finance and Economic Planning (Planning). *Prospects, Programmes and Policies for Economic Development 1982/83-1984/85.* Khartoum, Oct., 1982. (mimeo).

Ministry of National Planning Agricultural Section. *Recent Performance of the Agricultural Sector: An Analysis of Agricultural Production Trends and Policies in the Sudan.* Khartoum, Dec., 1979. (mimeo).

Murphy, J. and Sprey, L.H., *Monitoring and Evaluation of Agricultural Change.* July, 1981 (Draft).

National Committee for Aid to Refugees. *Background and Project Summaries. Vol. I.* Documentation for the June 20-23 Conference, Khartoum, 1980. (mimeo).

National Committee for Aid to Refugees. *Economics and Projects Implementation. Vol. II.* Documentation for June 20-23 Conference, Khartoum 1980. (mimeo).

National Committee for Aid to Refugees. *Project Proposals. Vol. III.* Documentation for the June 20-23 Conference, Khartoum, 1980. (mimeo).

National Committee for Aid to Refugees and UNHCR. *Planned Rural Refugee Settlements in Kassala Province: Report of a Technical Appraisal Mission.* Khartoum, December, 1980.

Office of the Commissioner for Refugees (COR), *Settlement of Refugees in the Sudan.* Khartoum, 1980 (typescript).

Ogborn, J., *Proposed Accord Programme for the Management of the Mechanized Refugee Farming System in the Qala en Nahal Resettlement Area.* Sept./Oct., 1980 (typescript).

Organization of African Unity. *OAU Convention Governing Specific Aspects of the Problem of Refugees in Africa.* Sept. 1969.

Osman, A.M., Karadawi, A., and Siddik, A., *The Outcome of the International Conference on Assistance to Refugees in Africa* (ICARA I): Sudan Experience, Khartoum, March 1984. (mimeo).

Saghayroun, A.A., 'Determinants of Fertility in Rural Sudan: Kassala Province as a Case Study.' Ph.D. Thesis, University College Dardif. July, 1982.

Sectoral Analysis of Resource Flows in the Refugee Settlement in Eastern Sudan: Office of Refugee Affairs American Embassy, Khartoum, Dec., 1983. (mimeo).

Sengal and Starck, *Nutritional Survey for Children under 12 Years in the Sudanese and Refugee Village of Aburakham,* Jan., 1983. (mimeo).

Spooner, B.C., *Accord Project Identification Mission.* Board Paper and Policy Recommendations, EA-A, March, 1981.

Spooner, B.C., *Qala en Nahal - Historical Review:* Current Status and Programme for Action: Agricultural and Socio-economic Study. EA-A, 1981 (mimeo).

Suliman, A.A., 'The Mechanized Crop Production Schemes: Their Development and the Economics of Production of Dura, Sesame and Cotton in the Gedaref Area'. Masters Diss. Faculty of Agriculture, University of Khartoum, 1977.

Tobisson, Eva, *Women, Work, Food, and Nutrition.* A Nordic Research Seminar. Uppsala 22-25 April, 1983.

Tuttas, G.H. and Gaymans, H., *Report on Mission to Gedaref Region.* UNHCR Branch Office, Khartoum: Feb/March, 1976. (typescript).

UNHCR/ILO. *Draft Report on the UNHCR/ILO Project on Income Generating Activities for Refugees in Eastern and Central Sudan.* Submitted to the Khartoum Workshop 17-20 April, 1983.

UNHCR. *The Use of Animal Power Cultivation in Refugee Farms and the Central Clay Plains of the Sudan* (typescript with no date).

Van der Kevie, W., and Buraymah, I.M., *Explanatory Soil Survey of Kassala Province:* A Study of Physiography, Soils and Agricultural Potential. Soil Survey Report No. 73. Soil Survey Administration, Wad Madeni, 1976. (mimeo).

Weaver, L.Jerry, *Donor Assistance to Refugees in the Sudan.* USAID, Khartoum 1982. (typescript).

West, C., *The Qala en Nahal Water System.* Anglia Consultants Cogeshall, Essex, U.K., May, 1981.

WFP, Letter of Readiness concerning WFP, Project 2503 - Assistance to the Settlements of Refugees - Vulnerable Groups. Gedaref, 1983.
Zaki, E.A.A., *Agricultural Pricing Policies of the Sudan*. Khartoum, 1983. (mimeo).

Published Secondary Sources - Books and Reports

Balamoan, G. Ayoub, *Peoples and Economics in the Sudan 1884-1956*. Cambridge, Mass.: Harvard University Centre for Population Studies. 1976.
Boserup, Ester, *Jorbruksutveckling och befolkningstillväxt*. Lund: CWK Gleerup Bokforlag, Lund 1965.
Beshir, M.O., *The Southern Sudan: Background and Conflict*. London, 1968.
Chambers, Robert, *Health, Agriculture and Rural Poverty. Why Seasons Matter*. Brighton: Discussion Paper IDS at the University of Sussex, 1979.
Chauhan, K.K.S., et.al., *Small Farmers Problems and Possibilities for Development*. Centre for Management in Agriculture, Indian Institute of Management, Ahmedabad, 1973.
Chayanov, A.V., *The Theory of Peasant Economy*. Ed. Daniel Thorner, Basile Kerblay, and R.E.F. Smith, 1966.
Freire, Paolo, *Education for Critical Consciousness*. London: Sheed and Ward, 1973.
Geertz, Clifford, *Agricultural Involution, the Process of Ecological Change in Indonesia*: Berkeley and Los Angeles: University of California Press, 1970.
Firebrace, J. and Holland, S., *Never Kneel Down. Drought, Development and Liberation in Eritrea*. Nottingham, Spokesman, 1984.
Galtung, Johan, *Theory and Methods of Social Research*. Oslo: Universitetsforl. 1969.
Gillette, Cynthia and Uphoff, Norman, *Cultural and Social Factors affecting Small Farmer Participation in Formal Credit Programmes*. Rural Development Occasional Paper No. 3, Cornell University, 1973.
Gemill, G. and Eicher, Carl, K., *A Framework for Research, on the Economics of Farm Mechanization in Developing Countries*. African Rural Employment Paper No. 6, East Lansing, Michigan, Department of Agricultural Economics. Michigan State University, 1973.
Holborn, L.W., *Refugees: A Problem of our Time: The Works of UNHCR, 1951-1972*. (2 volumes) Metuchen: Scarecrow Press, 1975.
ILO. *Growth, Employment, and Equity: A Comparative Strategy for the Sudan*. Geneva 1976.
el Jack, Ahmed, Hassan, *The Management of Resettlement Schemes in the Sudan*. Research Report No. 12, ESRC, Khartoum, 1982.
Khalil, S.E., Mohammed, *A Socio-economic Assessment of Family Labour Supply in New Halfa Irrigated Scheme*. Khartoum: Economic and Social Research Council, August, 1980.
Kibreab, Gaim, *African Refugees: Reflections on the African Refugee Problem*. Uppsala: SIAS, 1982. Trenton: Africa World Press of the Africa Research and Publication Project, 1985.

Kline, C.K., et.al., *Agricultural Mechanization in Equatorial Africa*. Contract Aid/ Afr-45g. Michigan State University, December 31, 1969.

Laing, R.G., *Mechanization in Agriculture in the Rainlands of the Anglo-Etyptian Sudan*, 1948-1951. Khartoum: Sudan Survey Department, 1953.

Lindberg, John, S., *The Background of Swedish Emigration to the United States. An Economic and Sociological Study in the Dynamics of Migration*. Minneapolis, Minnesota UP, 1930.

Lipsky, George, A., *Ethiopia: Its People, its Society, its Culture*. New Haven: Hraf Press, 1962.

Longrigg, Stephen, H.,*A Short History of Eritrea*. Westport, Connecticut: Greenwood Press, Publishers, 1945.

el Madi, S.M.A., *Introduction to the Land Law of the Sudan*. Khartoum: University Press, 1979.

Mellor, John, W., *The Economics of Agricultural Development*. Ithaca, New York: Cornell University Press, 1966.

Ministry of Interior. *The Regulation of the Asylum Act No. 45, Sudan Gazette No. 1162 Legis. Supp. 183*, 1974.

Ministry of National Planning. *Six Year Plan of Economic and Social Development 1977/78-1982/83. Vol. 1&2*. Khartoum, 1977.

Nobel, Peter, *Refugee Law in the Sudan* with the Refugee Conventions and the Regulation of the Asylum Act of 1974. Research Report No. 64. Upsala. Scandinavian Institute of African Studies, 1982.

Norman, D.W., *Economic Analysis of Agricultural Production and Labour Utilization among the Hausa in the North of Nigeria*. African Rural Employment Paper No. 4. East Lansing: Michigan, Department of Agricultural Economics, Michigan State University, January 1973.

Nutrition och lantbruk - Om samspelet mellan människan, jordbruket och födan. Arbetsgruppen för nutrition och lantbruk, U-landsavdelningen, Sveriges Lantbruksuniversitet, Uppsala 1980.

Nye, P.H. and Greenland, D.J., *The Soil under Shifting Cultivation*. Farnham Royal, England: Commonwealth Agricultural Bureau, 1960.

Pausewang, S., *Methods and Concepts of Social Research in Rural Developing Society: A Critical Appraisal Based on Experience in Ethiopia*. Munich: Meltforum Verlag, 1973.

Refugees and Development. Ed. Ernst E. Boesch, S. Armin and M.F. Goldschmidt. Intern. Conf. Organized by the DPF of the German Foundation for International Development (DSE), Berlin: Nomos Verlagsgesellschaft Baden-Baden, 13 to 17 September, 1982.

Rudengren, Jan, *Peasants by Preference?: Socio-economic and Environmental Aspects of Rural Development in Tanzania*. Stockholm: EFI, 1981.

Schumacher, E.F., *Small is Beautiful. A Study of Economics as if People Mattered*. London: Blond and Briggs Ltd., 1973.

Scott, James, C., *The Moral Economy of the Peasant Rebellion and Subsistence in South East Asia*. New Haven and London: Yale University Press, 1976.

Simpson, Sir John Hope, *The Refugee Problem. Report of a Survey*. London, Oxford UP, 1939.

Simpson, Morag and Khalifa, A.H., *A Study of Agricultural Development in the Central Rainlands of Sudan: an Interim Report*. Khartoum: ESRC, 1976 (b).

Spencer, Dunstan, S.C., *Micro-level Farm Management and Production Economics Research among Traditional African Farmers*. African Rural Employment Paper No. 3, East Lansing, Michigan, Department of Agricultural Economics, Michigan State University, September, 1972.

Stoessinger, John, George, *The Refugee and the World Community*. Minneapolis, Minnesota, UP 1956.

Sörbö, Gunnar, M., *How to Survive Development: The Story of New Halfa*. Monograph Series No. 6. Khartoum: University Press, Nov. 1977.

Trevaskis, G.K.N., *Eritrea a Colony in Transition*: 1941-52. Westport, Connecticut. Greenwood Press, Publishers, 1960.

UNHCR. *The Water Road: Highway to Regional Development at Qala en Nahal*. UNHCR Report 1972.

UNHCR/ILO. *Labour Markets in the Sudan*. Geneva 1984.

UNHCR. *Information, August 1982 No. 4*. UNHCR Branch Office, Khartoum.

UNHCR. *Refugees News from the UNHCR 1980-82 Refugees*. Geneva, 1983-85.

Ullendorf, Edward, *The Ethiopians. An Introduction to Country and People*. London: Oxford University Press, 1973.

Wallace, Wendy, *Gaining Ground: Refugees in Sudan*. A Report for Euro Action-Acord. London, 1985.

Zwingmann, C., and M. Pfinster-Ammende, ed. *Uprooting and after*. New York: Springer Verlag, 1973.

Journals

Agabawi, K.A., 'Some Developments in Rain-fed Agriculture in Central Sudan -II'. *Sudan Notes and Records* L (1969).

Agabawi, K.A., 'Some Developments in Rain-fed Agriculture in Central Sudan'. *Sudan Notes and Records* XLIX (1968).

Anker, Desmond, L.W., 'Some Effects of Farm Mechanization'. *International Labour Review* LXXI, 3 (March, 1955).

Awad, M.H., 'The Evolution of Land Ownership in the Sudan'. *Middle East Journal* 25, 2 (Spring, 1971).

Baker, Donald, G., 'Development Models and Strategies'. The Problem of Human Motivation. *Journal of Contemporary African Studies* 1,2 (April, 1982).

Beijer, G., 'Modern Patterns of International Migratory Movements'. *Migration*. Ed. J.A. Jackson. Cambridge University Press, 1969.

Bernard, W.S., 'Immigrants and Refugees: Their Similarities, Differences, and Needs'. *International Migration*, 14.4 (1977).

Burvill, P.W., 'Immigration and Mental Disease'. *Australian and New Zealand Journal of Psychiatry*, 7.3. (1973).

Clayton, Eric, S., 'Mechanization and Employment in East African Agriculture'. *International Labour Review* 105, 4 (1972).

Cervinka, Vaclav. 'Tractor and Implement Efficiency on Tropical Farms', *World Crops* XXIII, 3 (May-June, 1971).

Deutch, A.E., 'Tractor Dilemma for the Developing Countries', *World Crops* 24, 5 (1972).

Eitinger, L., 'The Incidence of Mental Disease among Refugees in Norway', *Journal of Mental Science* 105 (1959).

Gebre-Kiros, Fassil, 'Agricultural Land Fragmentation: A Problem of Land Distribution Observed in Some Ethiopian Peasant Associations'. *Ethiopian Journal of Development Research.* 2 (1980).

Gebre-Medhin, Jordan, 'European Colonial Rule and Transformation of Eritrean Rural Life'. *Horn of Africa* 6, 2 (1984).

Gould, W.T.S., 'Refugees in Tropical Africa'. *International Migration Review* 8.3. (1974).

Hansen, Art., 'Managing Refugees: Zambia's Response to Angolan Refugees 1966-1977'. *Disasters* 3, 4 (1979).

Hansen, Art., 'Refugee Dynamics: Angolans in Zambia 1966 to 1972'. *International Migration Review* 15.1 (1982).

Johnson, T., 'Eritrea Refugees in Sudan'. *Disasters* 3, 4 (1979).

Karpat, K.H., 'Social Effects of Farm Mechanization in Turkish Villages'. *Social Research* XXVII (Spring 1960).

Keddeman, W., 'A Survey of the Possibilities for Alleviating Rural Poverty', *Employment, Productivity, and Incomes in Rural Sudan.* Ed. Willem Keddeman and Ali Abdel Kadir Ali. ESRC and ILO, 1978.

Khan, Amir, U., 'Agricultural Mechanization: The Tropical Farmer's Dilemma'. *World Crops* 24, 4 (1972).

Kibreab, Gaim, 'The Problem of Refugees in Development Context in the Sudan'. Trenton: *Horn of Africa,* Special Issue, forthcoming.

Kibreab, Gaim, 'Sudan's Refugee Policy and its Settlement Programmes'. *Horn of Africa,* Special Issue, forthcoming.

Karadawi, Ahmed, 'Constraints on Assistance to Refugees: Some Observations from the Sudan'. *World Development,* Vol. 11, No. 6 (1983).

Kunz, E.F., 'The Refugee in Flight. Kinetic Models and Forms of Displacement'. *International Migration Review* 7 (1973).

Kolaja, et.al., 'A Sociological Note on the Czechoslovak Anti-Communist Refugee'. *American Journal of Sociology* 58 (1952).

Lee, E., 'A Theory of Migration'. *Migration.* Ed. J.A. Jackson. Cambridge University Press, 1969.

Mcfarquhar, A.M.M. & Hall, M., 'Mechanization and Agricultural Development: No Miracle in Africa'. *Options méditerranéennes* XVI (1970).

Melander, Göran, 'Refugees and International Cooperation'. *International Migration Review* 15, 1 (1980).

Murphy, H.B.M., 'The Extent of the Problem'. *Flight and Resettlement,* ed. H.B.M. Murphy et.al. Paris: UNESCO, 1955.

Nadel, S.F., 'Land Tenure on the Eritrean Plateau'. *Africa: Journal of the International African Institute* XVI No. 1 (1946).

Nadel, S.F., 'Notes on Beni Amer Society'. *Sudan Notes and Records* XXVI part 1 (1945).

O'Brien, Jay, 'The Political Economy of Capitalist Agriculture in the Central Rainlands of Sudan'. *Labour, Capital, and Society* 16, 1 (April, 1983).

Paul, A., 'Notes on the Beni Amer'. *Sudan Notes and Records* XXXI, 2 (1950).

Petersen, William, 'A General Typology of Migration'. *American Sociological Review,* 23.3. (1958).

Prins, Sal, A., 'The Individual in Flight'. *Flight and Resettlement.* Ed. H.B.M. Murphy et.al. Paris: UNESCO, 1955.

Robinson, R.D., 'Tractors in the Village - A Study in Turkey'. *Journal of Farm Economics* XXXIV (1952).

Rogge, John, R., 'The Qala en Nahal Resettlement Scheme'. *Sudan Notes and Records* 56 (1975).

Rose, I., Peter, 'Some Thoughts about Refugees and the Descendants of Theseus'. *International Migration Review* 15.1 (1982).

Seligman, Brenda, Z., and Seligman, C.G., 'Note on the History and Present Conditions of the Beni Amer (southern Beja)'. *Sudan Notes and Records* 13, 1 (1912).

Silkin, Trish, 'Eritrea': *Third World Quarterly.* 5, 4 (1983).

Simpson, Morag and Khalifa, A.H., 'Some Thoughts on Agricultural Development in the Central Rainland of the Sudan'. *Sudan Notes and Records* LVII (1976 a).

Smoke, David, R., 'Eritrean Refugees in the Sudan'. *The Journal of Modern African Studies* 20, 3 (1982).

Stouffer, S.A., 'Intervening Opportunities: A Theory relating Mobility and Distance'. *American Sociological Review* 5 (Dec. 1940).

Taylor, R.C., 'Migration and Motivation: A Study of Determinants and Types of Migration'. *Migration.* Ed. J.A. Jackson. Cambridge University Press, 1969.

van Wersch, Herman, J., 'Rural Development in Morocco: Operation Labour'. *Economic Development and Cultural Change* 17, 3 (October, 1968).

Wilson, Elmo, C., 'Problems of Survey Research in Modernizing Areas'. *Public Opinion Quarterly* XXII, 3 (Fall, 1958).

Newspapers and Periodicals

'Army Reverse Caused by Liberation Movements in Begemder and Eritrea Provinces'. *Keesing Contemporary Archives* XXIII (1 July, 1977):28422.

'Continued Guerilla Warefare in Eritrea'. *Keesing Contemporary Archives* XXI (4-10 August, 1975):27253.

'Emperor Haile Selassie's Visit. - Agreement on Eritrean Refugees in Sudan'. *Keesing Contemporary Archives* XVI (24 June-15 July, 1967):22104 A.

'Eritreagerilla hindras av regn'. *Svenska Dagbladet* 20 augusti 1970.

'Gerillakamp i Eritrea förlorat oberoende'. *Svenska Dagbladet* 27 april 1969.

Knutsson, K.E., 'Problemet Eritrea'. *Dagens Nyheter* 6 februari 1971.

Knutsson, K.E., 'Vad händer i Eritrea?' *Dagens Nyheter* 5 februari 1971.

'State of Emergency in Eritrea - Clashes between Government Forces and Eritrean Liberation Front'. *Keesing Contemporary Archives* XVIII (10-27 March, 1971):24507 A.

'Successful Government Offensive against Eritrean Secessionists', *Keesing Contemporary Archives* XXIV (15 December, 1978):29356.

'Vad händer i Etiopien?' *Aftonbladet* 15 mars 1969.

'Warfare between Eritrean Secessionists and Ethiopian Armed Forces'. *Keesing Contemporary Archives* XXI (24-30 March, 1975):27031.